CHANEL
THE LEGEND OF AN ICON

ALEXANDER FURY

CHANEL
THE LEGEND OF AN ICON

ASSOULINE

INTRODUCTION

The house of Chanel straddles the twentieth century, colossal. It represents modern fashion. Under its founder, Gabrielle Chanel, the style of the modern woman was invented, through the image of Chanel herself. Every marker and signifier of contemporary feminine dress can be traced back to her: notions of ease, unconstrained movement, pragmatism, and practicality. These are no longer even representative of a particular style; they have fused into the very meaning of clothing today. Fashion, she stated, must be logical—an idea that had never previously been posited in the decorative universe of female attire. She dressed women to be free, her emancipated clothes reflecting the shifting landscape of society around them. Her work fundamentally affected what we wear and how we wear it. The work of the house under her successor Karl Lagerfeld transformed fashion anew: Lagerfeld drew the template for a fashion designer reviving a staid, moribund house, transforming it through its own history. Just as Chanel created modern fashion, Lagerfeld in turn established the blueprint of the modern fashion house. She reshaped the clothing women wore, and he reshaped the industry that makes it.

Les Maisons Chanel et L. Rouff

In 1915, Gabrielle Chanel opens a couture salon in Biarritz on Avenue Édouard VII not far from the Hôtel du Palais.
Opposite: Portrait of Gabrielle Chanel, circa 1914.

Trying to compress a legacy of such magnitude into a single volume, however large, is a daunting, perhaps impossible task. Tackling this idea, one confronts a fundamental question: What does "Chanel" mean? How does one define "Chanel"? After one show, when asked what the collection was about, Lagerfeld responded with a Voltaire maxim: "Everything that needs an explanation isn't worth it," adding, "Look and you will get the message."[1] The same is true of Chanel, across the years: That Gabrielle Chanel's short, easy skirts and lightened fabrics enabled movement and went hand in hand with female emancipation is obvious; so is the fact that Lagerfeld's updates and tweaks to Chanel classics made them desirable, reflecting fashion as it shifted inexorably on its axis.

Nevertheless, there are elements that the world recognizes, always, as Chanel. Her suits, of course; her Little Black Dresses and quilted bags; her eased silhouettes; her love of camellias and bows, nubby tweeds, chiffon, tangles of faux jewelry among priceless real gems. The evocative fragrance of No. 5, a chemical scent in a modernist bottle, emblematic of Chanel's ideology; her hatred of nostalgia, in line with Lagerfeld's; her constant search for the new, another characteristic they shared. It was also important to express the remarkable popularity of her initially radical outlooks. Chanel No. 5 became and remains the most famous perfume in the world; the Chanel suit, decried by critics upon its appearance in 1954, is perhaps the most imitated designer fashion of all time. These ideas are reiterated again and again, by Gabrielle Chanel originally, then perpetuated by Karl Lagerfeld for more than thirty-six years.

"When Mademoiselle Chanel sketches her own frivolities," illustration by Christian Bérard, 1937.
The dress design in the center is a version of item 20, 1937.

This book is a literary exhibition, or museum-in-print: a curated selection, not exhaustive but informative, embedded in Chanel clothing. As an exhibition shows a particular point of view on an artist, so does this book, which showcases 100 items, 100 individual Chanel designs that together constitute the collective "Chanel." Some of this is unintentional: For instance, the color palette throughout is remarkably focused, and out of it emerges the Chanel spectrum, of pure black and camellia white, sandstone shades of beige maturing from wheat to blazing gold, blushes of pink, brilliant injections of red, touches of navy and cerulean. There are, of course, anomalies: Lagerfeld threw in some wild wolves, such as a poisonous, saturated slick of sequined yellow in 1991.

Gabrielle Chanel geared her garments inherently to the form in motion, an idea that determined many of her innovations, and ensures her work still looks relevant. To reflect that esprit, imagery has been included by the great photographers of their times—Edward Steichen, George Hoyningen-Huene, Cecil Beaton, Helmut Newton, Irving Penn, Peter Lindbergh—capturing Chanel's fashion designs worn by women. Women like Jacqueline Kennedy, Catherine Deneuve, Gloria Swanson, and of course the designer herself. "I designed dresses precisely because I went out, because I lived the life of the century, and was the first to do so," Chanel said. "I lived a modern life."

Because of this, early Chanel items are scarce. Made of working fabrics like cotton, wool, and jersey, they were not treated preciously by either their creator or their wearers. Our selection begins in 1920, with a Little Black Dress, naturally—albeit six years before it was named such by American *Vogue*. Worn with a jacket, an early ancestor of her suit, it still feels modern and wearable. These still-life images of Chanel garments showcase them as precious objects that have become testaments to the history of both fashion and culture, because examining the evolution of Chanel clothing is, in part, about examining the evolution of femininity and of societal attitudes about women. Although she never called herself a feminist, Chanel's clothes are about freedom, physical and ideological. Karl Lagerfeld's were too—freedom from respect, from tradition, from the past.

The selection is split almost exactly between pieces designed by Gabrielle Chanel and by Karl Lagerfeld. It was important, however, to include a piece from the interim—twelve years when, contrary to popular mythology, the house did not vanish nor close. Comparing the design of Chanel's immediate successor, Gaston Berthelot, to that of Karl Lagerfeld's debut, one understands better the sweeping away of cobwebs, Lagerfeld's revolution. Grouping items within this volume also forges unlikely comparisons. Lagerfeld's interest in elevating the ordinary—for instance, his Chanel-ized versions of sleeveless cotton tanks, denim jeans, leather jackets—is here automatically in conversation with Chanel's love of the modest, her use of men's undergarment fabrics to free women's bodies. At the time, Lagerfeld was critiqued for ignoring Chanel's legacy: In fact, he was continuing it anew. Chanel No. 5 is present in both eras, reflecting its endurance as the best-selling fragrance of all time. The original bottle is shown, as is its reincarnation in the 1980s, when its status was

Gabrielle Chanel photographed by Frères Séeberger. 1938.

significant enough to warrant a portrait by Andy Warhol. By that point, for Lagerfeld, it had become one of the visual codes of Chanel—he dressed his models in T-shirts marked with its logo, used its shape for jewelry and accessories. With Lagerfeld, No. 5 was always alive.

In compiling this selection—boiling down the history of Chanel to 100 key items spanning 1920 to nearly 2020—we thought it vital to tick off the universal components of Chanel's identity cemented in the wider culture. Alongside identifying the stylistic structure of Chanel, the other essential task was to demonstrate how, like a living, breathing organism, that structure has changed constantly. Many may assume Chanel's history to be static, knowing well the symbols, emblems, icons of its unmistakable style. Yet fixed though the idea is, "*le style* Chanel" has actually always existed in a state of constant reinvention, always moving with the times. It was essential both to reflect that evolution and to evaluate it—to demonstrate that the timeliness of garments labeled "Chanel" could, paradoxically, make the house of Chanel timeless.

When telling the story of the house of Chanel, by necessity one tells the story of fashion today. So much of fashion was not only invented by Gabrielle Chanel, but created in her image. It has subsequently been defined by the attitude and approach of Karl Lagerfeld, perhaps the last of the great couturiers, certainly the first artistic director, a role that would come to define the contemporary fashion landscape and that, like Chanel, he made in his own image. Understandably, books on Chanel have tended to focus on both—their fascinating public personae, the mystique around their private lives. This is the first to unpack the meaning of Chanel not through the designers but through the clothes they created.

☼

Fittingly, Chanel is a house of firsts. Gabrielle Chanel was the first to shorten skirts, to remove padding and frills and furbelows and streamline the figure. She put fur on the inside of coats, rather than the outside, literally inverting luxury. She made ersatz gems of paste and glass fashionable rather than tacky or poor; indeed, Chanel was arguably the first to champion the idea of modesty in dress, creating clothes that underplayed expense, that elevated the mundane, the everyday—even the unremarkable—into something unique. As *The New Yorker* wrote in 1931: "She has put the apache's sweater into the Ritz, utilized the ditch-digger's scarf, made chic the white collars and cuffs of the waitress, and put queens into mechanics' tunics."[2]

Those firsts came, first of all, from Gabrielle Chanel herself—a figure who, like no designer before or since, embodied both the aesthetic and the ideology of her clothes. Gabrielle Bonheur Chanel was born into poverty in the South of France, and abandoned to an orphanage in the convent of Aubazine at age 12 by her father, following the death of her mother. She glamorized this past frequently, excessively—romanticizing her upbringing, replacing the orphanage with "aunts," erasing or acquiring siblings, and shaving years off her age. Regardless, the austerity of the convent, the simplicity of the surroundings, the

Top row: Gabrielle Chanel's hands, photographed by André Kertész, 1938; Chanel on Lido Beach in Venice, circa 1930s; sketch of Chanel by Jean Cocteau, 1937.
Middle row: "Mademoiselle Chanel on the Lido—linen suit, pearls, enamel bracelets," illustration by Christian Bérard, from *Vogue* UK, June 1936; Chanel in her suite at the Ritz, photographed by François Kollar for *Harper's Bazaar*, 1937; Chanel with her friend Serge Lifar, principal dancer of the Ballets Russes, on the Lido in Venice, 1937.
Left: Chanel at work, 1937.

monochrome unadorned attire of the nuns, and the needlework Chanel was taught came to fundamentally shape her aesthetic. At age 18, she was first employed as a seamstress, and sang at a café-concert to supplement her income. She earned the sobriquet "Coco" during this time, a reference, perhaps, to two popular songs of the period—"Ko Ko Ri Ko" and "Qui qu'a vu Coco"—or to the word *cocotte,* which Chanel was. Her romances with wealthy men helped secure her financially; one of them, a scion of a British shipping merchant family, Captain Arthur Edward Capel, known as "Boy," supported Chanel's first boutique at 21 rue Cambon in Paris, opened in 1910 as Chanel Modes. At first she sold hats, in an era when no woman was properly dressed without one. Chanel's designs were extravagant but not elaborate, already hinting at the revolution to come. The hats sold well—the era's favored celebrities, demimondaine actresses such as Émilienne d'Alençon, Suzanne Orlandi, and Gabrielle Dorziat, bought them and brought success to the young milliner's nascent establishment. In 1913, Chanel opened a second boutique in the fashionable resort town of Deauville in Normandy. She decided to sell clothes using tricot jersey—a fabric hitherto used for the underclothes of laboring men—and sewn by her milliners rather than by experienced seamstresses. Thus she transformed, first from hatmaker to *couturière,* then to tastemaker. Her staff made simple clothing, such as dresses and loose jackets with wide sailor collars, whose ease fitted the seaside environs and, soon, whose sobriety suited wartime austerity. "I was witnessing the death of luxury, the passing of the nineteenth century, the end of an era," Chanel later stated.[3]

Not only witnessing but actively contributing to its demise, Chanel sounded the tocsin for the birth of a new age and, specifically, a new way of looking at clothes and at women. What she proposed was a modernized view of femininity, arguably resetting our perceptions of the female. Chanel's instinct was to strip women's clothes of the clamjamfry that had proliferated during the Belle Époque, when, as her archrival the couturier Paul Poiret commented, the S-bend shape of the corset and long skirts made the wearers look as if they were hauling a trailer. Chanel put women into clothes that emancipated their bodies, like suffrage through cloth. These were garments for an active life, a precursor to how women would feel, what they would want to achieve, during the next decade. The young *couturière,* with her shingled hair, raised skirts, and what Cecil Beaton later described as "her athletic, race-horse stride,"[4] became the ideal. She was her own best model and wore her clothes with an enviable ease. Luckily, women didn't have to envy; they could actually buy the garments. In 1915, Chanel opened her first couture establishment in another fashionable resort, Biarritz; three years later, she opened her business in Paris on the same street as her millinery shop, rue Cambon, this time at number 31. Here, she began to show her collections. Her revolution began on the beaches; by the early 1920s it was storming the Bastille of Parisian haute couture.

Chanel's revolution chiefly consisted of equality. Since the early nineteenth century, men had been dressing in sober suits engineered around their bodies with industrial precision. Men's clothes were modern machines for living; women's, by contrast, were decorative—corseted, crinolined, cumbersome. Chanel did away with all that, and ushered

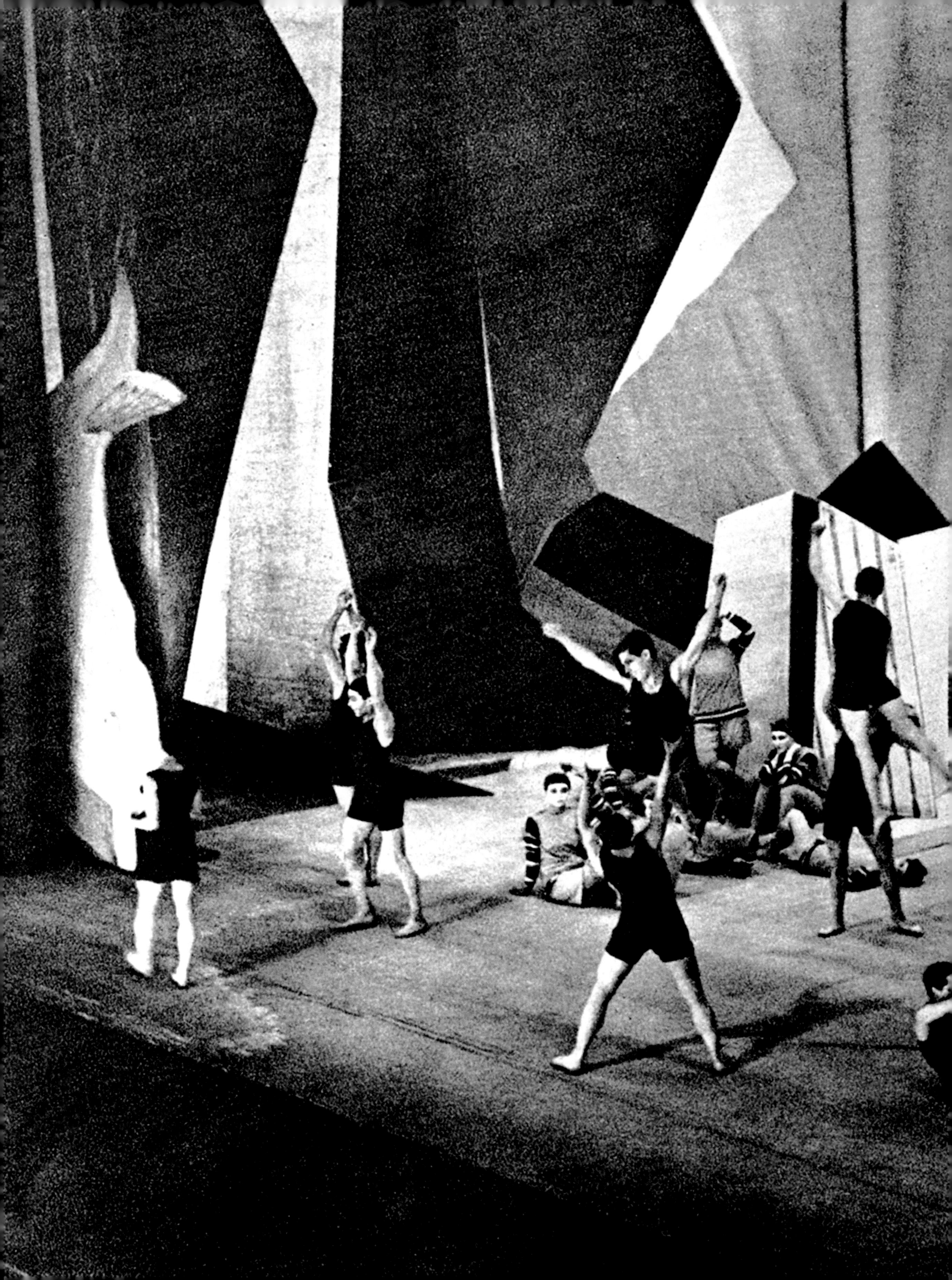

The ballet *Le Train Bleu*, by composer Darius Milhaud, performed by Sergei Diaghilev's Ballets Russes, with libretto by Jean Cocteau, curtain by Pablo Picasso, and costumes by Gabrielle Chanel, 1924.

women into the twentieth century, often by drawing from men's clothes, appropriating the fabrics and finishes, the ideal of simplicity. She proposed trousers, fishermen's sweaters, wide-cut jackets, many literally borrowed from her male partners, who in this formative interwar period included the French industrialist Étienne Balsan, the Duke of Westminster, Russian Grand Duke Dmitri Pavlovich, and the artist Paul Iribe. She continued to use jersey, even though grander stuff was available after 1918. The fabric became a signature of her house: Her dresses in tricot cost as much as other houses' embroidered and embellished styles. When commissioned in 1923 to design for the Ballets Russes, whose opulent exoticism had inspired Paul Poiret's Orientalist styles in the prewar years, she dressed the performers in striking contemporary sportswear. The performance played out against a curtain painted after a work by Pablo Picasso—whom Chanel knew, and to whom she can be seen as a fashion counterpart, just as she is allied with the Ballets Russes' reforming forces of Igor Stravinsky and Sergei Diaghilev.

Just as Picasso challenged our perceptions of the human figure and form, and Stravinsky broke apart music and Diaghilev redefined dance, so Chanel attacked and ultimately upended our ideas of the fashionable, even of luxury. Chanel used rabbit fur instead of precious chinchilla or sable, faux pearls instead of real; in the early 1930s she would advocate cotton, to the chagrin of the French silk industry, for she liked the way it took color. "People confuse poverty with simplicity,"[5] she later stated. An American client once delighted her by declaring, "To have spent so much money without it showing!"[6] Chanel stripped everything away, and in so doing introduced the idea of the couture house as transmogrifying force. Chanel's jersey was no different from a fisherman's except that it had been handled by Chanel. In a sense, this also underscored the power of taste—the one thing that an untrained, penniless orphan could have in abundance. Chanel's championing of what, despite her assertions, was ostensibly poor—humble textiles, lack of adornment, a penchant for beige (which she favorably compared to dirt)—underlined her own power. It wasn't what you wore, but rather *who*.

The launch of Chanel No. 5 in 1921 further accentuated this concept. While Chanel cannot lay claim to the first couture perfume—that distinction falls to her predecessor Poiret, and his Parfums de Rosine, launched in 1911 and named after his daughter—she was the first to place her own name on the bottle. She was also the first to eschew the idea of florid nomenclature—Rosine's first two fragrances, for example, were called Nuit Persane and Le Minaret—and instead simply named her debut fragrance, superstitiously, after a number she perceived as lucky: five. It was also the fifth sample created by perfumer Ernest Beaux that she tested. Chanel liked the chemical smell of the perfume, which abstractly reminded her of the soap she washed with as a child. She later declared it "a perfume such as has never before been made—a woman's perfume with a woman's scent."[7] Composed of over eighty ingredients, it had a complexity that was unique, as was its innovative use of synthetic aldehydes to intensify natural scents. Chanel led her clients by the nose: She sprayed her boutiques and salons with the fragrance before it was available, to engender curiosity, and wore the scent herself. Let it never be said that Chanel's genius lay only in design; she was, perhaps, the world's first true marketeer.

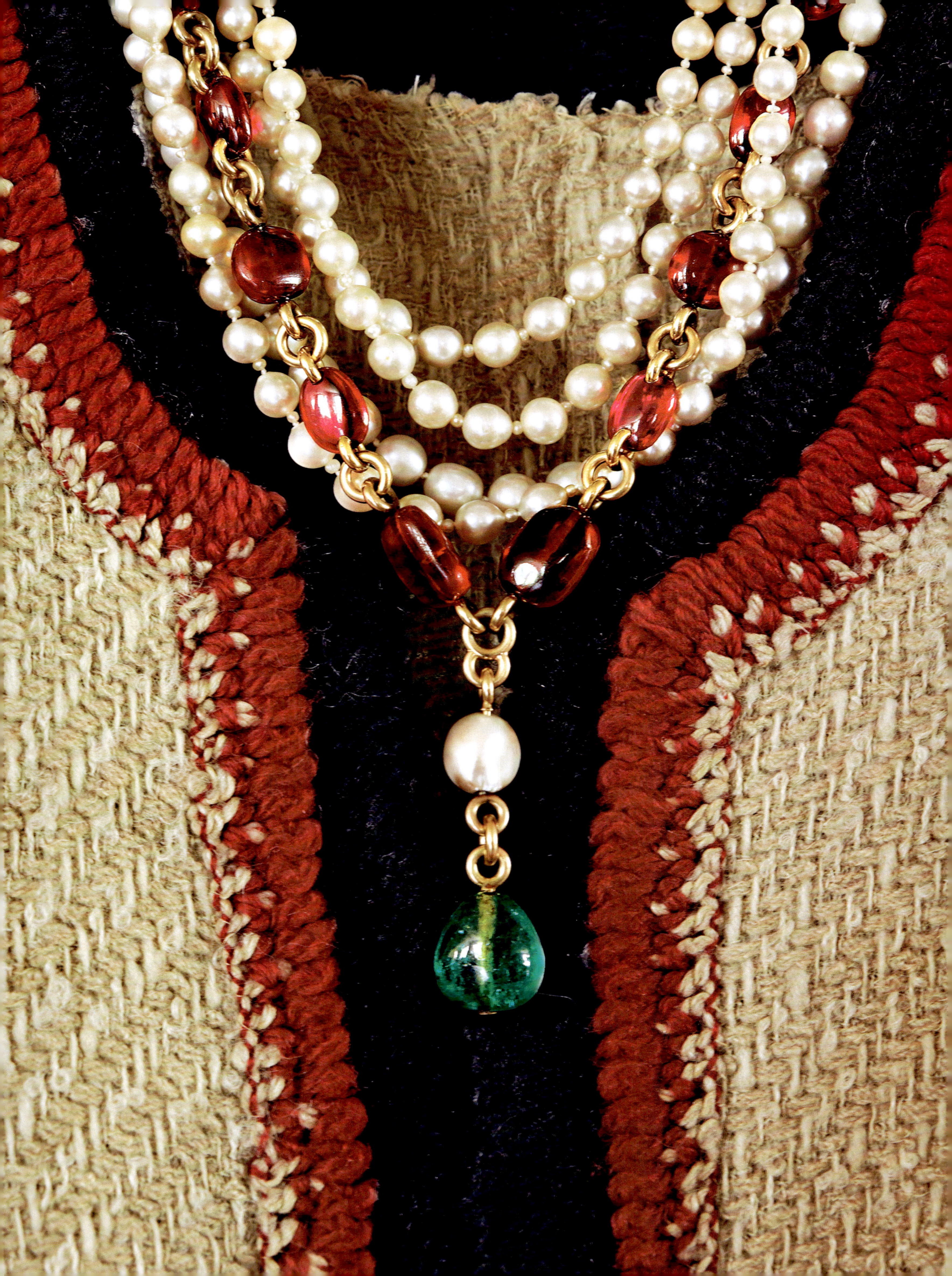

Illustration by Cecil Beaton for a set design for the Broadway musical *Coco*, starring Katharine Hepburn, 1969.
Opposite: From Gabrielle Chanel's own wardrobe, a classic tweed suit with
a favorite pearl necklace and a ruby-and-emerald necklace given to her by Paul Iribe.

In the same vein, the design of the Chanel No. 5 bottle was as important and revolutionary as the *jus* inside, the complexity of the formula belied by the stark simplicity, even austerity, of its packaging. Instead of baroque cut glass and elaborate colors, the shape was pure, almost medicinal, the packaging black and white. Multiple sources are cited for its shape, many pulled from the masculine realm of Chanel's moneyed lovers—liquor decanters, the cologne bottles of the men's shirtmaker Charvet. Regardless of its origin, the bottle transformed the appearance of modern perfumery. In 1959, its design was added to the permanent collection of the Museum of Modern Art in New York.

Chanel's hallmarks were plentiful, but more than the cloth or construction, the root of Chanel's style was embedded in the woman. Mademoiselle Chanel cut her own hair short, "because it annoys me,"[8] and popularized the suntan, both overturning the current ideals of beauty. Even more ephemeral were Chanel's notions of confidence, movement, and easiness, elements of her character that she transposed into dresses, reiterated so intently that they developed into a style. Many of her innovations were born from her personal ideas of attractiveness, of what suited her, which she assumed other women would want as well. Chanel's remarkably long life—she died in 1971, aged 87—afforded her an unfair advantage: She could constantly tell new generations of journalists that she had invented everything.

She did so in the 1950s when, at age 70, she re-opened her fashion house on rue Cambon. Her instinct was to rail against the male-dominated styles of postwar haute couture: "Dior doesn't dress women, he upholsters them,"⁹ she once stated. Her comeback collection, presented in 1954 on February 5—that lucky number again—was criticized for its resemblance to prewar styles: Chanel was decried as a figure from the past, fast disappearing into it. Nevertheless, she persevered—again, convinced that women would want what she did. She was correct.

No further proof is needed than the Chanel suit: First proposed in the 1920s, evolved in the 1930s, and resurrected in 1954, it became a uniform for generations of women. Her first outfit of that Spring 1954 collection was a suit in jersey. Despite its place in the running order, it was called, of course, "No. 5." That Chanel suit, *the* Chanel suit, every Chanel suit, proved a precise, concise exegesis of Chanel's philosophy of fashion, an evolution of every opinion and conviction she had about clothing and style. Chanel herself wore the suit 24/7: In the 1920s and 1930s she was seen in her own evening wear, in layers of lace and tulle, velvet and frills, but in her later years she is universally clad in variations of her tweed cardigan-jacket and just-below-the-knee skirt, day and night. Softly tailored, quilted to the lining with no interfacing, and held straight by the weight of a gilt chain sewn into the hem, the jacket is light, supple, and easy. Often, the suits were trimmed in three-dimensional *gallon* braid, serving as a graphic decorative device but also adding to the structure of the jacket on the edges and on pockets, which always were functional. Of particular note were the sleeves (narrow, always three-piece, to create a slight natural curve) and the high U-shaped armholes that Chanel obsessively ripped apart and refitted with her own hands, shredding the seams (and often drawing blood from the model inside them) to fastidiously reset the sleeve head. The perfection

Following pages: Chanel chats with actress Jeanne Moreau in her apartment on rue Cambon, 1960.

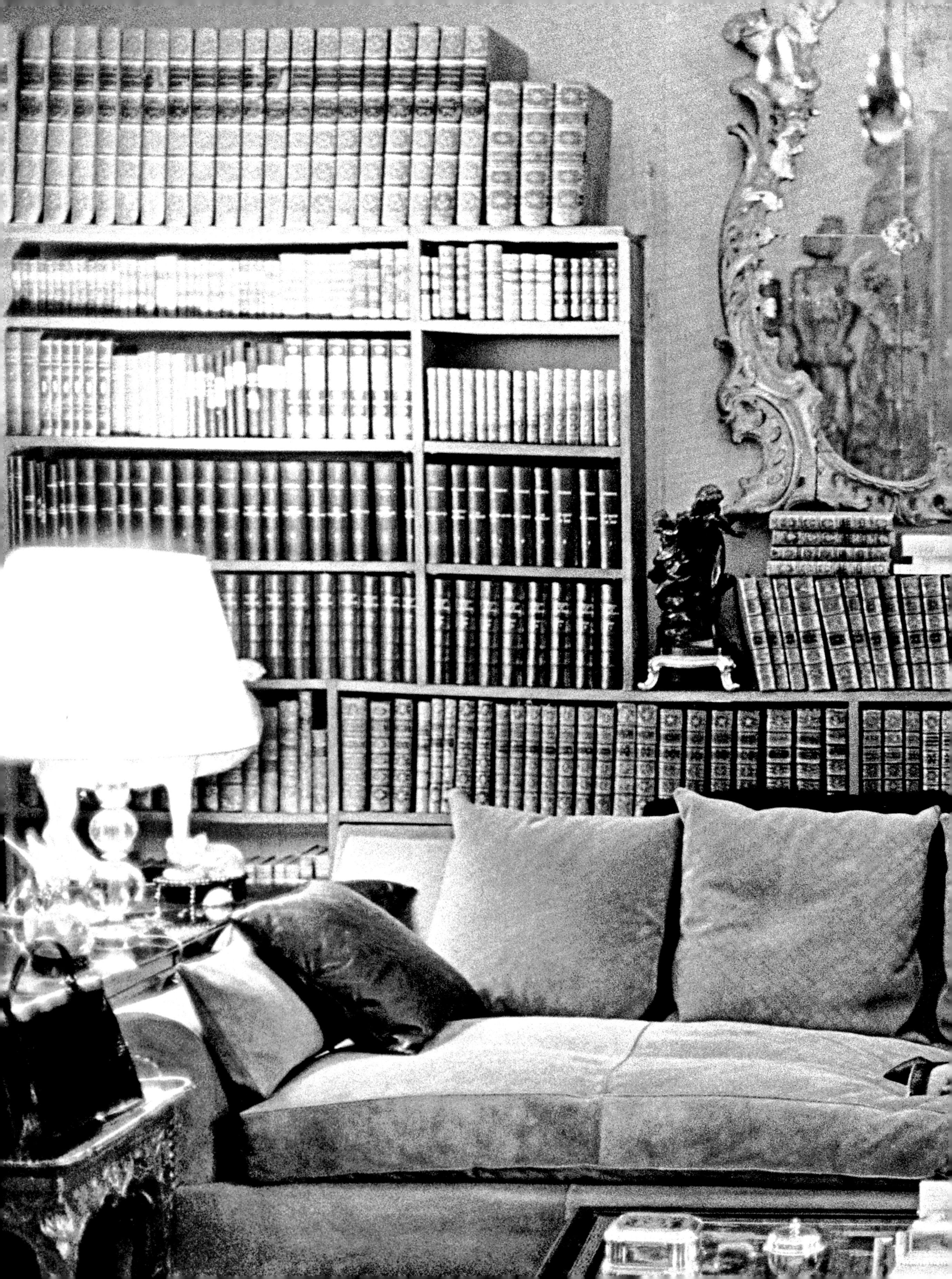

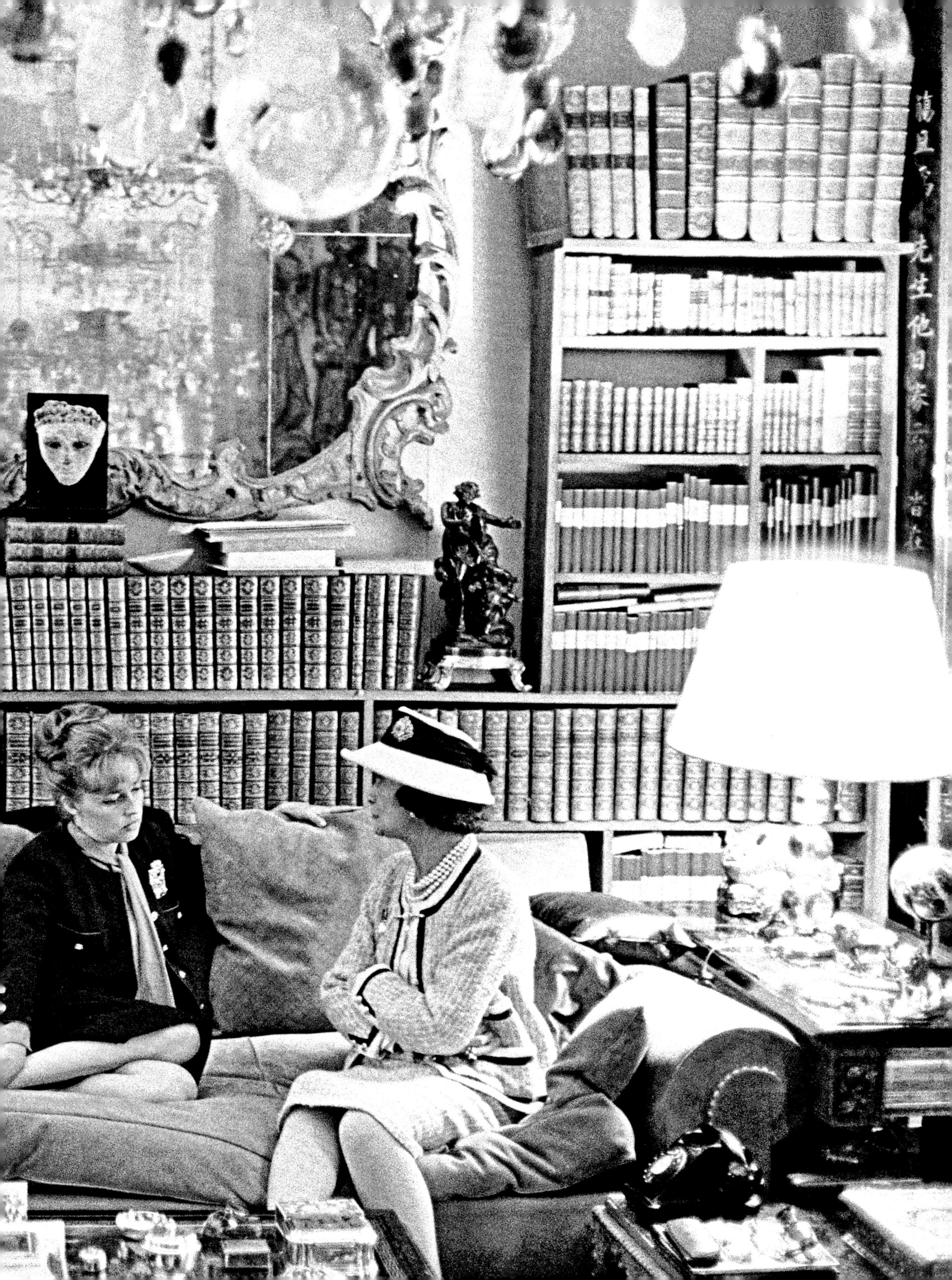

of sleeves, for Chanel, was vital, for they facilitate a woman's freedom of movement. Like the seemingly endless reworking of her signature sleeves, the 1950s and 1960s were for Chanel a search for perfection through refinement, a period of subtle evolution and reevaluation, tinkering with elements, distilling the essence of this timeless look.

The ensemble, by the end of the decade, would be completed by two additions: the 2.55 handbag, a quilted model with chain shoulder strap that left the hands free to get on with life, and almond-toed, two-tone shoes in beige leather and black satin. As a uniform, it collided the oft-irreconcilable demands of elegance and practicality. It was worn not just by society women, but by everyone—from nurses to teachers to presidents' wives. For many, the single most memorable image of the aftermath of John F. Kennedy's assassination on November 22, 1963, was his wife, Jacqueline, in her bloodstained suit. More than fashion, or even style, it had simply become clothing. Throughout those decades, it was rabidly copied, officially and not. "Along with plagiarism go admiration and love,"[10] said Chanel herself. Chanel loved her suit. She made it, sold it, and wore it ceaselessly until her death in 1971.

A hundred years, give or take a few months, after the birth of Gabrielle Chanel, her fashion house was reborn under the deft hands and eagle eye of Karl Lagerfeld, who presented his first haute couture collection for the house on Tuesday, January 25, 1983. A German, born in Hamburg in 1933—but, in a manner similar to Gabrielle Chanel, he drew a pall over that date and his past in general—Lagerfeld was an unlikely successor. Although trained in couture's hallowed halls, he soared to prominence via the fast-paced world of 1970s ready-to-wear, with designs defined by their witty panache and healthy disrespect for rules, boundaries, or conventions. His work for Chanel would establish the blueprint for the resuscitation of a fashion house, both the origins and the attitude. Like Chanel, Lagerfeld changed fashion forever.

"Everybody told me then not to touch it,"[11] Lagerfeld said of the house of Chanel. He only accepted the creative leadership the second time it was offered, late in 1982, when Gabrielle Chanel had been dead for eleven years. The house was effectively dead, too; the creative reins had been first handed to Gaston Berthelot, a former Dior designer, then to Jean Cazaubon and Yvonne Dudel, former assistants to Mademoiselle, as Chanel was known. They followed her aesthetic without great change—the house itself cited in 1971 that Berthelot would not create original designs, but would continue to follow the styles established by Mademoiselle Chanel. Under their watch, the house slid into quiet complacency—Chanel ready-to-wear had launched in 1978 to little attention (it had just eighteen U.S. stockists in 1982); the perfume sold, but it had wound up in duty-free and discount stores, steeply marked down. Yet Lagerfeld saw something, somewhere, buried deep, that interested him. "This was a challenge that I thought was exciting," he later recalled.[12]

Hindsight reveals the wealth of the inspirational seam running through Chanel, but at the time it was difficult to see why Lagerfeld might be entranced. Chanel was a sleeping beauty, a giant slumbering under a thick dust of time, with a whiff of No. 5 hanging about it. Moreover, Chanel's stylistic trademarks—the first-radical-then-polite tweed suits, wide-brim hats, and low-heeled shoes—were seen as old-fashioned and passé next to the attention-grabbing ready-to-wear fashions of the 1970s and 1980s, many of which had originated with Lagerfeld, hence the questions when he took on Chanel's mantle. Never mind that in 1983 ready-to-wear and haute couture were seen as separate entities, the former commercial fodder, the latter true creative expression. That hegemony had been challenged, first by Yves Saint Laurent's declaration in 1971 that haute couture was "a museum…a refuge for people who do not dare to look life in the face and who are reassured by tradition,"[13] and latterly by the emergence of the *créateur*, ready-to-wear designers who designed with the kind of flair and invention previously only afforded to couture. Lagerfeld was the first of this breed. Still, to hand him the reins of a couture house was, literally, unprecedented, almost obscene. It caused a sensation in the chichi salons of the Seizième. "I knew he was the one," Alain Wertheimer told American *Vogue* in 1989. With his brother, Gérard, Alain owns the controlling interest in the house of Chanel. His father, Pierre, alongside his brother, Paul, established Société des Parfums Chanel in 1924, to distribute Chanel fragrances. The Wertheimers had also underwritten half the costs of Gabrielle Chanel's comeback in 1953. "People before had tried to revive Chanel with respect," Alain continued. "But you can't stand still, in fashion or in business."[14]

In no small part, Karl Lagerfeld was brought into Chanel for business, to generate publicity, because the all-important sales of No. 5 were flagging. No one could have predicted how he would reenergize not only the label

Gabrielle Chanel with model Suzy Parker, photographed by Richard Avedon in Paris, January 1959. Parker's suit is item 34, 1959.

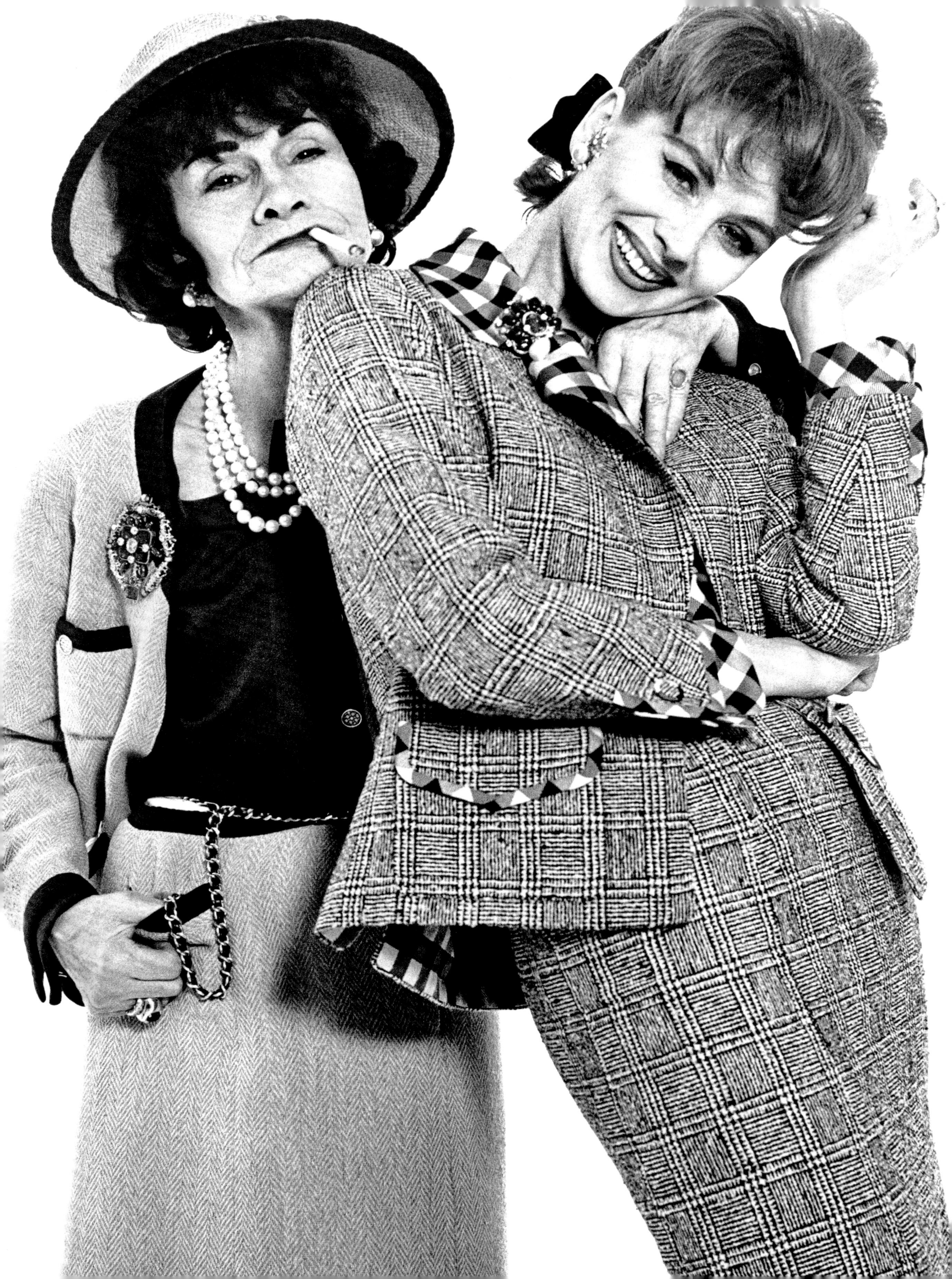

specifically, but haute couture in general, and how his work would shape the direction of fashion as a whole. Without Lagerfeld and Chanel, the landscape of modern fashion would be radically different. Lagerfeld established the modus operandi of the industry today—take an age-old, old-age house, raze it to the ground, and rise from the ashes with new fashionable ideas, imbued with the spirit of the antecedents but embedded in the shape of the now. The fashion world of the twenty-first century is dotted with success stories that owe an undoubted, undeniable debt to Chanel's forward thinking and to Lagerfeld's Brobdingnagian talent.

"I don't reinterpret the past. I'm pretentious enough to say that we invent something for today, that people can identify as Chanel, even if she never did it," Lagerfeld once told me. "There are lots of things people think are native to the house which are born since I'm here. My job is to make believe. There is no other way for a fashion house to survive."[15] Chanel did not merely survive; it thrived. Under the artistic leadership of Karl Lagerfeld, Chanel became the most successful fashion house of the last century, with more than 300 stores across the globe by 2018. What Lagerfeld's endless invention, reinvention, and reinterpretation achieved was the reactivation of the legacy of Chanel for today, the imbuing of styles of the past with a modernity that made us look at the old anew. Generally taste has turned toward seeking out the original, via vintage fashion. Specifically, it is through Lagerfeld's constant revisiting and reevaluating of the Chanel suit, for instance, that ensured it has never been consigned to the dustbin of history. By using it as a foundation for the new, he kept the original constantly in fashion. It was the timeliness of Lagerfeld that made Chanel, perversely, timeless.

Many perceived Lagerfeld's styles as parody rather than homage: *The New York Times* dubbed him "The Designer Who Destroys the Past,"[16] and he was accused of jackbooting his way through Chanel's philosophy of dress. Certainly, he held no truck with the notion of "respect," as Alain Wertheimer identified. Nevertheless, his clothes from that very first collection could be immediately "read" as Chanel, and still can be. What Lagerfeld did—cleverly, even with a touch of genius—was to tinker with those aforementioned elements of the then passé *jolie madame* Chanel aesthetic (bouclé, boaters, camellias, chain-hem jackets) but combine them in different manners, echoing fashionable tastes. That approach echoes, indefatigably, Gabrielle Chanel's own assertion: "Fashion should express the place, the moment."[17] Hence the Chanel suits in Lagerfeld's first collection of 1983 had roomier armholes and wider shoulders, an assertive bent, shaping up to the silhouette of the developing decade. Later, he would show the suits' tweeds combined with leather and denim, rescaling the gilt chains to echo the fashionable rap styles of the early 1990s, jangling against Ping-Pong ball–size pearls and worn over the littlest of black dresses with thigh-gripping miniskirts. The timeless thus became timely. "A very static image has emerged based on Chanel's last years," Lagerfeld told *Women's Wear Daily* before his first show, adjusting clothes in the Chanel studio behind a sign that still read *Mademoiselle—Privé*. "I've looked over her whole career and found something much more interesting."[18] He continued to look, to find, and to reinvent for thirty-six more years.

Alongside Chanel, Karl Lagerfeld designed for the houses of Fendi (1965–2019) and for Chloé (1963–1983 and 1992–1997). His approach could be

Following pages: Inès de la Fressange in a fitting with Karl Lagerfeld at the Chanel atelier, 1984.

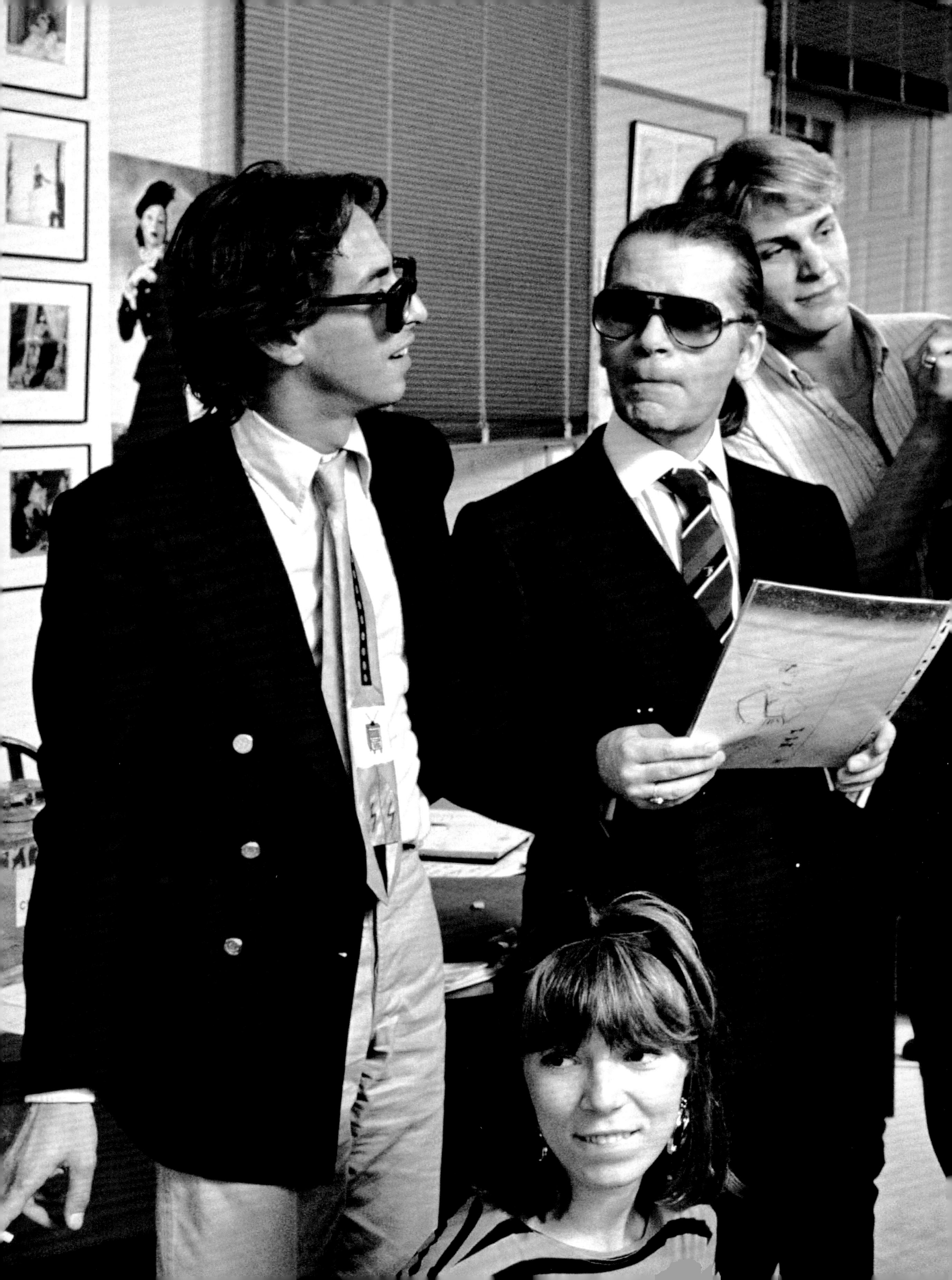

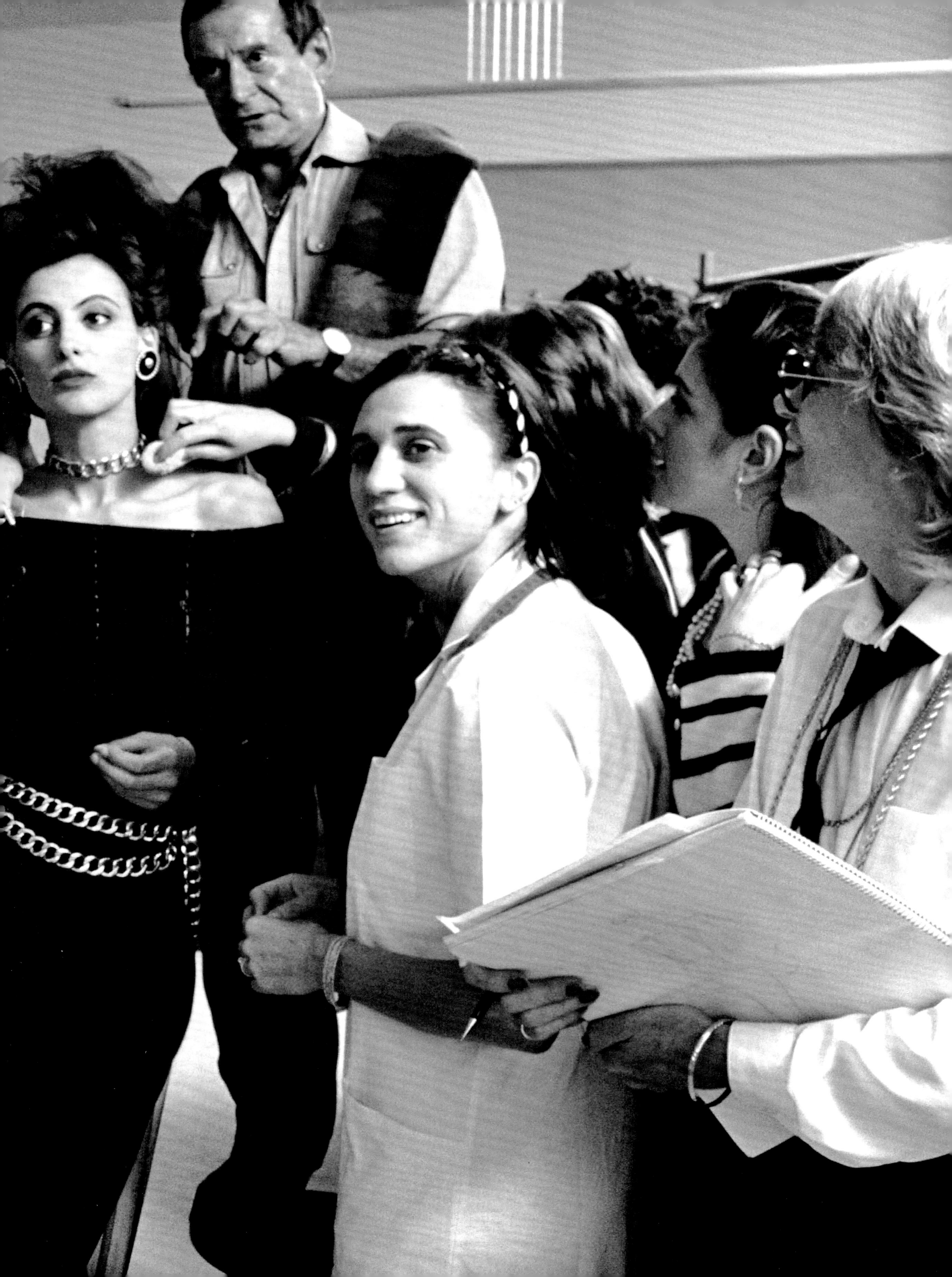

The building blocks of classic Chanel chic.

compared to Cerberus, the triple-headed Hound of Hades of Greek mythology, who guarded the mouth of the Underworld to prevent the dead from rejoining the living. With his restless, relentless search for modernity, his disavowing of the past and constant pushing forward, Lagerfeld did the same. He refused to let the ghost of the past haunt him, or us, or fashion as a whole.

Yet Lagerfeld's work did not ignore history; by contrast, he demonstrated a supreme knowledge of the past. He once asserted that his archive of materials about the life and work of Gabrielle Chanel was superior to that of the *maison* that bears her name—which could be apocryphal but is probably true. That intimate knowledge of Chanel allowed him to rip apart, to entirely reinvent. Respect and reverence are restraining; Chanel herself felt no affection for past modes and manners. Hence Lagerfeld's linking of themes and ideas was intuitive, instinctive; a flower may lead to a movie, which may lead to a woman in the 1920s. It is only through the power of knowing—knowing everything, or thereabouts—that Lagerfeld could make such extraordinary leaps of inspiration and collide seemingly disparate sources, to create a fusion that felt fresh, new, and never-before-seen, even if elements were drawn from the grand arc of history.

Many have leapt to the conclusion that Lagerfeld's anti-nostalgia was anti-history—that those account for two of his three heads, all three staring ceaselessly forward. But in fact, one head was always glancing backward, assessing and reevaluating, drawing pieces from the past that could be relevant today. And then, when their moment was over, they were discarded, or at least shoved to the back of his mind. Karl Lagerfeld was the ultimate Zen designer—no muss, no fuss. How very Chanel.

※

Yet, familiar though it may seem, Chanel's work is often contradictory, even paradoxical—as this book demonstrates. Alongside the established imprimaturs of Chanel are the lesser known—the romance of her creations in the 1930s, in which long skirts and lace ruffles replace the streamlined short jersey dresses of the 1920s. Chanel was, in her personal life, an incurable romantic; this sensibility drifted into the 1950s, as seen in her slipstream dresses of billowing chiffon draped to midcalf. And while she was known for elevating faux gemstones, she also explored the most precious of fine jewelry—platinum and diamonds—in an extraordinary 1932 collection inspired by her lucky stars. As Lagerfeld himself put it before his first presentation for the house in 1983, "Even if she never did it this way, it's very Chanel, no?"[19]

That, essentially, was at the root of Lagerfeld's approach to Chanel's mythology—inventing ideas she perhaps never thought of, but conceivably could have. It underpinned the conceptualization of his globe-trotting Croisière and Métiers d'Art collections, interseasonal presentations in May and December showcased in far-flung locations, in some way tethered to the legacy of Gabrielle Chanel. The link was increasingly tenuous, a measure of Lagerfeld's confidence in his own creativity, moving farther and farther away from the history of the house, recognizing that in playing with codes

Model-muse Inès de la Fressange poses in Chanel's rue Cambon apartment, 1984.

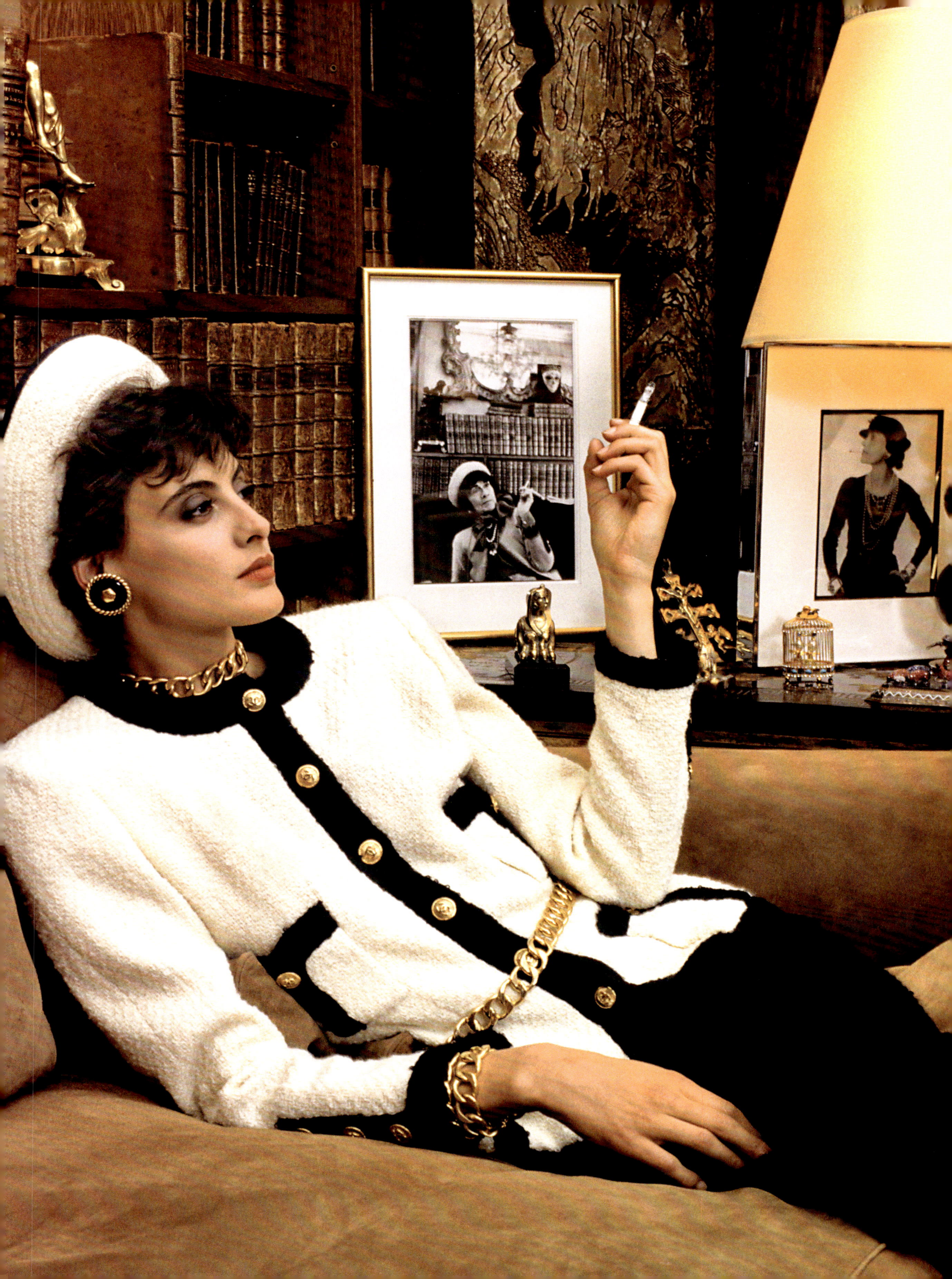

Top row: Cara Delevingne and Karl Lagerfeld walk the Chanel Spring 2015 ready-to-wear show finale; Lagerfeld with Kate Moss at the Chanel Autumn 2009 ready-to-wear show.
Middle row: Lady Amanda Harlech and Lagerfeld attend the Rose Ball at the Monte Carlo Sporting Club, 2007; Lagerfeld with Chanel fashion studio director Virginie Viard and his godson Hudson Kroenig at the Chanel Métiers d'Art show at the Metropolitan Museum of Art in New York City, December 2018.
Left: Vanessa Paradis with Lagerfeld at Paris ready-to-wear fashion week, March 2010.

thoroughly cemented in the annals of history, almost anything could be Chanel—a name that rapidly became an adjective. Everything from a fabric to a trim, to a gemstone could be and often was described as "Chanel."

Karl Lagerfeld's interpretations of the concept of "Chanel" roamed ever wider. "Somehow, with Chanel…her interests were so wide and varied, there's always a link,"[20] says Lady Amanda Harlech, who worked with Lagerfeld from 1996 to 2019. His febrile exploration of those interests also brought up ideas amusing, unexpected, even impudent. His work not only referenced the garments Gabrielle Chanel created, but also her entire environment, her universe. He created earrings and bags shaped like Chanel No. 5 bottles, an entire haute couture collection inspired by Gabrielle Chanel in a Watteau-inflected costume for a 1939 ball thrown by Comte Étienne de Beaumont, evening dresses and jackets embroidered with the patterns of her Coromandel screens. Indeed, in his taste for grand luxe, Lagerfeld was perhaps more akin to Chanel's taste in interiors than her fashion. Those interiors, her private realm, her personal sphere, Lagerfeld sought to project, to encapsulate for a new generation for whom the *legend* of Gabrielle Chanel was perhaps more seductive than the clothes she actually produced. He was also, notably, creating clothing geared to his time—an era in which fashion became a spectator sport and the designer a celebrity and performer. "People in the street didn't know about Chanel. People today know about Chanel," Lagerfeld said.[21]

Times change, and fashion changes with them. Chanel is Chanel—which is, as Karl Lagerfeld once signed a drawing, "always and never the same."

> "A Scheherazade is very easy. A Little Black Dress is very difficult."
>
> Gabrielle Chanel,
> quoted by Paul Morand, *The Allure of Chanel*

1920

1 DAY DRESS AND JACKET, HAUTE COUTURE, SPRING 1920. Gabrielle Chanel transformed black, traditionally worn for mourning, into a color of fashionability. Her "Little Black Dress"—a phrase coined in the mid-1920s, but an idea present in her earliest designs—transformed the way women dressed. It epitomizes Chanel's revolutionary approach to fashion: Akin to Adolf Loos's declaration that ornament is crime, she eschewed extraneous embellishment to emphasize the woman over the dress. Here, decoration is pared back to a simple row of functional faceted black buttons and the lustrous sheen of silk satin.

Chanel No. 5 was originally created as a limited edition for customers of the boutique, and until 1924 it was only available to Chanel clients. The original bottle's gently curved edges and thin walls were too delicate for distribution,

1921

2 CHANEL NO. 5 PERFUME. Chanel's foray into perfume also showed a willful disregard for convention. "I do not want a woman to smell like a rose," she said in an age when that was precisely what all other couturiers proposed. Chanel's debut fragrance broke every rule: It liberally used aldehydes, giving it a smell of soap rather than florals. The novel, unadorned bottle was inspired by men's toiletry flasks and whiskey decanters, a stark contrast to elaborate crystal flacons. Also unlike other perfumes with evocative, romantic names, she stripped the title back to a number: five. It was the fifth formula presented to her, and her lucky number.

circa 1924

3 DAY DRESS, HAUTE COUTURE. Among Chanel's earliest and most inventive designs, she used wool jersey, traditionally a fabric used for men's underwear, to create dresses that had the practicality and ease of sportswear. This example has buttons, but the stretch inherent in the knit means it could also be pulled on over the head, like a sweater. The only decorations are a braided trim in the same fabric—which also serves a function, as button *rouleaux*. These striking early Chanel outfits combined simplicity with stylishness and a new, modern sense of pragmatism.

Illustration of dress designs by Chanel, from *Vogue*, April 1, 1927.

1925

4 EVENING DRESS, HAUTE COUTURE. Chanel's cocktail dresses of the 1920s were the uniform of a new idea of modern woman, dubbed flappers in America and the UK, and *garçonnes* in France. The latter is particularly evocative, both as descriptor of the short boyish haircut and slender, androgyne body of the fashionable ideal, and ideologically denoting a woman with the kind of liberty previously only afforded men. Chanel's evening clothes, often with layers of handkerchief hems in fluid fabrics like chiffon, maximized the locomotive impact of the energetic dances of the period, physically expressing the newfound freedom.

Marion Morehouse, wife of poet E.E. cummings, models a black sequined dress by
Chanel, photographed by Edward Steichen for *Vogue*, 1926.

1925

5 EVENING DRESS, HAUTE COUTURE. Chanel's clothes appeared straightforward, but their simple exteriors belied complex construction techniques possible only in haute couture. By the start of the 1930s, she employed 2,400 people in twenty-six ateliers, whose expertise enabled the creation of clothes like this—which look easy but were anything but. This brief evening dress in a soft shade of rose-beige is created from petals of chiffon curving around the figure and increasing in size toward the hem. They are reminiscent of the petals of the camellia, a flower which Chanel would later adopt as one of her many signatures.

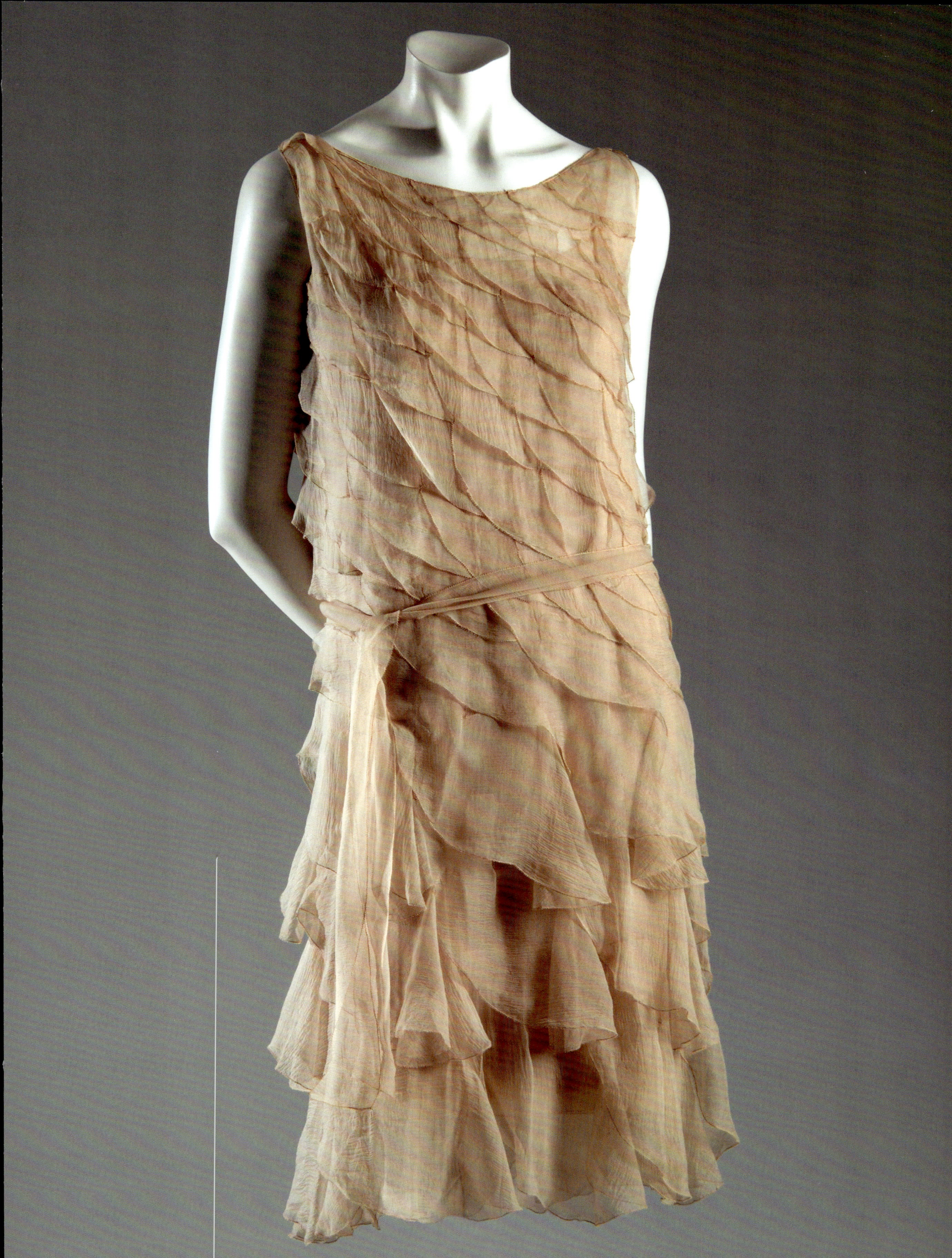

Gabrielle Chanel models her own clothes and costume jewelry, 1928.

1926

6 DAY SUIT, HAUTE COUTURE. Decades before the term gained popular use, Chanel's techniques were those of deconstruction—removing extraneous layers, stiffenings, and fastenings to streamline not only the look but also the construction. This is an early example of the famous Chanel suit in unlined wool jersey, twinned with other distinct tropes of the house: a fabric corsage and a string of artificial pearls. The striped jersey beneath recalls the Breton stripes often worn by French seamen, which first inspired Chanel's use of the fabric a decade earlier.

1926:

THE CHANEL "FORD"

which Vogue said then all the world would wear.

From Cecil Beaton's personal scrapbooks, a photo of Gabrielle Chanel and a fashion sketch from 1926.

1926

7 LITTLE BLACK DRESS, HAUTE COUTURE, AUTUMN 1926. *Vogue* hurrahed the black dresses of this collection as "The Chanel 'Ford'—the frock that all the world will wear." In wool jersey and silk satin, this day dress is simple to the point of austerity, its adornment confined to its structure of pleated skirt, blouson back, and self-fabric belt. Unique among couturiers, Chanel was unconcerned when copies of her designs appeared across the globe. Saying "Every imitation has its basis in love for the original," she viewed copies as publicity, and got immense satisfaction from the idea that she dressed the whole world.

1926

8 EVENING DRESS, HAUTE COUTURE. Chanel reveled in contradiction: Undoubtedly best known for striking simplicity, true of much of her daywear, she did not ignore embellishment for evening. Many of her cocktail dresses and gowns were exuberantly decorative. Her favored designs in the 1920s were fashionably Art Deco, using metallic sequins and embroideries, seen in this gold-and-black slip dress. The pattern of these sequins and the slender silhouette are reminiscent of the skyscrapers that were beginning to redefine city skylines.

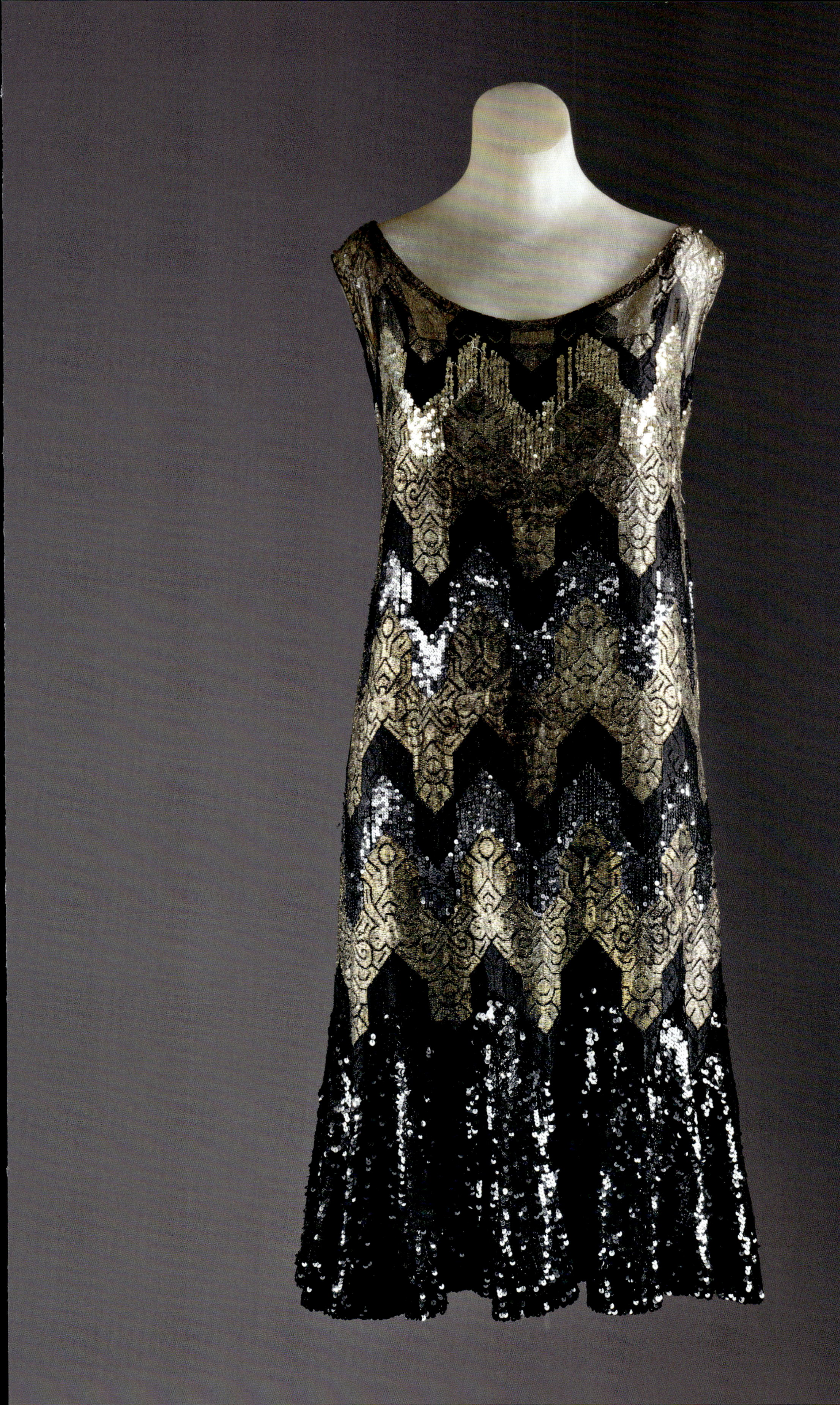

1927

> **❝ I always wanted to design dresses that women could wear for years. ❞**
>
> Gabrielle Chanel,
> quoted in "Chanel dit non," *Marie-Claire* (France), March 1967

9 EVENING DRESS, HAUTE COUTURE. This dress epitomizes Chanel's signature ease, often present in her daywear but here shown for evening. It also showcases her love for marrying simple, even plain designs with extravagant textiles, to give a restrained sense of luxury. In the same period, Chanel produced dresses in lustrous velvet and satin, as well as a number entirely hand-embroidered. This example is covered with a mosaic of gold-tinted beads, but the preciousness is lightened by the easy tie sashes and buckle belt. The rounded, unadorned neckline is also a feature of Chanel's 1920s clothes.

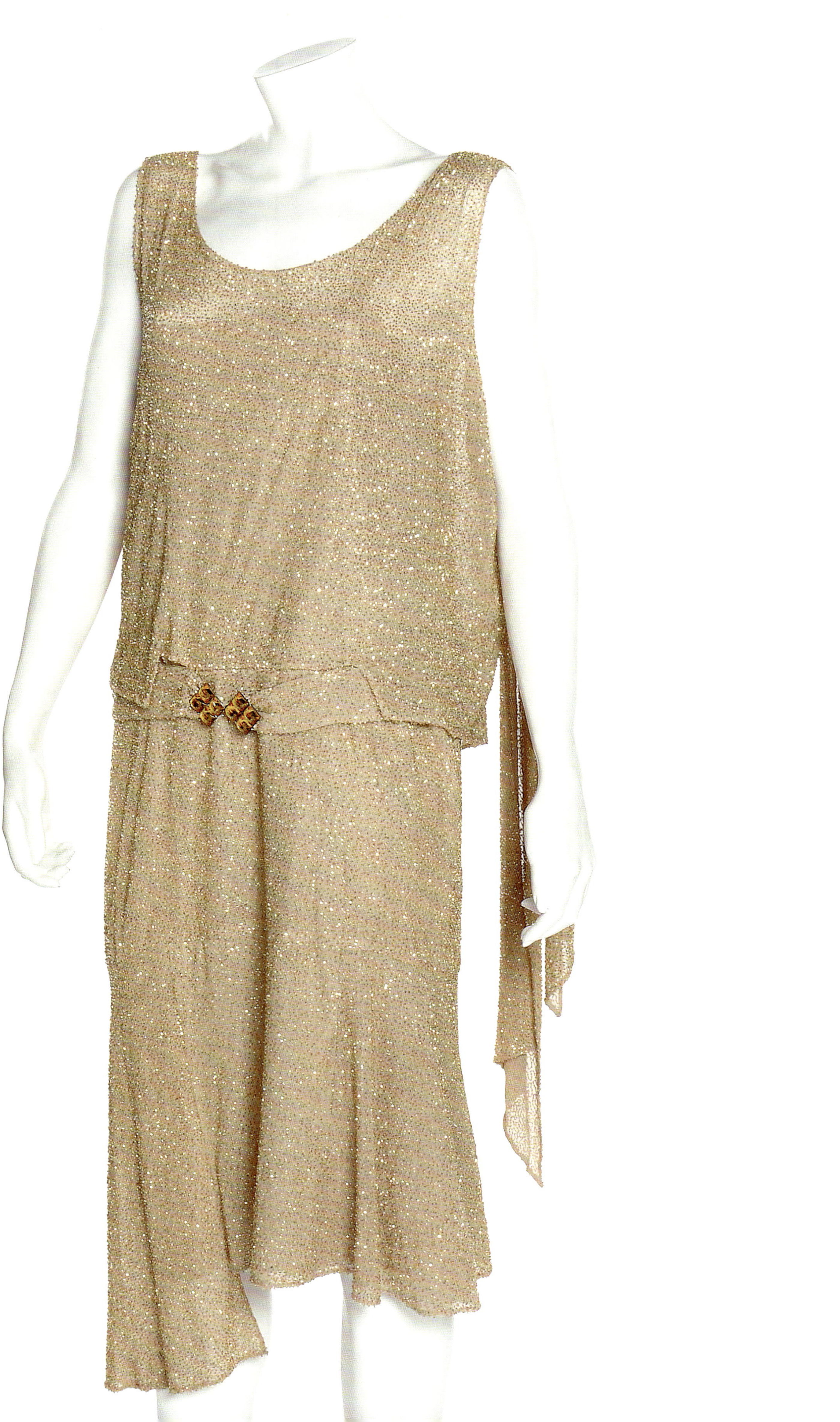

1928

10 "ICELAND" EVENING DRESS, HAUTE COUTURE. AUTUMN 1928. The late 1920s was a period of transition, with hemlines falling and waists rising, a move away from the flapper silhouette that Gabrielle Chanel helped define toward a romanticism that would characterize much of the 1930s. Although this dress retains a linear shape, the tiered skirt—each layer stiffened with horsehair for emphasis—reflects the general uncertainty around hemlines, and a white satin ribbon is tied at the natural waist. The fabric, a silver-beaded lace, is an early example of a textile that would become a new Chanel signature in the coming decade.

Model Jule Andre photographed by Edward Steichen for *Vogue*, 1928.

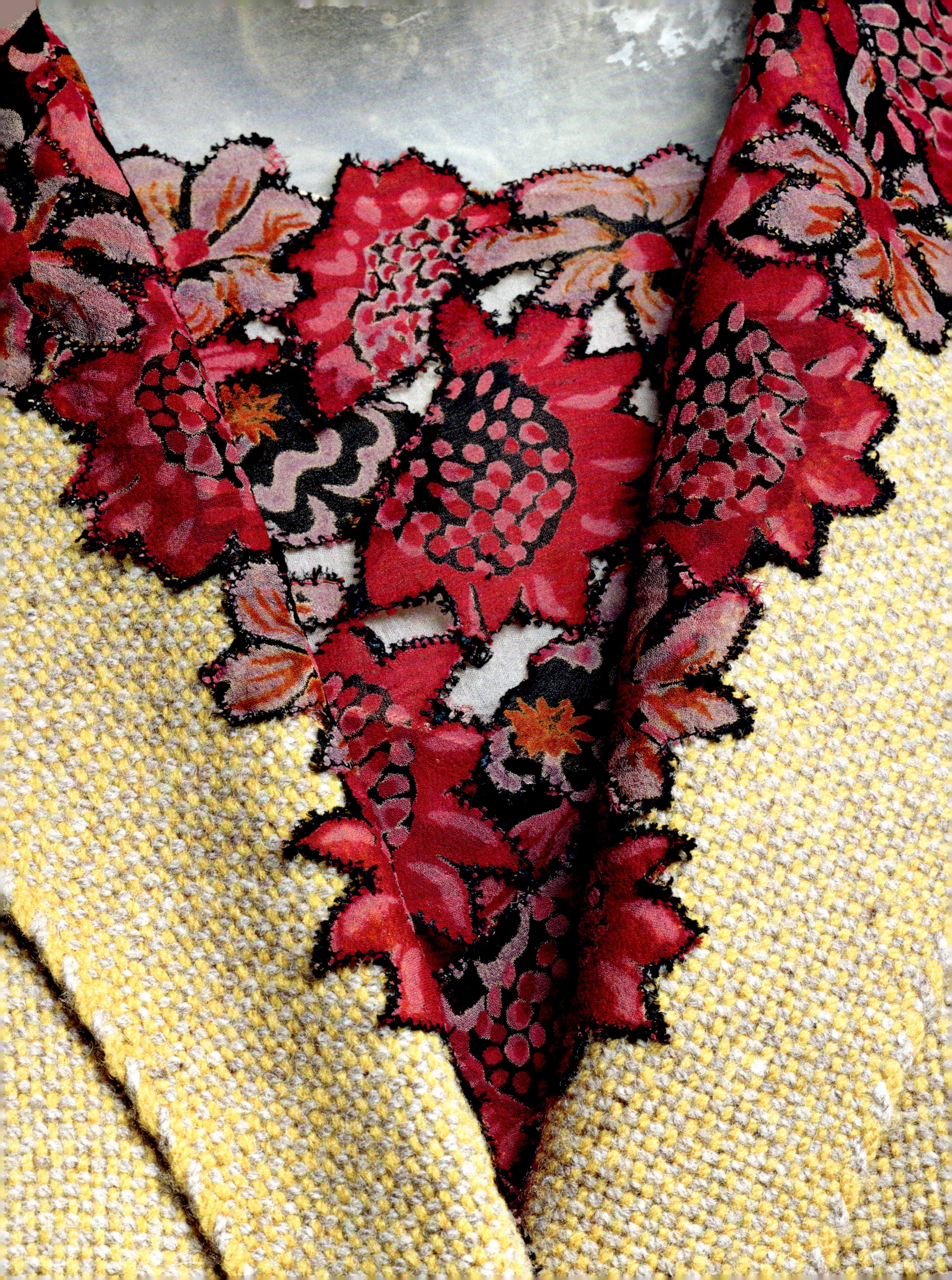

1929

11 DAY DRESS AND COAT, HAUTE COUTURE. A characteristic feature of many Chanel designs was the lining—focusing extravagance inward, for the wearer's private enjoyment, rather than projecting it outward. Often, a decorative printed lining to a jacket or coat would be matched to the dress or blouse beneath, giving the ensemble a streamlined air of dynamism. In this example, the floral silk chiffon itself has been cut out and appliquéd to the cuffs and lapels of a pale wool coat, anchoring the lining in place and simultaneously affording a frisson of decoration, albeit functional.

1930

12 EVENING DRESS, HAUTE COUTURE. The romance of Chanel's 1930s gowns was as much a reaction to the mood of the times as was her Little Black Dress. After the stock market crash, many yearned for escapism, dreaming of better things. Hollywood movies indulged audiences with epic fantasies; Chanel offered willfully romantic dresses at odds with her reputation for modernism. Those instincts, however, were still present: this dress, entirely of silk lace, is constructed with remarkable simplicity, with rows of vertical stitching rather than old-fashioned stiffening or wires to hold the flounces in place.

circa 1930

13 EVENING DRESS, HAUTE COUTURE. Lace became a Chanel signature during the 1930s. Although initially appearing anathema to her adoption of masculine fabrics and stark simplicity, the idea of a fabric whose decoration is keyed into the material itself, rather than superficially applied, ties fundamentally to Chanel's design philosophy. Here, the idea of construction as decoration is pushed further with inset ribbons of silk satin spanning the body horizontally and wittily "tied" into a bow under the bust—a reflection of Chanel's love of Breton-stripe jerseys (item 6, 1926). The decreasing scale of the bands also flatters the figure.

circa 1930

> " I love luxury. It lies not in richness and ornateness, but in the absence of vulgarity. "

Gabrielle Chanel,
quoted in *The New York Times,* July 29, 1961

14 EVENING JACKET, HAUTE COUTURE. Gabrielle Chanel's apartment at 31 rue Cambon was a riot of rich texture, crammed with *objets* and *bibelots* from across the world. She had particular affection for Asia: Her private rooms were paneled with Coromandel lacquer screens. Other than the muted palette of browns, blacks, and mother-of-pearl iridescence, these items rarely influenced her clothes. This evening jacket is a notable exception—boldly patterned silk gauze embroidered with metallic threads, it is reconfigured from a traditional Chinese robe but shows her signature simplicity and exactitude in the matching of its intricate motif.

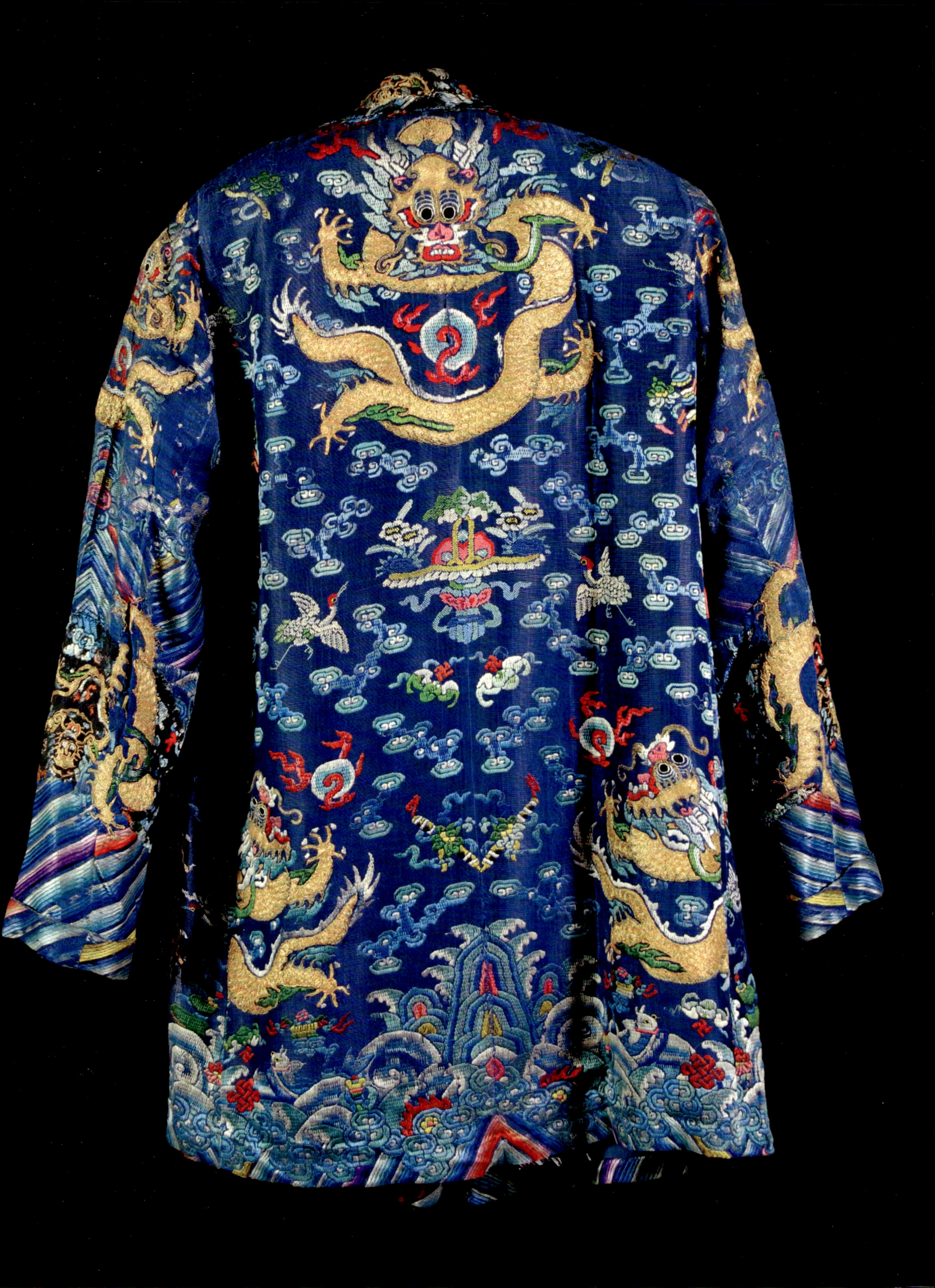

Gabrielle Chanel and Italian jeweler Fulco di Verdura, 1937.

1930

15 ENAMEL CUFF BRACELETS. Chanel collaborated with Duke Fulco di Verdura in the creation of ostentatious fake jewelry—a notion that Chanel not only popularized but legitimized in fashionable circles. The addition of dramatic faux bijoux to her austere designs was calculated, to give decorative richness. These enamel bracelets, designed to be worn in pairs, were set with deliberately mismatched semiprecious stones in Byzantine motifs. Worn often by Chanel herself during the 1930s—both day and evening—they rapidly became recognizable imprints of an expanding Chanel style.

ANOTHER big fashion "scoop" for PHOTOPLAY! Once again we are able to give you an exclusive preview of the Chanel-designed clothes that you will see Gloria Swanson wear in "Tonight or Never." And, according to our reviewers, Samuel Goldwyn has made a picture worthy of the clothes.

Look at those wing-like draperies! Who but Chanel would add them to a black velvet evening gown? Who but Gloria could wear them so smartly? Both front and back decolletages are tricky. Those are jeweled clips on the shoulder. Note the straighter line, too

Chanel goes in for sleeves in a big way, it seems. Huge muffs of fur match a face-framing collar on the short satin jacket which accompanies this regal white satin evening gown. That train is dramatic, isn't it?

52

Gloria Swanson wearing Chanel costumes for the film *Tonight or Never*, from *Photoplay* magazine, January 1932.

1931

16 EVENING DRESS, HAUTE COUTURE. In March 1931, Chanel traveled to Hollywood to design costumes at the behest of Samuel Goldwyn at United Artists. Chanel was the first couturier to do so, a response to the quickly changing fashions of 1929–30, when the sudden drop in hemlines rendered many film costumes obsolete. She was offered $1 million a year to design the on- and off-screen wardrobes for stars including Ina Claire and Gloria Swanson, who wore this glamorous gold embroidered dress. Chanel designed costumes for three Hollywood pictures: *Palmy Days* (1931), *Tonight or Never* (1931), and *The Greeks Had a Word for It* (1932).

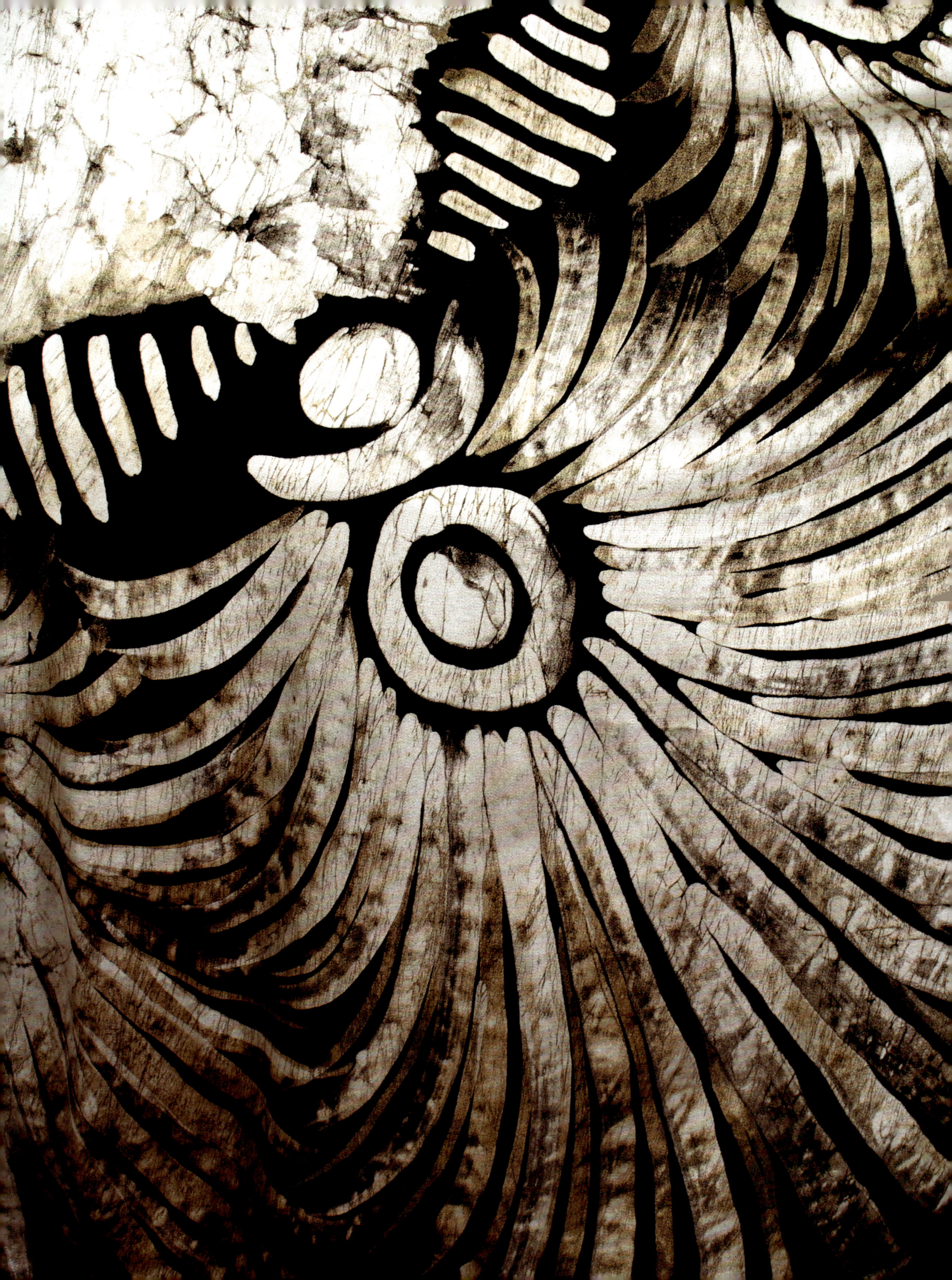

1931

17 EVENING CLOAK, HAUTE COUTURE. By 1930, Chanel was one of the largest couture houses in Paris—and the single most profitable. Through the following decade, Chanel expressed a new sense of luxury in her designs—perhaps paradoxically in response to the hardships of the Great Depression. This cloak is trimmed in sable—previously a fur Chanel had eschewed in favor of rabbit, stating, "I had decided to replace expensive furs with the humblest hides." The pattern is a batik-style print, and its arrangement around the hem attests that the fabric was specially made for this piece.

1932

> " I wanted to cover women with constellations! With stars! Stars of all sizes! "
>
> Gabrielle Chanel

18 COMÈTE NECKLACE. In the depths of the Great Depression, Chanel bucked her own trend for fake gems and launched her first fine jewelry collection, created from platinum and diamonds set in the forms of stars. The jewelry was articulated to drape softly around the body, as Chanel declared she loathed clasps. The means of display was also novel: shown on lifelike wax mannequins instead of in velvet-lined coffers. The exhibition was to show Chanel's prowess and to generate interest in the ailing diamond industry; an entrance fee was charged, which was donated to charity.

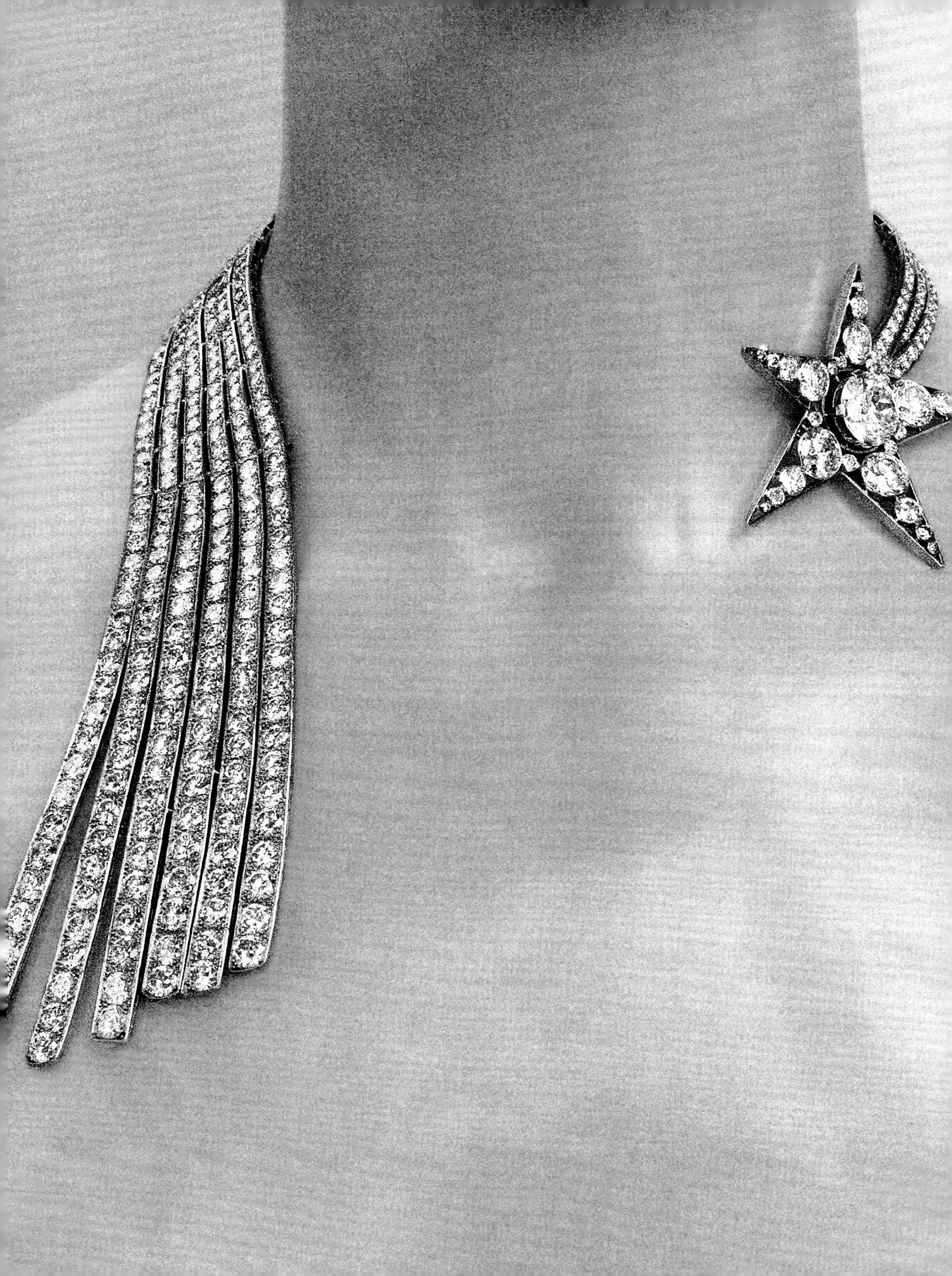

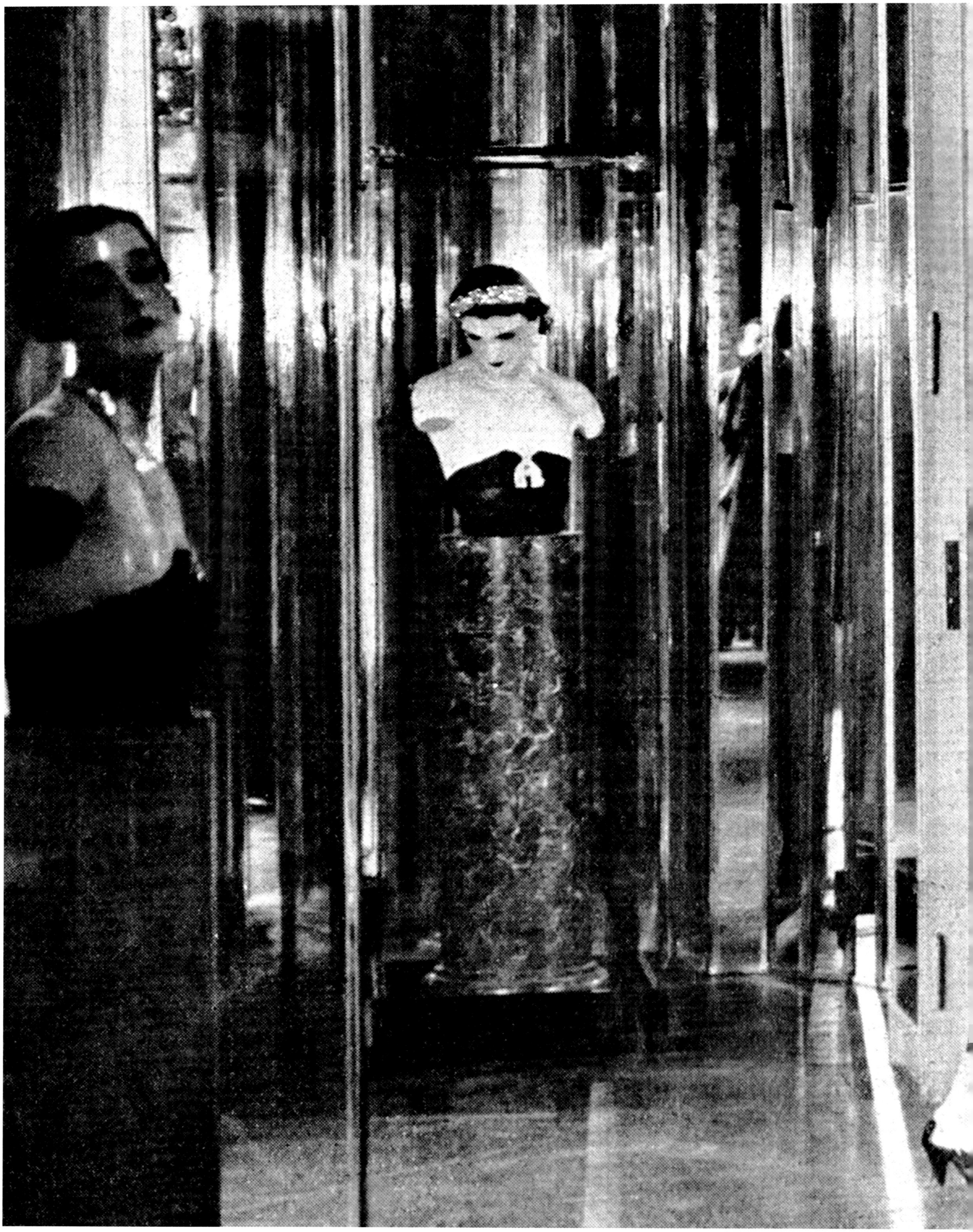

The *Bijoux de Diamants* exhibition, photographed by André Kertész for *Vogue Paris*, January 1933.

circa 1932

19 EVENING ENSEMBLE, HAUTE COUTURE. In the 1930s, Chanel elongated her Little Black Dresses into elegant gowns that count among her finest designs. More traditionally feminine than her work from the previous decade, these garments referenced the slender, bustled silhouettes of the late nineteenth century, an inspiration for many couturiers of the period. Yet she continued to experiment, drawing ire from the French silk industry for her use of humble fabrics for evening. Here, cotton tulle is cut into a dreamy dress—the picot-edged ruffles are featherweight yet voluminous, giving drama to the skirt and matching short cape.

1937

20 EVENING ENSEMBLE, HAUTE COUTURE, AUTUMN 1937. Chanel often took inspiration from Gypsy styles—the tiered skirt and bolero jacket here are reminiscent of Andalusian costume. Chanel's 1930s collections often featured gathered skirts and puff-sleeve blouses, in which one can detect the lines of Spanish or Romany and Slavic folk styles—the latter possibly influenced by her affair with Grand Duke Dmitri Pavlovich in 1920–21. Rather than specific regional references, it was a picturesque idea of Gypsy dress that Chanel's work evoked—the notion of the "noble peasant" also explored in avant-garde art of the period.

1937

> " True elegance consists in not being noticed. "
>
> Gabrielle Chanel,
> quoted in "L'élégance et le naturel,"
> *La Revue des Sports et du Monde,* October 1934

21 DAY SUIT, HAUTE COUTURE. Even as she explored a new taste for decoration through the 1930s, Gabrielle Chanel always returned to the stark and severe. Executed in dark linen, unadorned and plainly cut, this style can be seen as a hangover from the convent habits of Chanel's childhood—she was raised from the age of 12 in an orphanage in Aubazine, where she learned to sew, and whose values of frugality impacted her nascent aesthetic. This outfit, another evolution of Chanel's emblematic suit, also recalls a maid's uniform, a revolutionary proposal for wealthy women, summing up another of her maxims: Elegance is refusal.

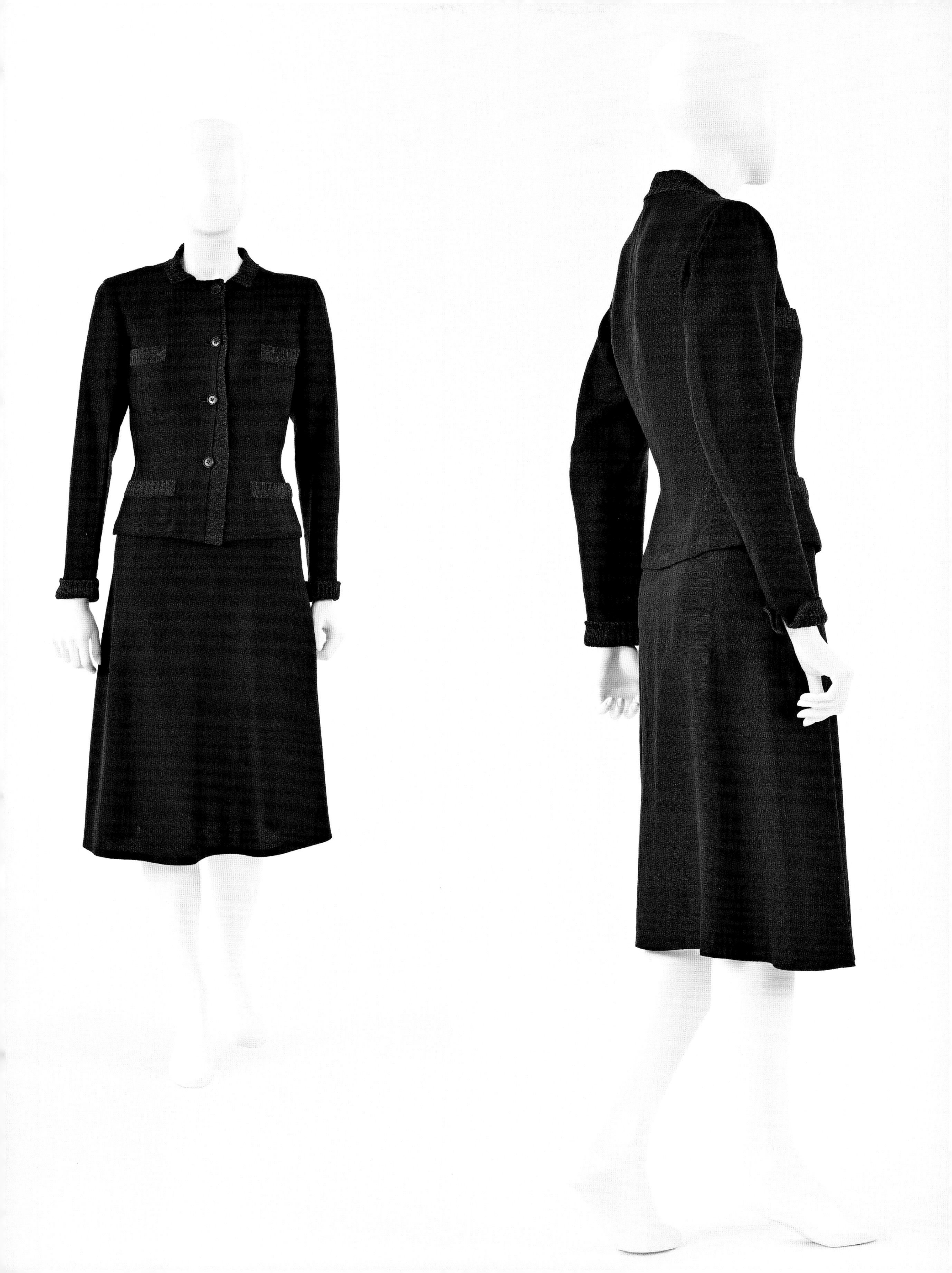

circa 1937

22 EVENING DRESS, HAUTE COUTURE. Fabric flowers have always been a Chanel signature; later, she would pin only camellias to her suits, but in the 1920s and 1930s she often trimmed evening gowns with varied corsages, in matching or contrasting tones, to animate her linear styles. This dramatically simple black silk lace gown is enlivened by a corsage of violets, gardenias, and chrysanthemums in raw-cut linen—the quintessentially Chanel contrast of black and white. This is also a rare example of a Chanel dress featuring a boned bodice, here a necessary device to support the low back and off-the-shoulder neckline.

Illustration of Chanel evening frocks, from *Vogue* UK, July 8, 1936.

1938

> ❝ The point of jewelry isn't to make a woman look rich but to adorn her—not the same thing. ❞
>
> Gabrielle Chanel,
> quoted by Axel Madsen, *Chanel: A Woman of Her Own*

23 EVENING DRESS, HAUTE COUTURE. Although Gabrielle Chanel would introduce her chain belts in the 1950s, through the 1930s she experimented with the notion of this functional accessory as a point of interest and decoration. This lace gown, in Chanel's favored beige, is clasped by a vaguely floral Art Deco jewel set with rhinestones and blue glass. The cut of the dress also streamlines the fabric against the figure, in contrast with her more romantic ruffled designs of the period. Chanel was photographed wearing dresses in similar styles at her apartment at rue Cambon, acting as her own best model.

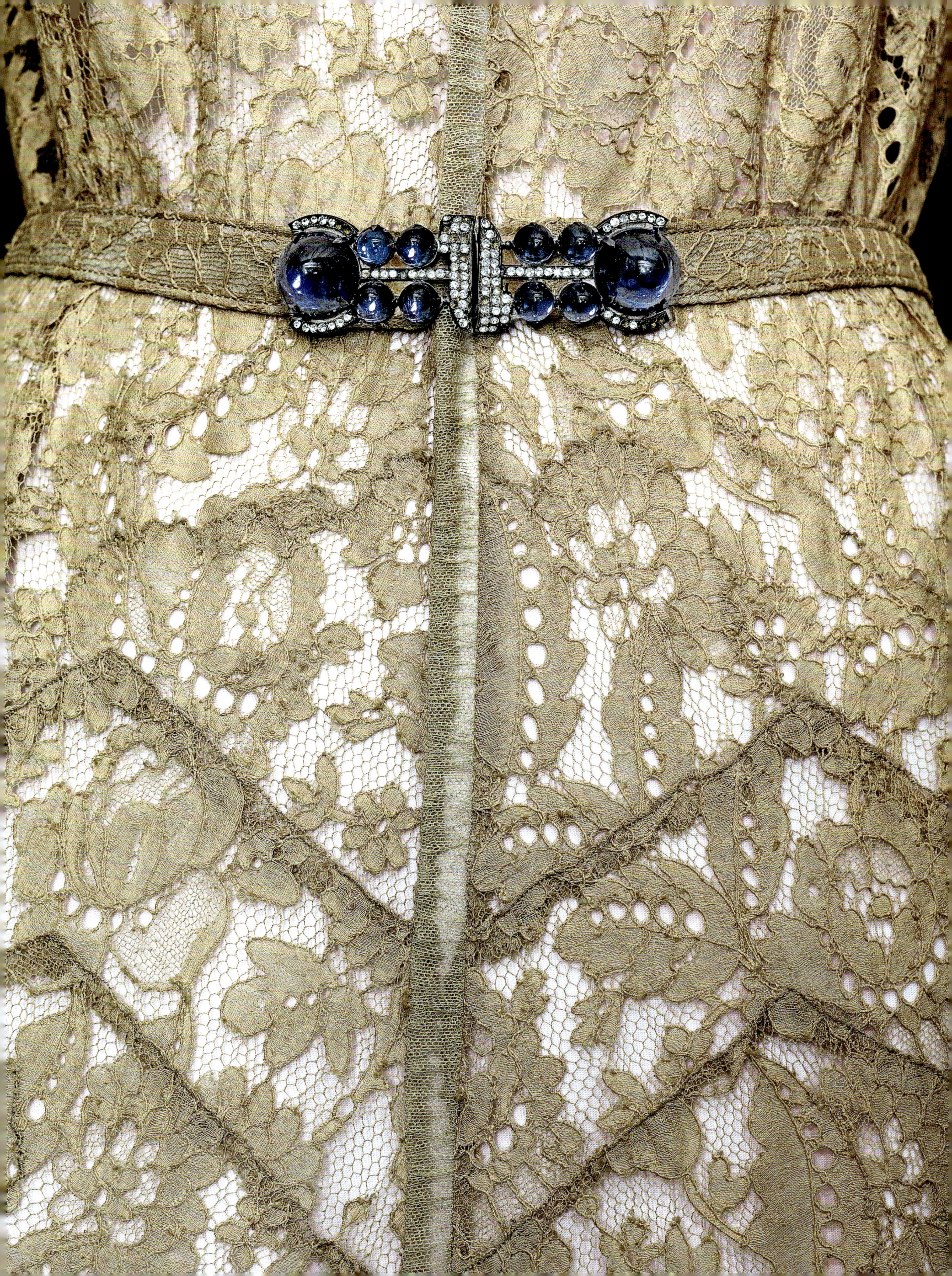

1938

> ❝ No need to be a genius to create fashions; you just need professional experience, and a little taste. ❞
>
> Gabrielle Chanel,
> quoted by Françoise Giraud,
> "La femme de la semaine: Chanel," *L'Express,* August 17, 1956

24 EVENING DRESS, HAUTE COUTURE, AUTUMN 1938. Inspired by the Fountain necklace in Chanel's 1932 *Bijoux de Diamants* exhibition (item 18, 1932), created in collaboration with the artist—and Chanel's lover—Paul Iribe, this dress features a flow of sequin embroidery across silk tulle. One of a trio of dresses in different colorways, this example has a restrained tonal embroidery that chimes with Chanel's continual urge to pare back, as does the simple camisole-strap shape. Notably, Chanel's embroidered evening dresses of the 1930s were shown with minimal or no jewelry, the embellishment instead applied to the garment itself.

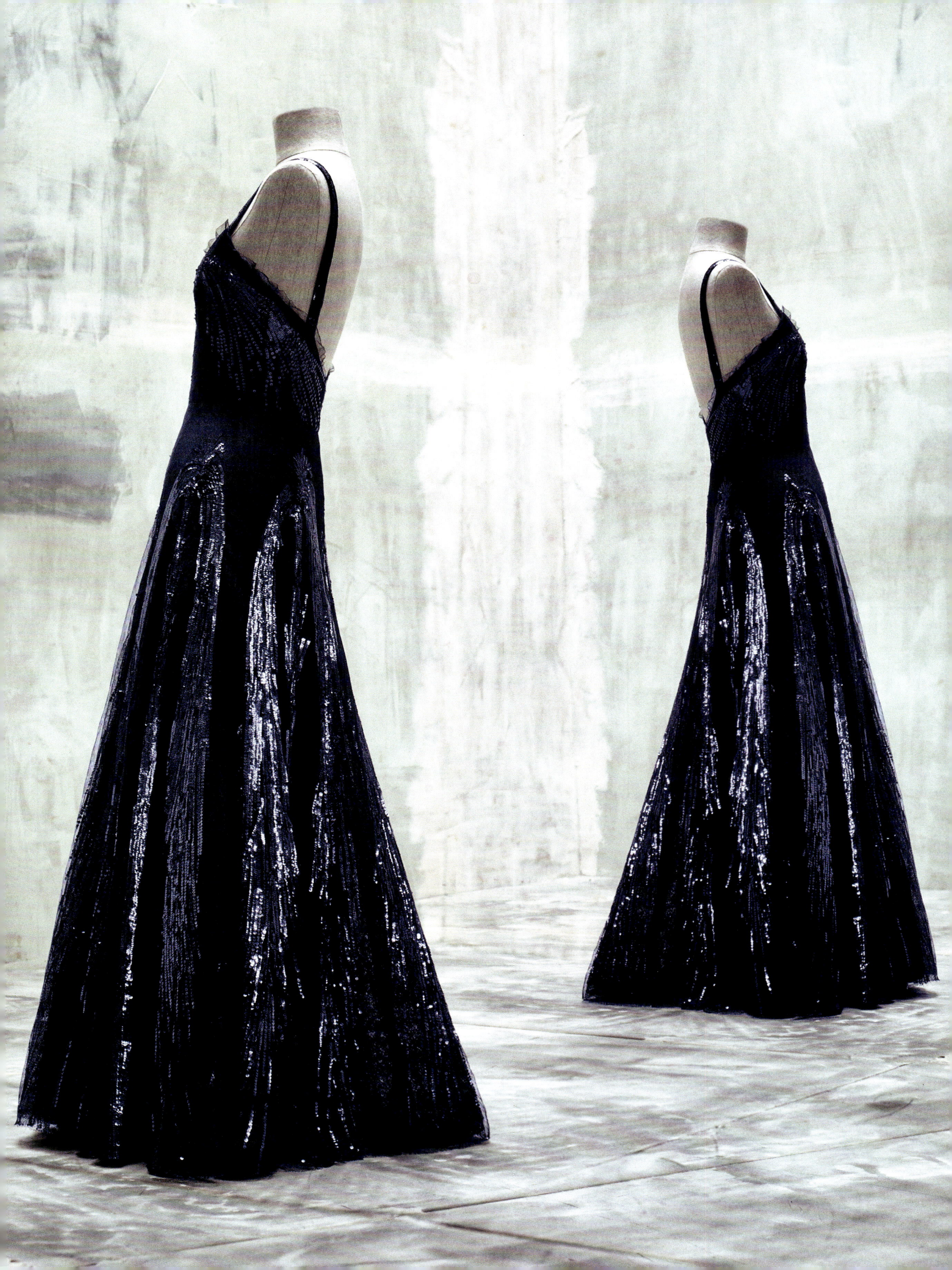

Gabrielle Chanel photographed by George Hoyningen-Huene, 1939.

1939

25 THEATER SUIT, HAUTE COUTURE. AUTUMN 1939. As war crept closer, Paris couturiers indulged in fantasies of other cultures and eras. This velvet evening suit, from the final collection Chanel presented before the outbreak of conflict in Europe in September, references the work of Watteau and eighteenth-century male attire. Once owned by the legendary Diana Vreeland—then fashion editor of U.S. *Harper's Bazaar*—the suit is executed in her favored shade of red, while Chanel herself owned and wore a version in black (*opposite*). After showing this collection, Chanel closed her couture operation until 1953.

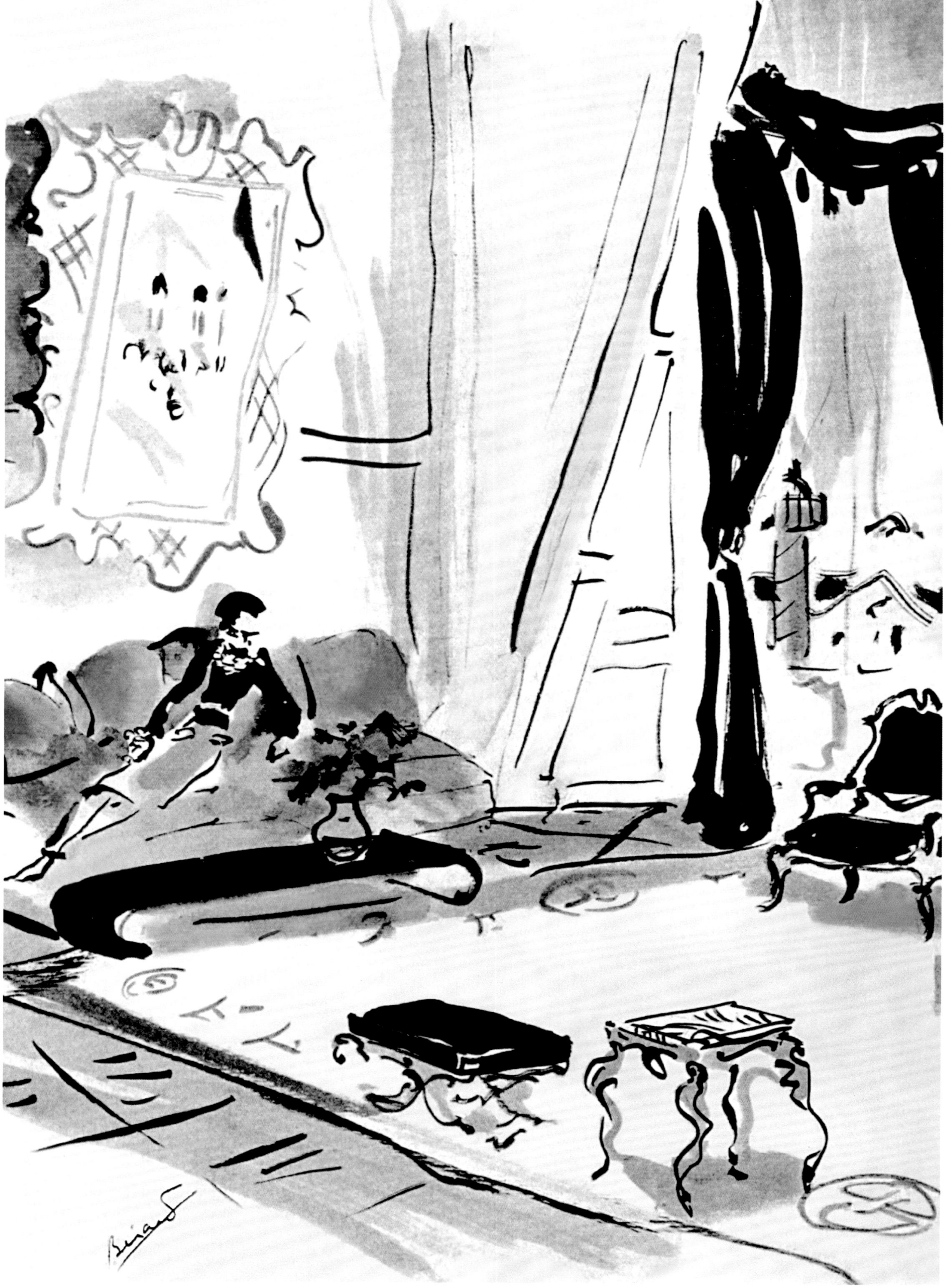

GABRIELLE CHANEL

Chanel, the winner of this year's Neiman-Marcus Award, has, in the last three years, reimposed "the Chanel look" on women who knew it before and has imposed it on a whole new generation who never heard of it before. The woman behind "the Chanel look" is small and ageless with snapping black eyes, a wide beguiling grin, and a little-boy figure. She leads a moderate life, eats the simplest food at regular hours (she refuses to dine any longer at Balenciaga's house because his late Spanish dining hour doesn't please her), and walks in the woods for exercise with the relaxed grace of a gazelle. She wears her own simple, easy Chanel clothes better than anyone else in the world. The silk blouse and jersey skirt she is wearing in this picture, with the addition of a jersey jacket, is typical of what she has worn forever; but on her it always has a contemporary look. She invented the "Chanel stance," a way of standing with hips forward, stomach in, shoulders relaxed, one foot forward, one hand plunged in a pocket, and the other hand gesticulating as she talks. She is temperate in everything but talk. This she does with a witty river of words tumbling out in theories about life, clothes, friends, places, art, or in amusing anecdotes about fascinating people.

When Chanel reopened her Rue Cambon shop three years ago, she stood up against the most virulent criticism the French press could print. What small applause she had came from America, a sort of creeping appreciation that gained by word of mouth, and from a few faithful customers who were happy to wear her easy clothes again. Chanel herself, a wily and articulate fighter, was quick to turn the criticism into a controversy. She challenged the press, saying, "I design clothes that make women look young; easy clothes in which women can move and feel free. I'm not trying to hide them in ridiculous fashions!" Women began to think there was something in what she said, the buyers and press took a second look—and the Chanel boom was on. Chanel shrugged her shoulders and grinned. She had loved the fight.

Coco Chanel lives against a background of beige, with rich treasures in antique bronze lions, Coromandel screens, ancient Chinese animals, modern sculpture, Louis XV furniture, and mountains of books. She built a fashion empire on jersey and lace. She made fake jewels elegant by designing them colorfully and boldly and by wearing them herself with her own fabulous real jewels. She taught women the comfort of an easy, unclinging skirt; how important a pocket, a belt, or a bow could be to fashion. She made the earring an everyday accessory and the long string of pearls and colored beads the rage. She made jersey handbags in which a woman could find what she needed. She designs with a woman's instinct for women's needs. Chanel richly deserves a reward for many things but, above all, for making women feel the rightness of youthful, easy, understated fashion and for having the generosity to say, "I like to be copied," and to mean it.   —Bettina Ballard

Article from *Town & Country* magazine, September 1957, congratulating Chanel on winning the Neiman Marcus Award for Distinguished Service in the Field of Fashion.
Opposite: Drawing of Chanel in her suite at the Ritz, by Christian Bérard, 1937.

1954

> **"Women think of every color, except the absence of colors. I have said that black had everything. White too. They have an absolute beauty."**
>
> Gabrielle Chanel,
> quoted by Paul Morand, *The Allure of Chanel*

26 LITTLE BLACK DRESS, HAUTE COUTURE, SPRING 1954. After fifteen years away from fashion, Gabrielle Chanel reopened her couture house, and on February 5, 1954, presented a new collection, thus reviving her ethos and identity, although her styles had evolved: Her clothes were a logical, pragmatic counterpoint to the corseted and petticoated propositions of male couturiers, whom Chanel accused of "upholstering" women. This Little Black Dress, juxtaposing luxurious black silk velvet with humble ivory cotton organdy, was purchased and worn by another enduring icon: Marlene Dietrich.

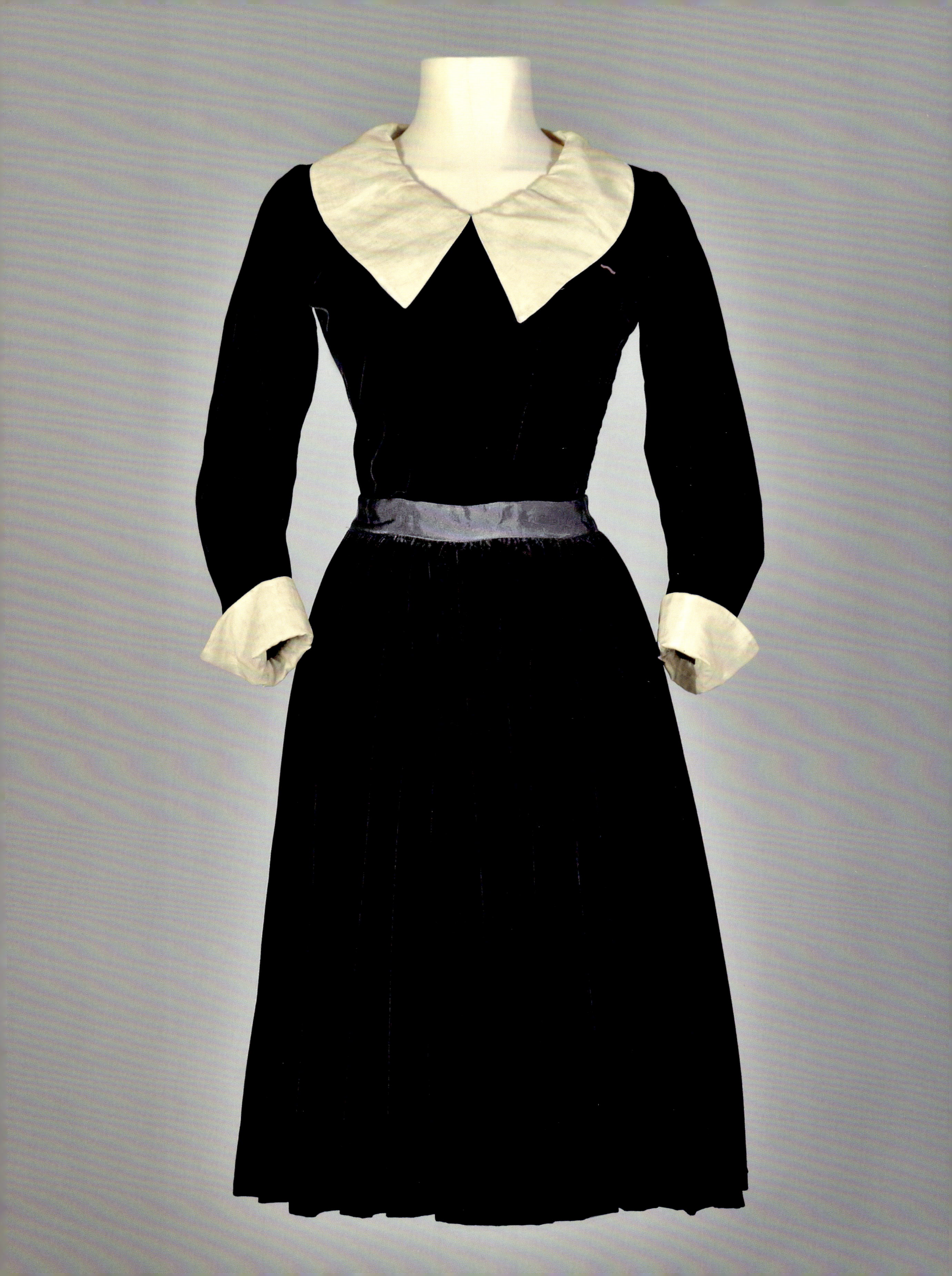

1955

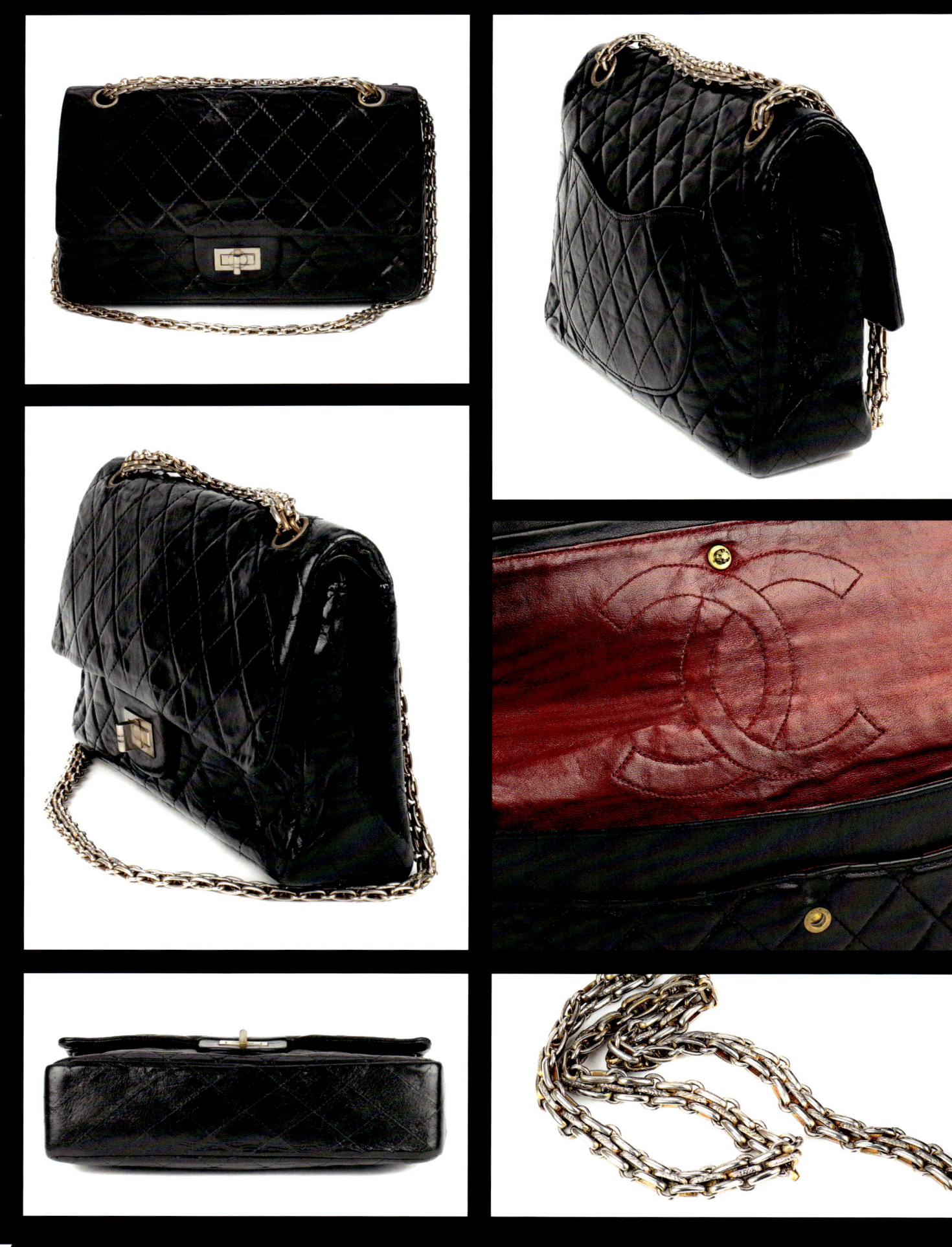

27 **2.55 HANDBAG.** Chanel first designed shoulder bags in the 1920s, influenced by soldiers' knapsacks. When her fashion house reopened, she revisited the idea, combining mythology with practicality: Named simply 2.55, after the month and year it was launched, its burgundy lining and chain strap were suggestive of the uniforms and chatelaines of her Catholic upbringing; the adjustable strap could be suspended from the hand or the shoulder, affording freedom; and the contrast lining allowed the wearer to easily locate belongings. The leather or jersey exterior, quilted in diamonds or chevron stripes, referenced the structure of Chanel's suits, and also riding clothes.

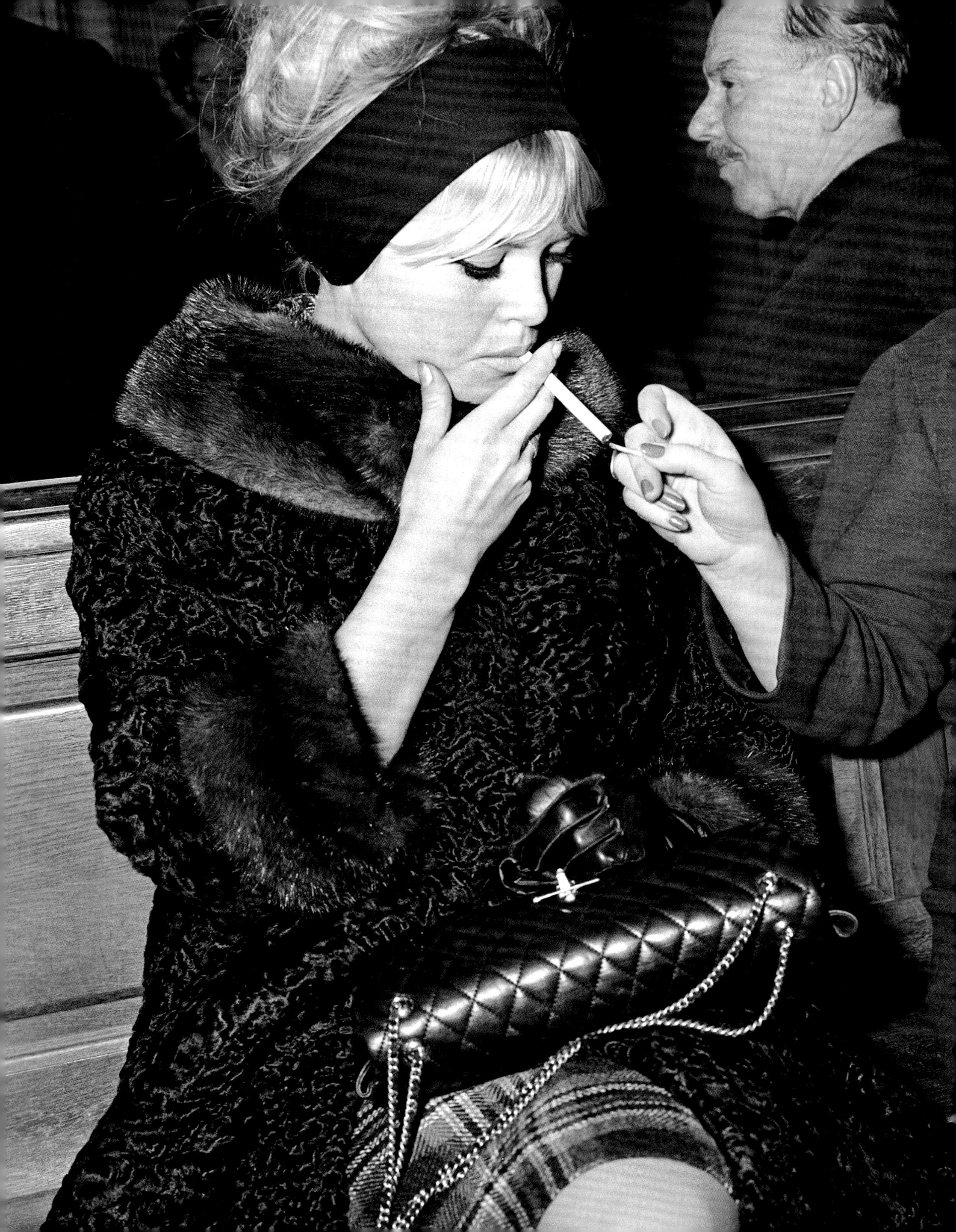

1956

> ❝ I believe that style belongs to the street, in everyday life, like a revolution. That's the real style. ❞
>
> Gabrielle Chanel

28 COCKTAIL SUIT, HAUTE COUTURE, AUTUMN 1956. Originally devised as early as 1916, with her "entire sports costume" of one-piece dress and jacket, the Chanel suit was introduced in its pure form in her comeback collection of February 1954. Its format was already set: a loose-waisted jacket with high armholes and slender sleeves, worn with an easy skirt just below the knee. For the rest of her life Chanel would continue to refine this system for dressing, subtly evolving new shapes and cuts, but setting herself apart from the vagaries of fashion, silhouette, and hemline. Here, the Chanel suit is proposed as cocktail attire, richly lined in white satin.

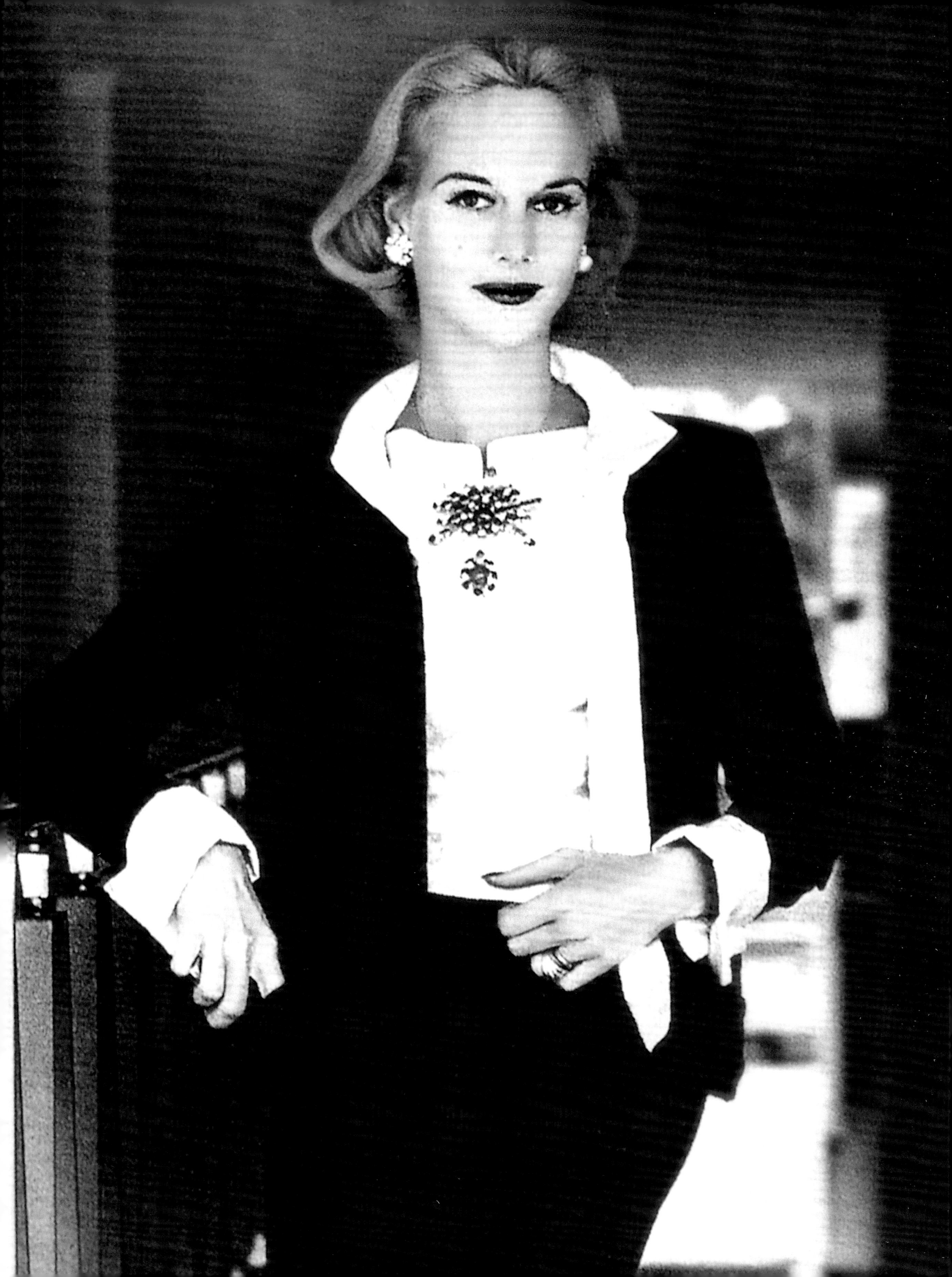

1956

29 EVENING DRESS, HAUTE COUTURE. Chanel favored neutral, masculine, and monochrome colors, but she also had a fondness for brilliant scarlet lipstick. Indeed, as early as 1926, when her Little Black Dress first found fame, *Women's Wear Daily* dubbed a shade "Chanel Red." Soft, billowing chiffon, worn by model Suzy Parker, creates a seductive image of femininity. Yet this dress is eminently practical—the flowing cape covers the upper arms, which Chanel reasoned were what women felt most uncomfortable about in later life. The cape is also shorter at the front than the back to allow movement.

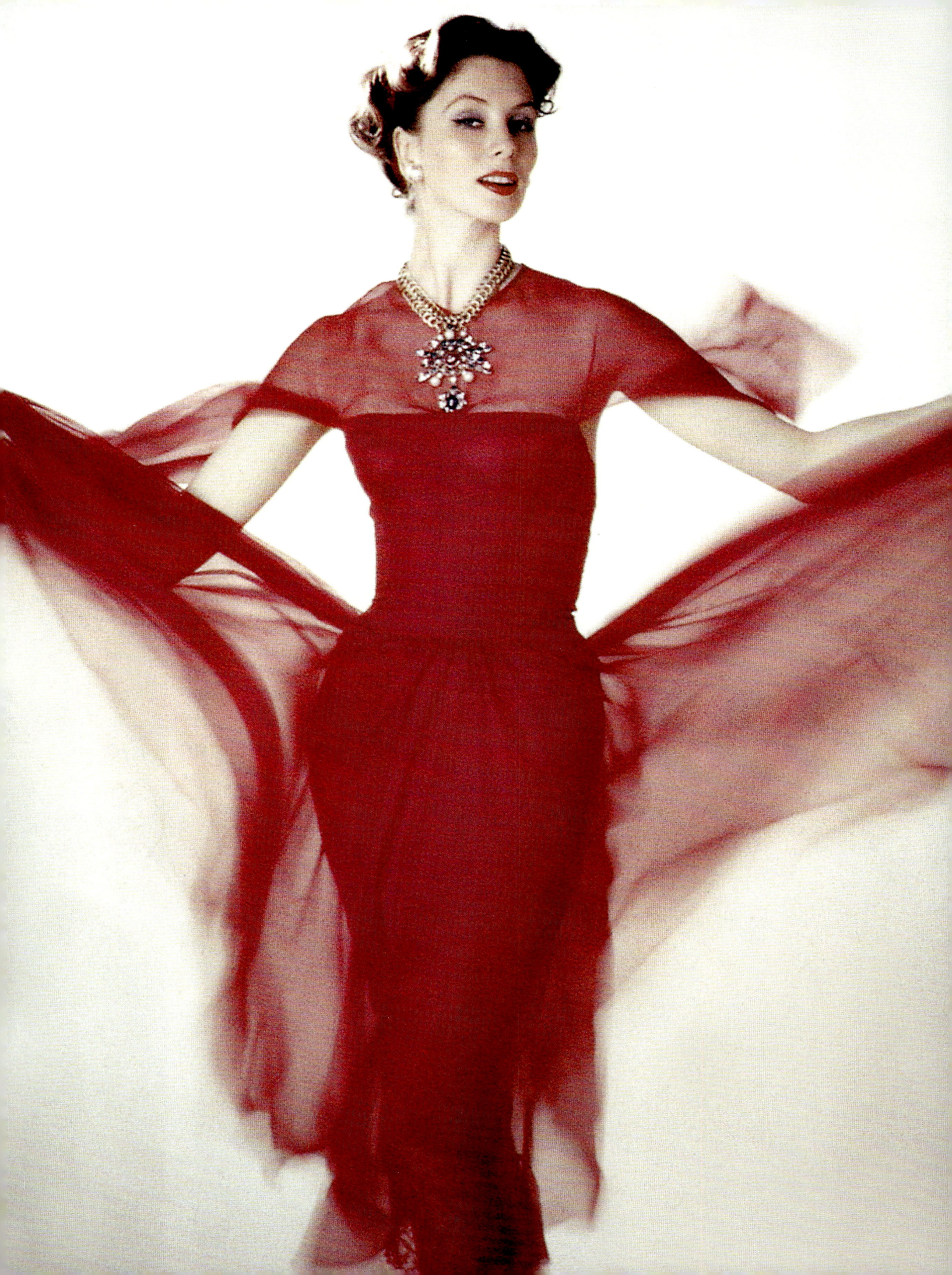

1957

30 COCKTAIL DRESS, HAUTE COUTURE. Although Gabrielle Chanel proposed an alternative to the highly structured postwar styles of Parisian couturiers like Christian Dior and Jacques Fath, she also created dresses that melded her aesthetic with the shifting tastes of the times. These cocktail dresses in chiffon and lace reference the Gypsy-influenced styles of Chanel's 1930s modes (item 20, 1937), but the full skirts and gently pinched waists also bear the undeniable imprint of the 1950s. Here, Chanel is fitting Princess Odile de Cröy, a model of her *cabine*—at this time, models worked exclusively for a single fashion house.

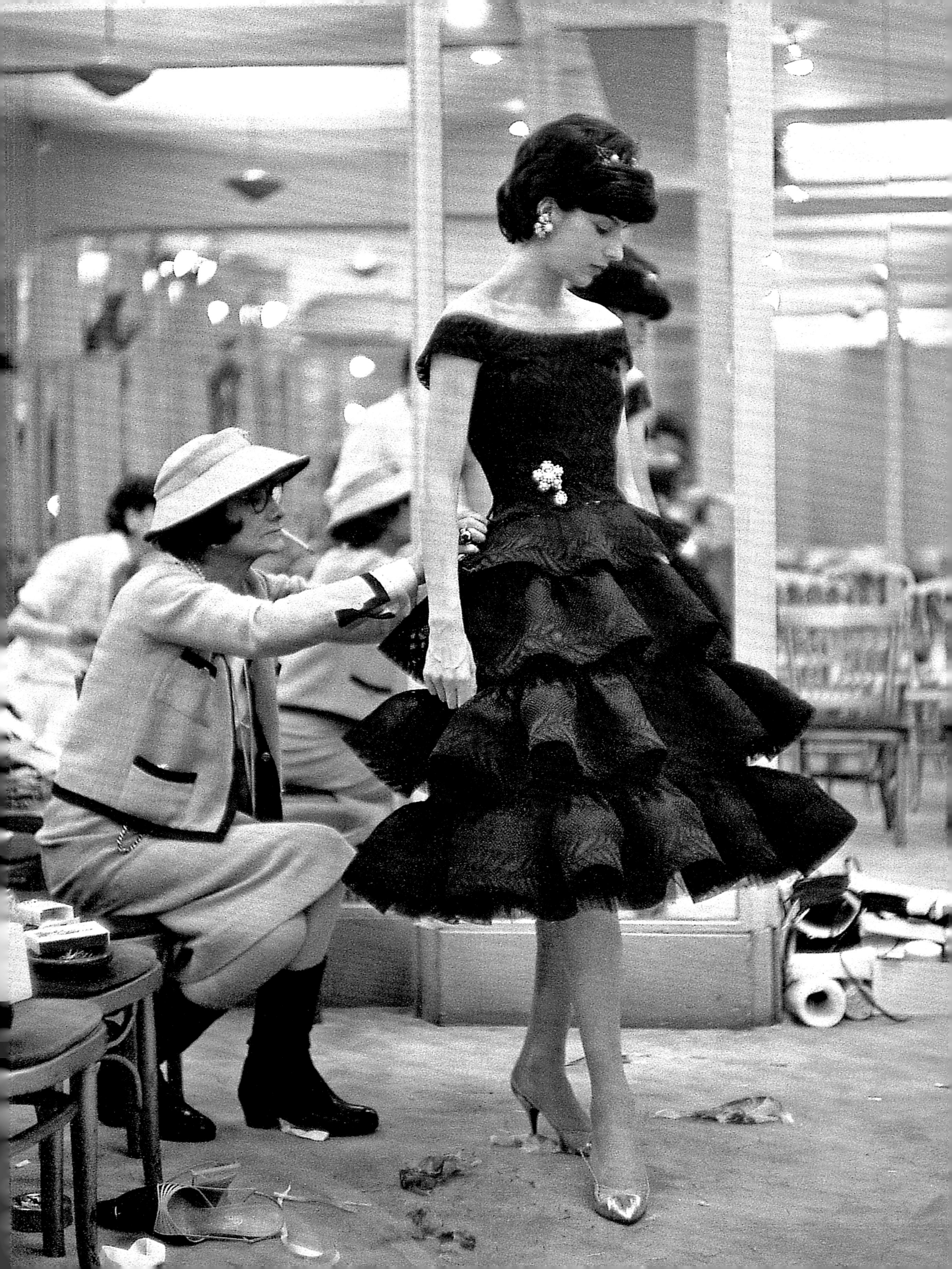

1958

31 LEATHER AND SATIN SHOES. Chanel designed these famous two-tone pumps in 1958, executed with the couture shoemaker Raymond Massaro. A low heel allows easy movement, as does the elasticized sling-back strap, the first application of this element to shoes without a buckle. The design of the shoe creates not one but two optical illusions: Instead of an impractical high heel, it is the vamp of the shoe, in beige leather, that serves to elongate the leg, ending with an emphatic black satin toe cap, which is gently rounded rather than sharply pointed, flatteringly shortening the foot.

1958

32 DAY SUIT, HAUTE COUTURE, AUTUMN 1958. Chanel wanted fashion to be logical, hence her timeless legacy of the sensitive, sensible Chanel suit, filled with details to ease everyday life that could, arguably, only be fully appreciated when worn and lived in. An idea explored by Chanel since the early 1900s, many of its composite parts are in place here—more about attitude than look or materials. Chanel asserted that pockets should always be functional and that a button should never be used without a buttonhole; she cut her skirts gently flared, sometimes with a central front panel with two pleats, to facilitate movement.

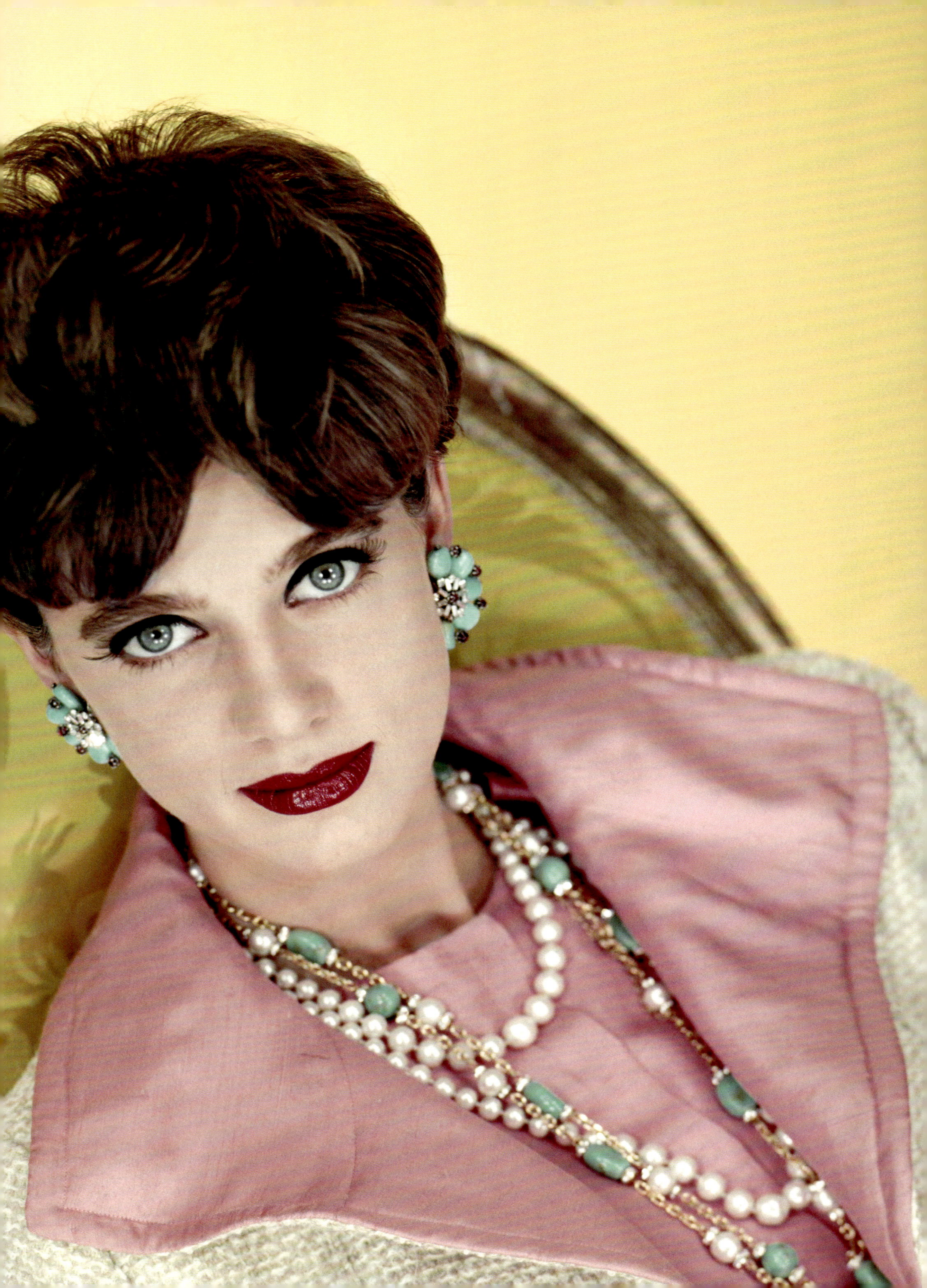

1959

33 COSTUME JEWELRY. "I started creating costume jewelry because I felt it was refreshingly free of arrogance," Chanel once said. In 1954, she began to work again with Gripoix, which had created bijoux for her in the 1930s, and forged a new relationship with jeweler Robert Goossens, then just 27. She repurposed his chain necklaces as belts, which became a house identifier, alongside designs inspired by Renaissance or Byzantine shapes, such as this Goossens brooch. Influenced by Chanel's mixing of real and simulated jewels in her own attire, pieces often combined precious stones with glass, blurring lines between real and make-believe.

1959

34 DAY SUIT, HAUTE COUTURE, AUTUMN 1959. Chanel loved checked fabrics, and here uses two types—a bold Vichy and a subtle Prince of Wales—exploring their graphic qualities while showcasing her ateliers' skill. The Vichy check of the matching jacket lining and sleeveless blouse also trims the patch pockets and cuffs. All patterns are perfectly matched across lapels and bias-bound pocket edges, the apex of each curve ending in an identical black stripe. The Prince of Wales check also matches across sleeve-head, pockets, and the line where the jacket meets the skirt, in a remarkable display of finicky perfectionism and couture prowess.

1960

35 EVENING SUIT, HAUTE COUTURE, AUTUMN 1960. This ensemble demonstrates Chanel's affinity for elaborate fabrics married to simple silhouettes for evening, by the 1960s often proposed with Asian-inspired brocades and figured lamés. This brief dress and boxy jacket hark back to clothes she created during the 1910s, and the first incarnation of the Chanel suit. The jacket is free from fastenings except the self-tie bow, while the straps at the back of the dress recall racer-back swim attire. The gently flared box-pleat skirt was a shape Chanel explored during the 1960s, to allow movement and create surface interest without embellishment.

1960

36 DAY SUIT, HAUTE COUTURE. Frequently Chanel trimmed garments with grosgrain ribbon or ribbed knit to both decorative and practical extent, to reinforce edges against daily wear and to offer a graphic focal point. The signature low-slung pockets were purportedly positioned to best hold packets of her omnipresent cigarettes. Gabrielle Chanel herself wore these suits as a uniform, and many of the innovations were born from her personal experience as a wearer: In this model, a tab attaches the blouse to the skirt, holding it securely in position, a feature introduced around 1957.

circa 1960

37 DAY SUIT, HAUTE COUTURE. *Tailleur* is the French term for a suit, but Chanel's are not tailored in the traditional sense. A lifelong proponent of softness in her coats and jackets—she removed linings as early as the 1910s, to give pieces suppleness and lightness—from 1959 Chanel pioneered a technique of quilting the lining directly to the outer fabric, without an interlining, lending structure to the jacket and stabilizing the wide-woven bouclé tweed, whose surface in turn hides the stitching. A chain is sewn into the hem to weight the fabric and hold it straight. Even today, Chanel tailoring still uses these methods, unlike those of any other couture house.

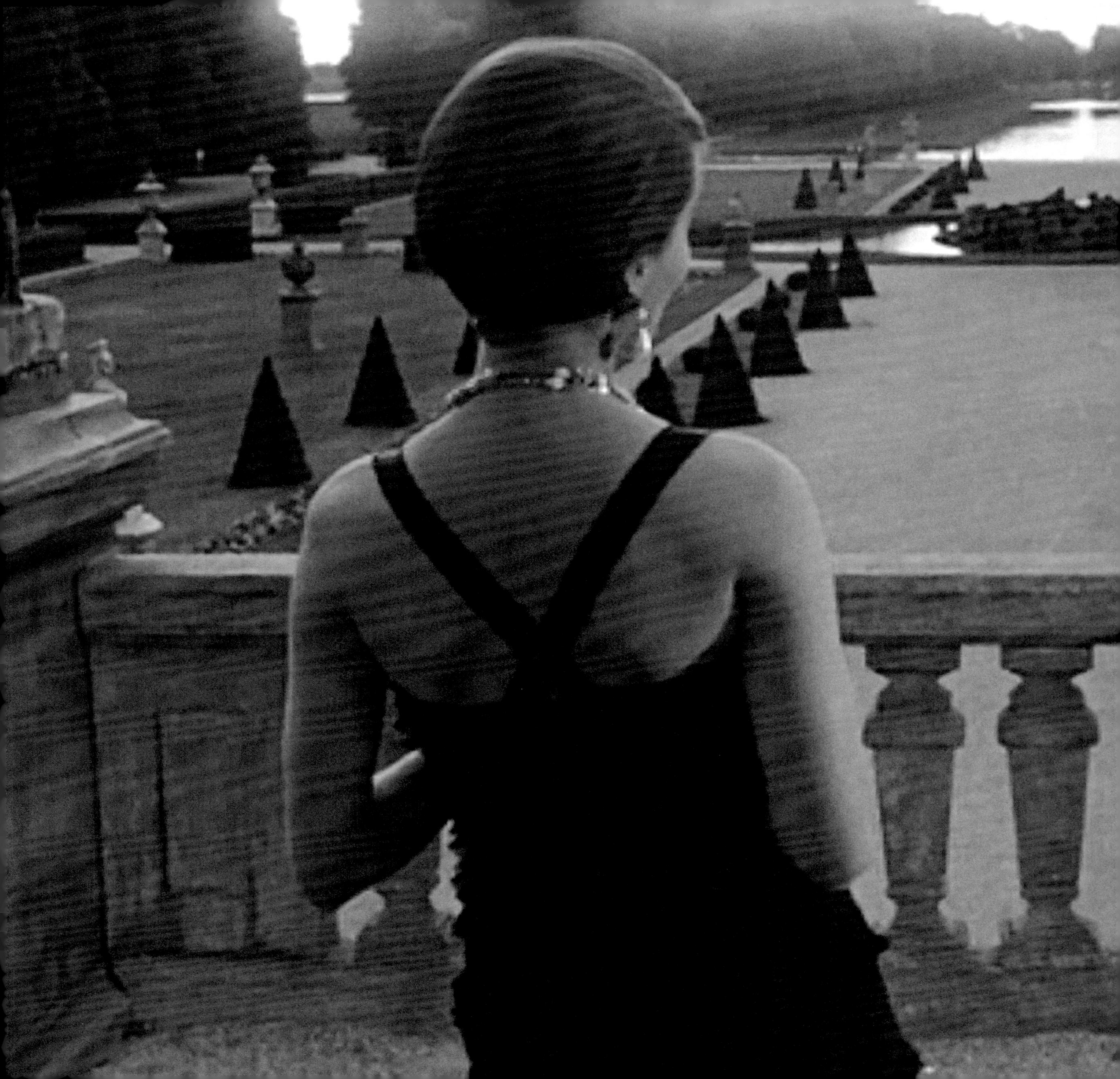

Film still from *Last Year at Marienbad*, directed by Alain Resnais, starring Delphine Seyrig and Giorgio Albertazzi, 1961.
Seyrig's costumes were designed by Gabrielle Chanel.

> "The dress shouldn't wear the woman; it's the woman who should wear the dress."
>
> Gabrielle Chanel,
> quoted by Antoinette Nordmann, "Je ne suis qu'une petite couturière," *Elle* (France), September 9, 1957

Delphine Seyrig wearing a dress designed by Gabrielle Chanel in the film *Last Year at Marienbad*.

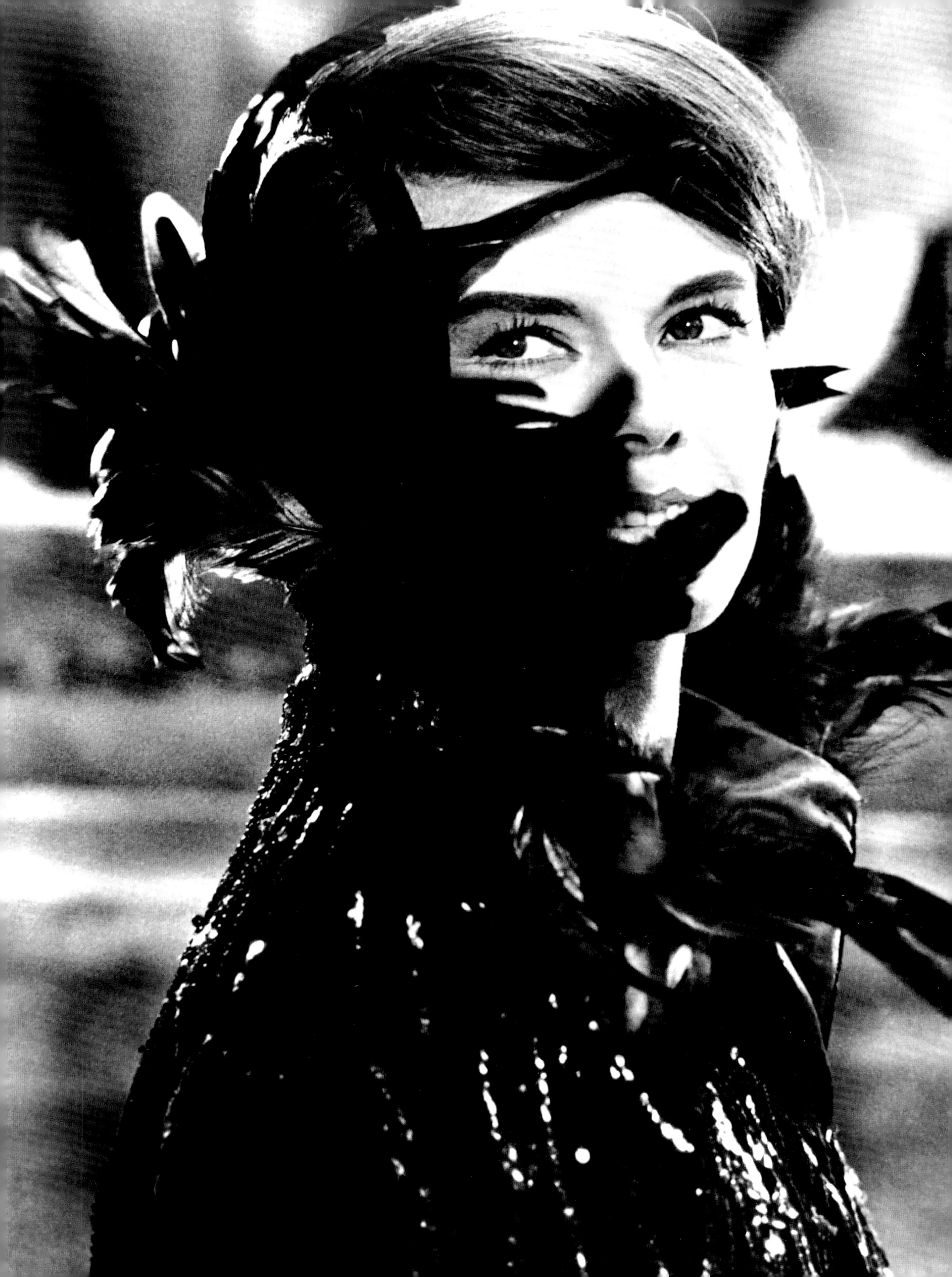

1961

38 EVENING DRESS, HAUTE COUTURE, SPRING 1961. "Underwear as outerwear" was a phrase coined in the 1980s, but it was an idea Gabrielle Chanel was fascinated by and brought to the fore in her designs. She originally drew her trademark jersey from men's underclothes, and often incorporated elements of dishabille into her designs. This dress, with its fine chiffon fabric and Chantilly lace hem, resembles elevated lingerie. It also demonstrates the timelessness of Chanel's style, even beyond her signature suit—it is strikingly similar to a design shown five years earlier (item 29, 1956) and could be worn today.

circa 1962

39 LITTLE BLACK DRESS, HAUTE COUTURE. In the second stage of her career, Gabrielle Chanel continued to use construction methods as a means of creating decorative interest, especially on her spare Little Black Dresses: Throughout the 1950s and 1960s appear dresses apparently magically constructed from horizontal bands, like layered ribbons. Delphine Seyrig's dress from the 1961 film *Last Year at Marienbad*, in linear strips of pleated chiffon and satin ribbon, was based on a style from Chanel's Autumn 1960 collection; two years later, the horizontal emphasis and tiered fabric of this cocktail dress reiterate this key notion.

114

1962

40 DAY SUIT, *BOCCACCIO '70*. Luchino Visconti first met Chanel after he moved to Paris in 1936, at the age of 30. She introduced him to Jean Renoir, who would become his mentor, and she and Visconti became lifelong friends. In *Boccaccio '70*, an anthology of four films directed by Mario Monicelli, Federico Fellini, Vittorio De Sica, and Visconti, the director not only asked Chanel to costume Romy Schneider's character, Pupe, a *bourgeoise* wife, but also to coach her in her ideas of elegance. In Schneider's first shot in the film—wearing a Chanel suit and clutching a cigarette in a richly appointed interior— she appears an avatar of Gabrielle Chanel herself.

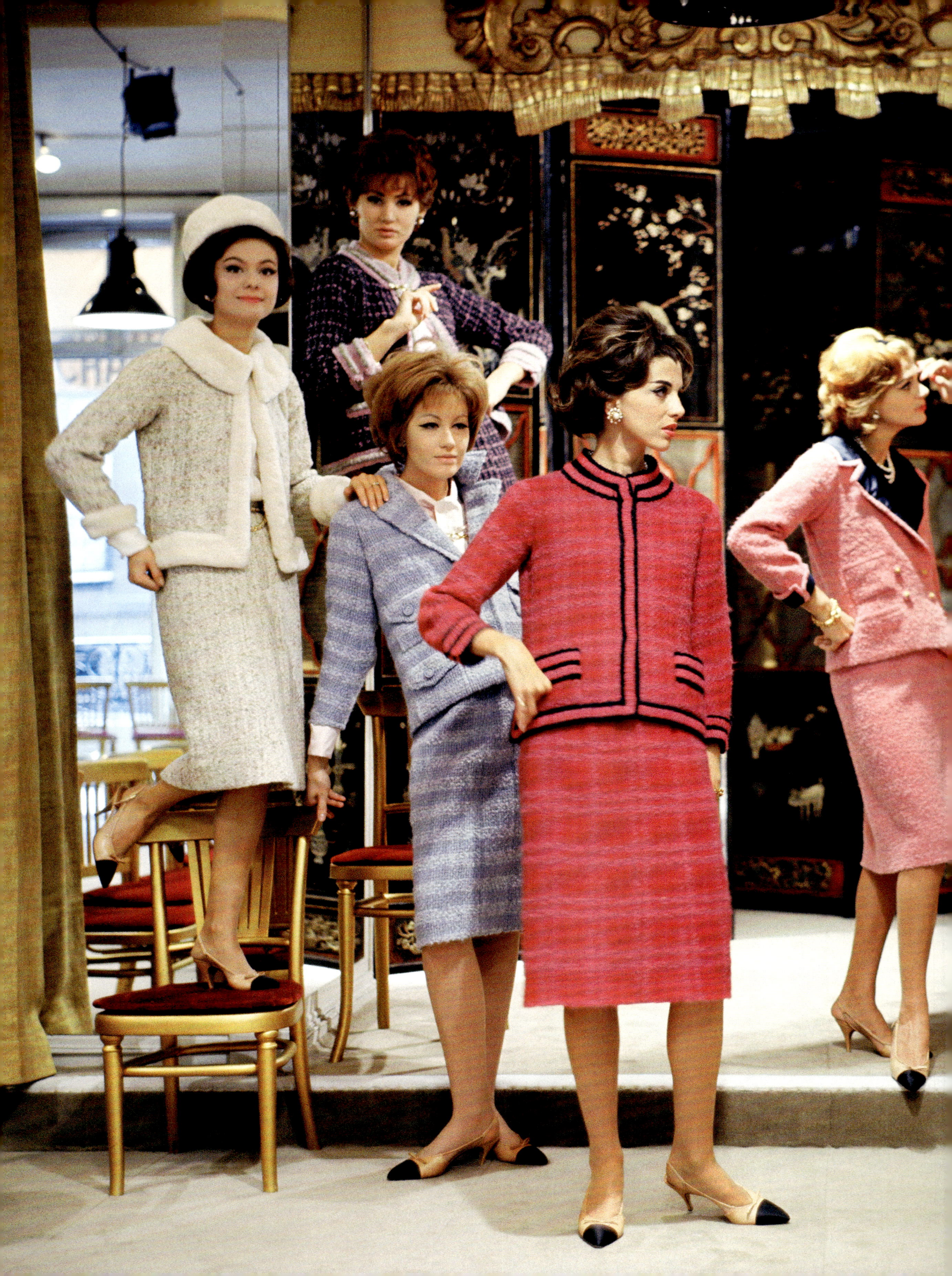

Models wearing Chanel suits, circa 1961.

1963

" **Simplicity is the keynote of all true elegance.** "

Gabrielle Chanel

41 JACQUELINE KENNEDY'S SUIT. On November 22, 1963, U.S. president John F. Kennedy was assassinated. First Lady Jacqueline Kennedy was wearing a bright pink suit, a licensed reproduction from Chez Ninon on Park Avenue, derived from Chanel's 1961 collection, chosen for its visibility. Under these unimaginable circumstances, Mrs. Kennedy insisted on wearing the bloodstained suit for the swearing-in of Lyndon B. Johnson and the flight back to Washington, D.C., with her husband's body. Preserved since 1964 in a climate-controlled vault in the National Archives, the suit cannot be displayed until 2103, by instruction of Caroline Kennedy.

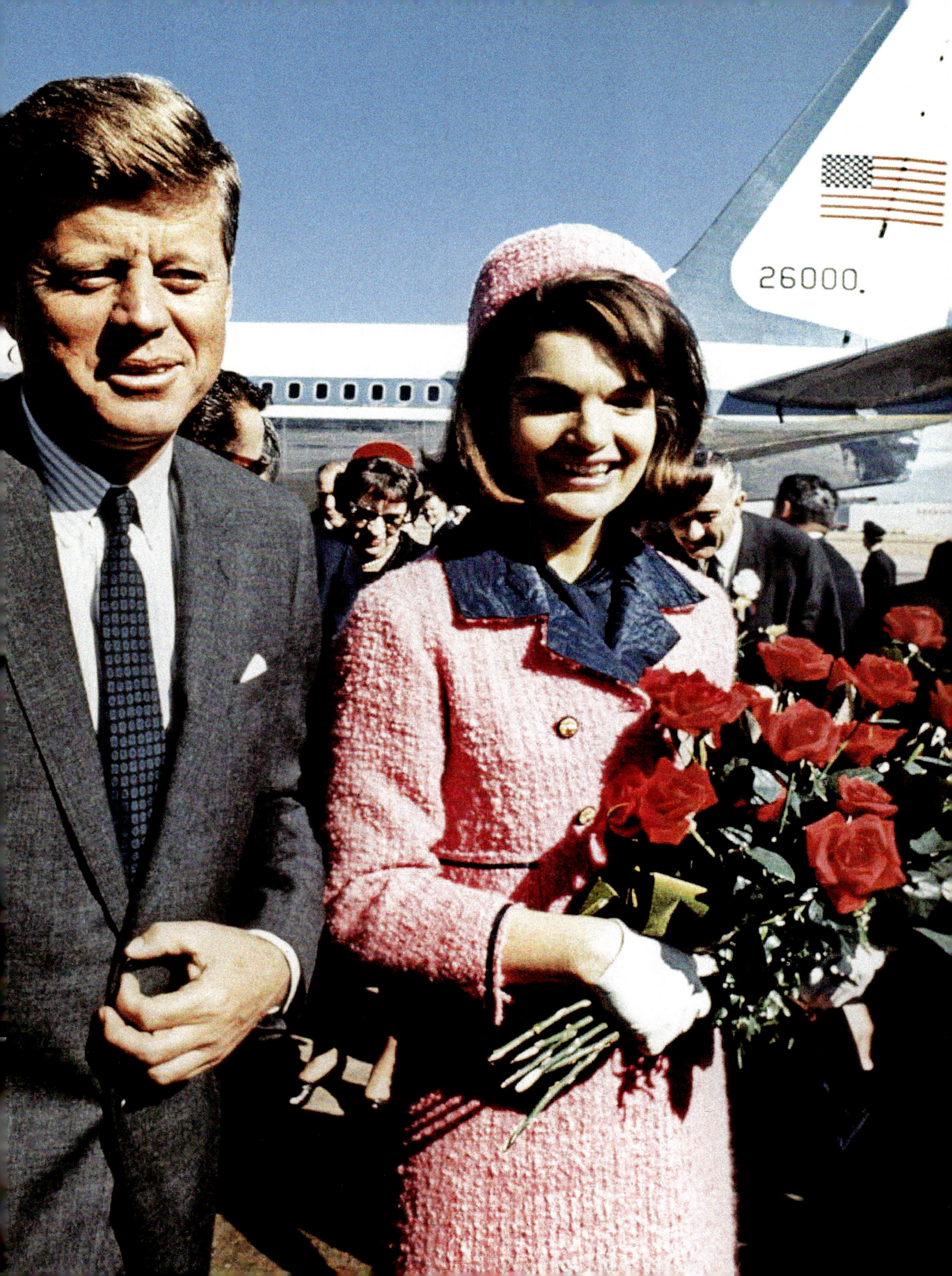
26000.

1963

42 LITTLE BLACK DRESS, HAUTE COUTURE, SPRING 1963. Actress Catherine Deneuve wears a distillation of Chanel style: a chaste black dress with white collar and cuffs. The style is strikingly similar to a costume she would wear in Luis Buñuel's 1967 film *Belle de Jour*, designed by Yves Saint Laurent, who often professed his admiration for Chanel. Of Saint Laurent, Chanel stated archly, "The more he copies me, the better taste he displays." Her iteration of this dress features a camellia and bow at the waistline, to soften and feminize the strictness. After Chanel's death in 1971, Deneuve became the face of Chanel No. 5.

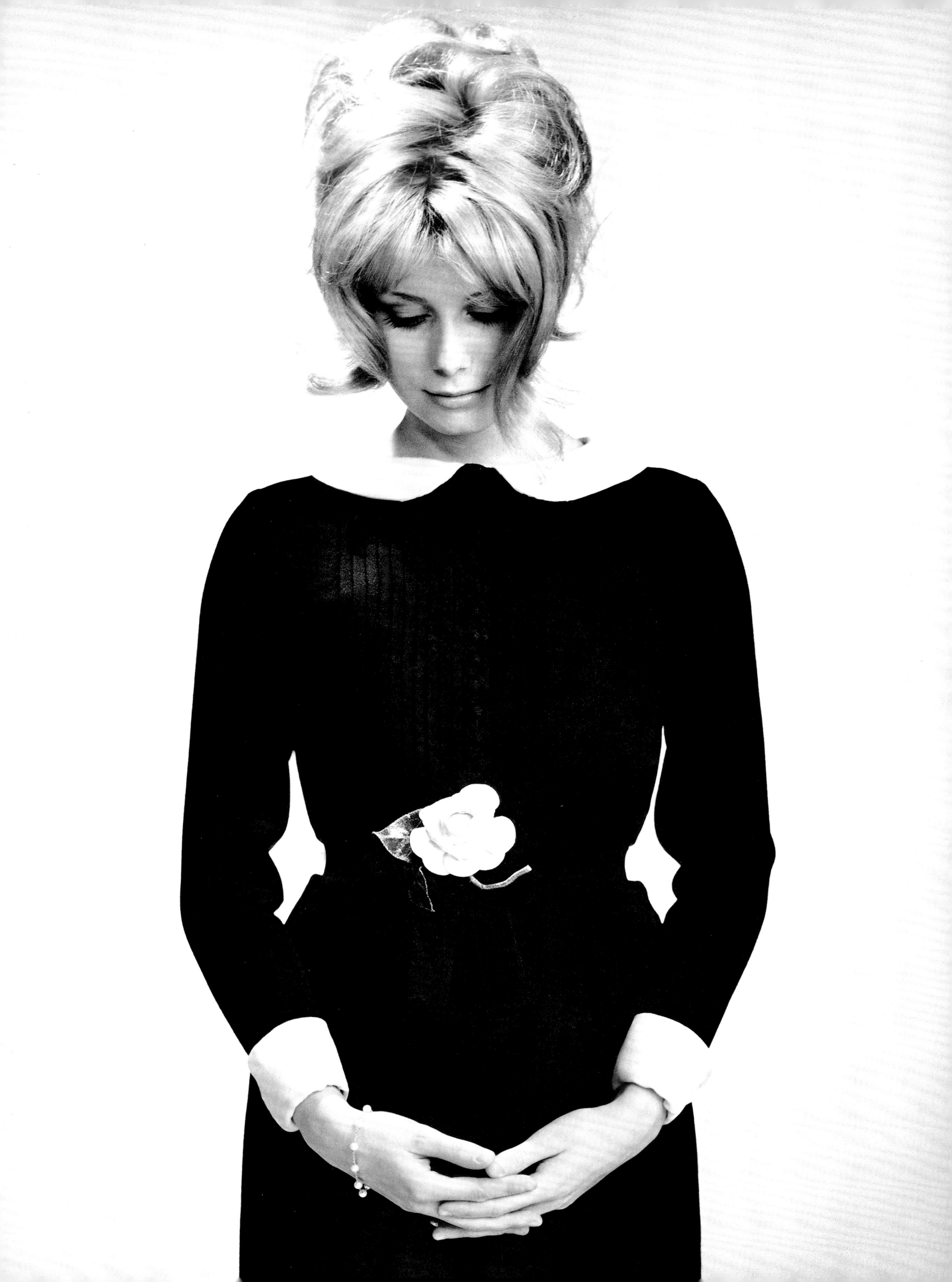

circa 1964

43 EVENING SUIT, HAUTE COUTURE. Although Gabrielle Chanel's evening versions of her eternally appealing suit were often executed in finer and more elaborate fabrics than for day, they retained her signature pragmatism. This jacket is lined in ivory silk damask, the body done in a clipped silk and synthetic pile suiting that lends the black a lustrous quality. The cuffs are decorative—Chanel often included detachable cuffs, and sleeveless blouses allowed her to fit the jacket armholes as closely as possible while still permitting movement. The flared panel in the skirt's center front is a detail Chanel introduced in the late 1950s to allow free locomotion.

late 1960s

44 EVENING ENSEMBLE, HAUTE COUTURE. In 1946, contemplating a career that had potentially run its course, Gabrielle Chanel stated that she had "imposed black; it's still going strong today, for black wipes out everything else around." Twenty years later, following her return to couture, she continued to create outfits that explored the depth and richness found in her favored non-color, particularly in contrasts of black on black. The silk matelassé fabric gives the color a three-dimensional quality, accentuated by a pair of black silk bows emphasizing bust and waist, running counter to the flattened fashions of the period.

Gabrielle Chanel on the mirrored staircase at 31 rue Cambon, circa 1950.

1964

45 DAY COAT, HAUTE COUTURE. In the 1920s, Chanel had championed "poor" furs such as rabbit and squirrel instead of sable and chinchilla. Further challenging the idea of the fur coat as status symbol, she often used the fur as the lining to plain wool coats—putting the luxury on the inside, to be appreciated only by the wearer. She continued to explore this notion in the 1960s, here using a humble shearling to line a long wool bouclé tweed coat, cut as easily as a bathrobe. This style represents a fusion of her pre- and postwar aesthetics—a fur lining to a coat styled as a facsimile of her universally adopted braid-trimmed suit (*at right*).

1966

46 DAY SUITS, AUTUMN 1966. Chanel's lack of ornament focused attention on the fabric, cut, and finish of her garments—the latter two were impeccable, even if the former was humble. This was how she elevated her suits from imitators, who by the 1960s were legion. Compare a Chanel suit (*at left*) with a licensed copy from Ohrbach's department store, executed in the same nubby tweed but quite different. The matching of plaid across body and arms, two-piece collar, four individual pockets, and double-button cuffs all signify the quality of the original. "It's totally pointless to take out a patent on a dress," stated Chanel. "It's admitting you've run out of ideas."

1967

47 EVENING ENSEMBLE, HAUTE COUTURE, SPRING 1967. This is Chanel in exuberant evening mood—utilizing a sculpted gold lamé by Bucol, one of her frequent suppliers of fantasy fabrics, alongside jersey from Lesur and Gerondeau, and tweed from Linton. Chanel frequently elevated her simple silhouettes via extravagant textile treatments, to transform them into cocktail or evening attire: This example teams a brief jacket with a wraparound square-shoulder dress, the edges formed in gold embroidery. Here, the lining of the jacket does not match the dress, as is the usual Chanel mode, but rather contrasts, serving as further embellishment.

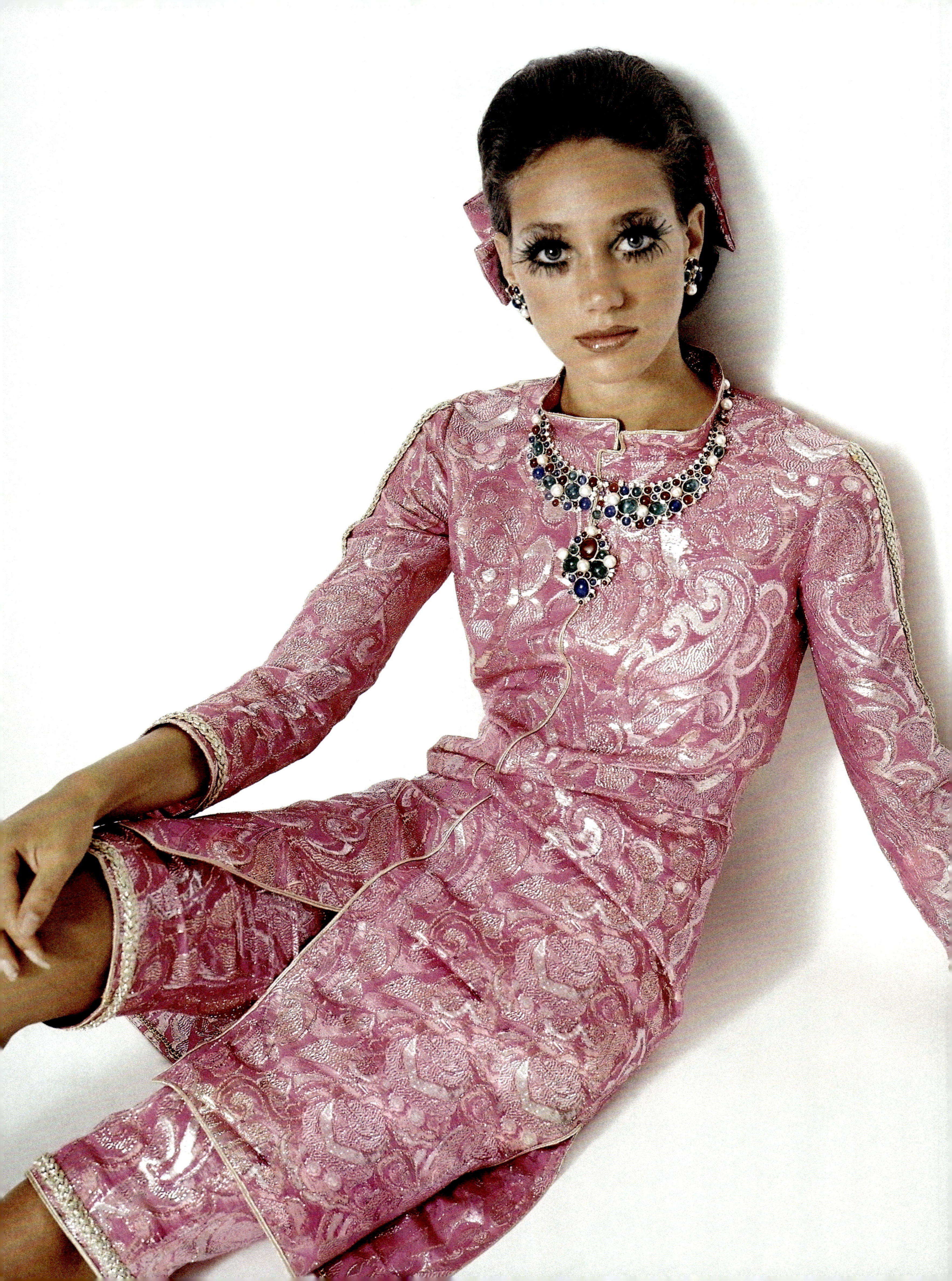

1968

48 COCKTAIL ENSEMBLE, HAUTE COUTURE, AUTUMN 1968. An outré example of the influence Gabrielle Chanel drew from the East, this style reflects Indian dress, described by *Vogue* as "the romantic air of a young Rajput prince." Again, Chanel borrows garments from menswear, still revolutionary at a time when women wearing trousers could be refused entry to restaurants. As in the previous example, braid is used to trim the outside seam of the sleeve—an idea Karl Lagerfeld would revisit (item 70, 1990). Interestingly, this ensemble is modeled for *Vogue* by Marisa Berenson, granddaughter of Chanel's great rival, Elsa Schiaparelli.

1969

49 COATDRESS, HAUTE COUTURE, AUTUMN 1969. Owned by the Duchess of Windsor, this tidy brocade coatdress combines economy of detail with elaborate fabric. The pattern demanded precision cutting and tailoring to match along all seams as well as the front closure. Chanel's lifelong interest in Asia chimed with popular culture in the late 1960s: A year before this, the Beatles traveled to India and unleashed a wave of enthusiasm for the music and styles of the subcontinent, manifested in couture by Saint Laurent and Ungaro. "I know how to express my times," Chanel once said. "Fashion should express the place, the moment."

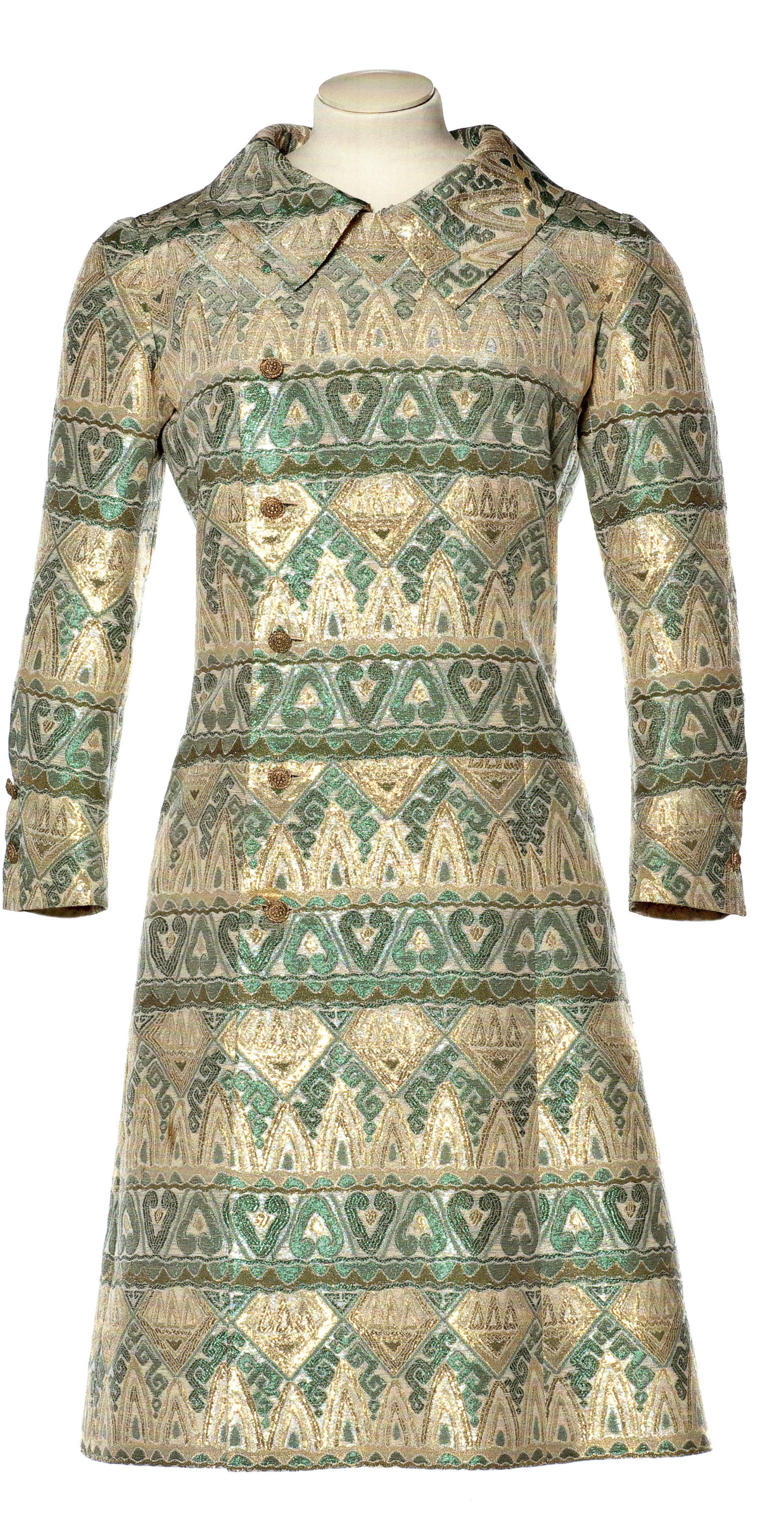

1972

50 DAY SUIT, HAUTE COUTURE, AUTUMN 1972. Gabrielle Chanel died on January 10, 1971, in her suite at the Ritz in Paris: Her final collection was presented posthumously on January 25, and each model wore a discreet black bow as sign of mourning. Contrary to popular mythology, the next creative head of Chanel was not Karl Lagerfeld, but former Dior designer Gaston Berthelot. He was tasked with continuing in the Chanel tradition, rather than making radical changes—including executing orders for designs created before Mademoiselle's death. "They give you a feeling of security," said *The New York Times* of clothes such as this suit.

WWD

FRIDAY, JANUARY 22, 1971
WOMEN'S
THE RETAILER'S DAILY NEWSPAPER
Vol. 122, No. 15
20 CENTS

JAN 26 1971
The Joseph Schaffner Library

Italy Couture Fails to Win U.S. Dollars

ROME (FNS Cable) — Americans drastically cut their Italian couture buying this season. They were here mainly to window shop next season's rtw.

Valentino is the only Italian who fits the real couture definition, making Italy a one-house market, but that's only part of the slack buying story. It looks like Saks Fifth Avenue's policy of putting all the emphasis on European rtw appeals to other stores as well.

Saks president Gordon Franklin declared unequivocably that his 10-man team was here only to "explore the couture with an eye to rtw buying next April."

See ITALIAN, Page 6

NLRB Defines Salesman Role

NEW YORK — The National Labor Relations Board has ruled that independent traveling salesmen representing various companies are not employes of any one firm and are not entitled to participate in an election to name a union as a bargaining agent.

The decision, by Region Two of the NLRB, involved the Sternberg Knitting Co., manufacturer of children's wear, versus District 65, Wholesale, Retail, Office and Processing Union, National Council Distributive Workers of America and Alliance for Labor Action.

While the decision affects only the 14 sales representa-

See NLRB, page 6

The Blind Are Also Color Blind

You can make their world a little brighter when you buy this award-winning 12"x18" poster (at $1.00 each) with its relevant message. All proceeds from the sale of posters donated in full to the Foundation For The Junior Blind. Order posters from Foundation For The Junior Blind, c/o Funky, 1053 S. Main St., L.A. 90015. Thank you.

Drawing by Kenneth Paul Block

CHANEL ADVANCE

PARIS—

COCO CHANEL ALWAYS BELIEVED IN CIVILIZED CLOTHES.

And WWD shows one of her Civilized suits, finished just before she died, in advance of her last collection which will be shown to press and buyers Tuesday.

This season, Coco was thinking padded shoulders — this model has a subtly widened shoulder and skirt for a new balance. Chanel called it her "safari suit."

"I don't know why, but the fabric makes me think of deserts, of sand, of Morocco," Chanel said just a few weeks ago. She liked this brilliantly striped black, mauve and yellow wool (Bucol) so much she shaped it into this suit and several coats.

Pants Business Hits Roadblock

A NATIONAL SURVEY

Pants business at dress and coat resources has slackened off, except for the sale in HotPants as an item.

In the higher price and couture area, pants have stopped selling. While they still represent a substantial amount of volume among lower and moderate price dress producers, the pace of sales has started to level off.

Sportswear manufacturers remain the chief segment of the apparel field that hasn't felt a pants squeeze. The category is still the biggest volume-puller, they contend.

One-piece shirtwaist and chemise dresses, and skirts in longer lengths are moving up quickly as fashion challengers. HotPants are already showing advance signs of being a summer winner. Knickers have been a disappointment to manufacturers and retailers.

Pants will continue as a staple item, a basic category according to those polled. Volume and profits are predicted more on items and an ability to spot trends, sources maintained.

In the designer area, pants business is a thing of the past. "If you show buyers pants now, they don't want to see them," said Calvin Klein. "They've been pantsed to death. They want dresses. They'll try HotPants or even knickers. It's getting to be an item business."

See PANTS, Page 15

FOCUS

Apollo 14 Faces Major Crossroad

By MARY BUBB

CAPE KENNEDY, Fla. (FNS) — In the 10-year span between Freedom 7 and Apollo 14, America's space program and astronaut Alan Shepard have come a long, long way.

The United States is well ahead in the space race with Russia, has placed four men on the moon and gleaned tremendous scientific and technical knowledge from a program costing nearly $22 billion.

The country now stands at a new crossroad with Apollo 14, slated to blast off for the moon Jan.31. It is the most costly ($400 million), the most dangerous and potentially the most scientifically rewarding mission to date. Failure of this mission could sound the death knell to the remainder of the Apollo program and strongly influence the future prospects for Space Shuttle and space station ventures now plodding along at a snail's pace.

Experts say a serious problem in Apollo 14 could wipe manned space flight right off the books for a number of years.

See APOLLO, Page 13

White Stag To Sell Chains Private Label

PORTLAND, Ore. (FNS) — White Stag Manufacturing Co., which historically has avoided distribution to national mail order chains is forming a division to sell private label sportswear to Sears, Roebuck, Penney's and Montgomery Ward.

Harold Dolgenow, senior vice-president, who will be responsible for the yet unnamed division, projected the company will do about $5 million in annual sales in its second year of business with the big

See WRITE, Page 35

EVER THINK ABOUT HOW YOU COULD GET YOUR FIRM'S NAME ON THE FRONT PAGE OF WWD?

think about it.

Women's Wear Daily, January 22, 1971: Gabrielle Chanel's final designs.

> **Let them copy.
> My ideas belong to everyone.
> I refuse no one.**
>
> Gabrielle Chanel,
>
> quoted in "Fashion Was Her Pulpit,"
> *The New York Times,* January 1971

Illustration of Gabrielle Chanel and Karl Lagerfeld, by Donald Robertson.

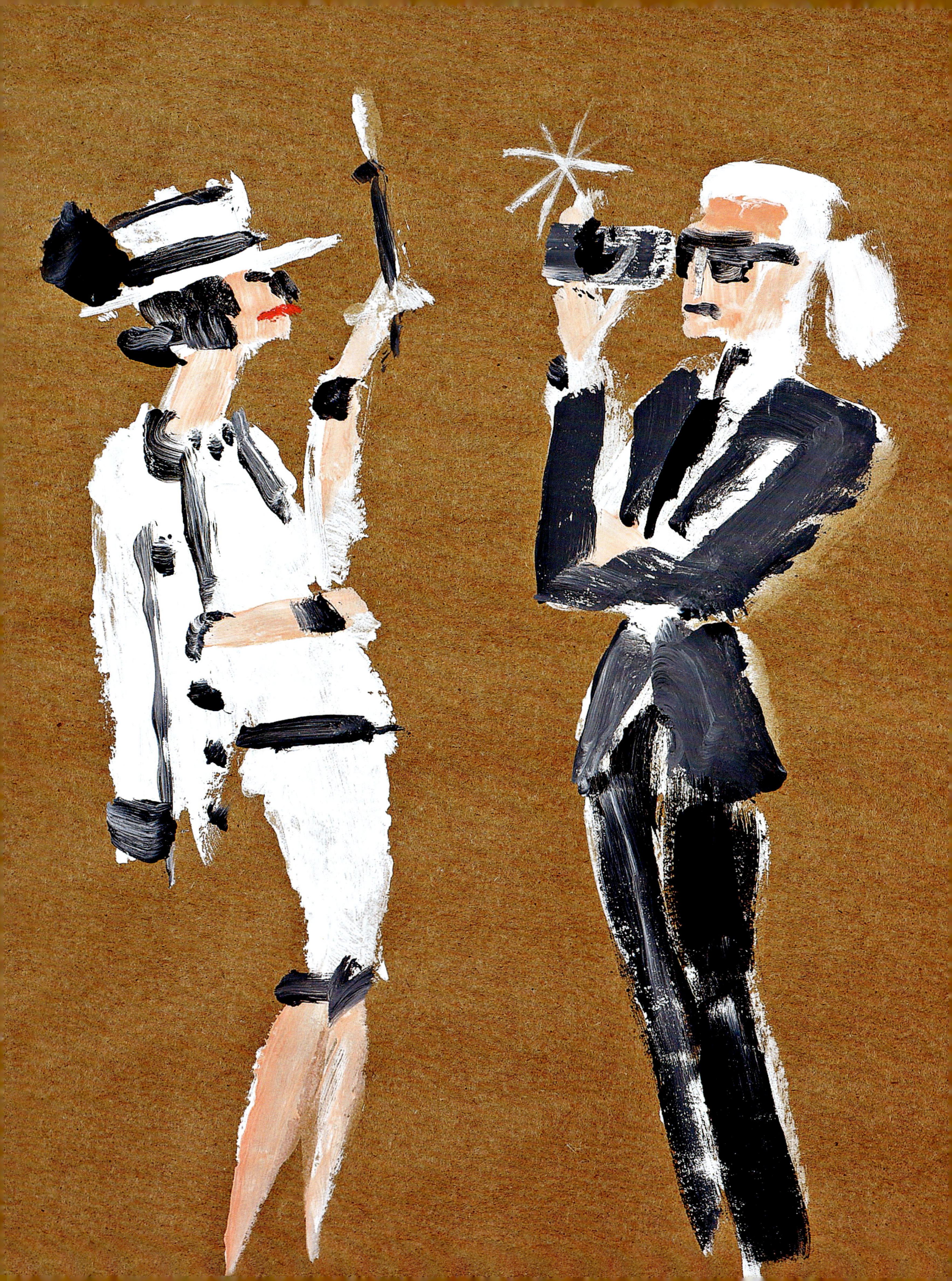

FIRST LOOK AT PARIS

CHANEL WWD

WEDNESDAY, JANUARY 19, 1983
VOL. 145, NO. 13   50 Cents

Lagerfeld tackles couture

PARIS — The sign on the design studio's door still reads "Mademoiselle — Prive," but inside is a remarkably tanned, newly trim Karl Lagerfeld nervously admiring his careful rendition of the chanel suit he will present in his first couture collection for the house on Tuesday, Jan. 25.

It was at Lagerfeld's insistence that the ghostly reminder of Coco Chanel remains outside his newest part-time office, and he works deep into the night, hoping to live up to the hallowed name while keeping aloft his own reputation. For Chanel, and myriad other clients, he is working "16 hours a day and delighted to do it."

Under Lagerfeld's weighty and controversial

See CHANEL, page 4

Coast firms see summer orders late

By ROB GOLUM

LOS ANGELES — Summer apparel orders are expected to arrive later than a year ago, manufacturers here say, but many anticipate at least a modest upturn in unit sales. And, if business opens up, dollar sales may be higher too.

For the most part, manufacturers are cautious because summer lines have been on the road only a week or two, and makers are hesitant to project for the short selling season. Nevertheless, there is a better feeling than existed a few months ago when spring lines were opened. That business finished flat to slightly

See COAST, page 43

Photo by GUY MARINEAU

Designer Karl Lagerfeld recasts Coco Chanel's famous suit

Store sales for week steam ahead, page 8

Copyright © 2013 Fairchild Fashion Media

"Lagerfeld Tackles Couture," *Women's Wear Daily*, January 19, 1983.
Opposite: Karl Lagerfeld on the mirrored staircase at 31 rue Cambon, photographed by Helmut Newton, 1983.

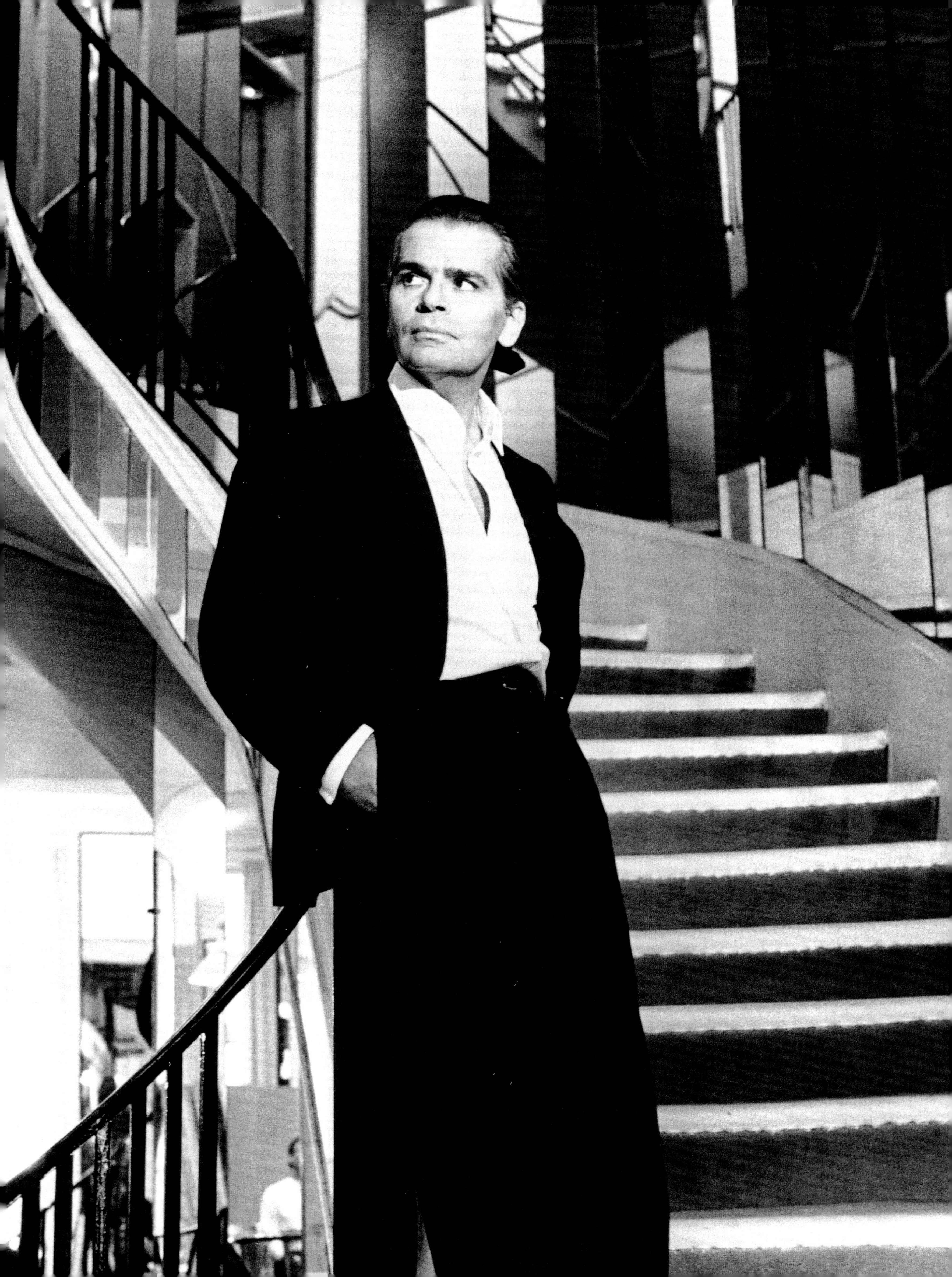

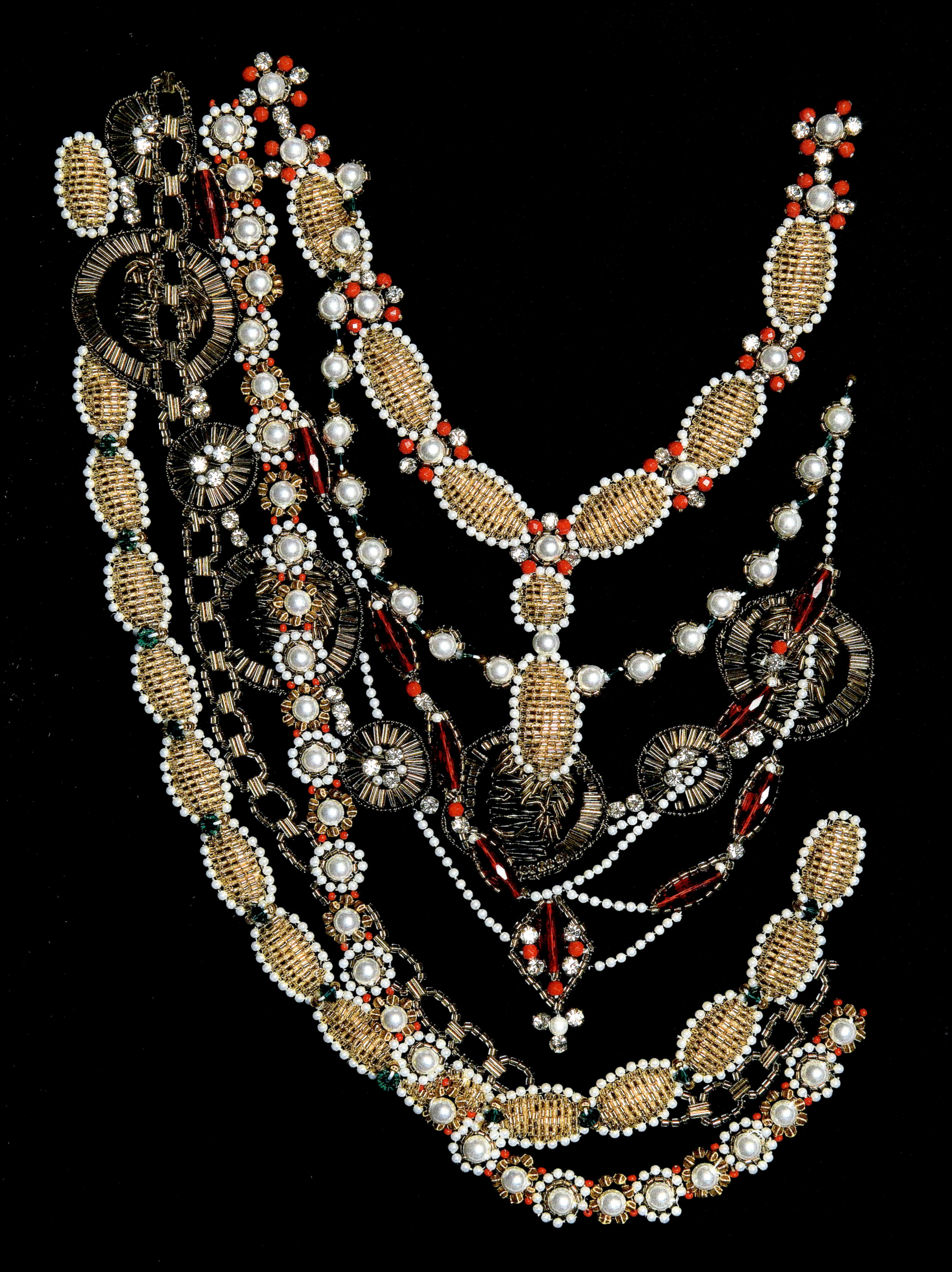

1983

51 EVENING DRESS, HAUTE COUTURE, SPRING 1983. Presented in the mirrored salons of 31 rue Cambon, Karl Lagerfeld's first couture collection for Chanel established his blueprint for reviving the house—treating recognizable emblems of Chanel's style with unimagined irreverence. This silk crepe dress epitomizes his approach: Chanel's signature faux bijoux, inspired by a Horst portrait of Chanel herself, are re-created as sumptuous trompe l'oeil embroidery by François Lesage. The dress marries a pop interpretation of Gabrielle Chanel's style with enduring elegance—both chic and tongue-in-cheek.

1983

52 CLASSIC HANDBAG. From the outset, Karl Lagerfeld's revitalization of Chanel was head to toe: He executed his own versions of the house's two-tone shoes, changing the last and the heel height. Later, he would tweak colors and even add plastic, platform-sole variations in the 1990s. And he reworked the original 2.55 (item 27, 1955) for the 1980s. The quilting, rectangular shape, and chain strap were all in place, although the latter became flashier, more visible, in leather-twined gilt chain, and the plate lock was replaced with one flaunting the double-C logo. Designed in 1983, this style, called the Classic, joined the 2.55 as a bestseller.

Sketch of the Classic handbag on quilted leather.

1983

53 DAY SUIT, HAUTE COUTURE, SPRING 1983. In his first couture collection, Karl Lagerfeld inevitably took on the challenge of reinventing the Chanel suit for a new era. Rather than thinking it timeless, Lagerfeld decided Chanel had to move with the times, to evolve its signature look. This suit, in Chanel-red tweed with wide-brimmed straw boater-style hat to match, hews close to Chanel's legacy of narrow shoulders and tight-fitting sleeves rather than the wide shoulders of the 1980s. Yet the prominent use of the golden double-C buttons first introduced by Chanel in the late 1950s is an indication of things to come.

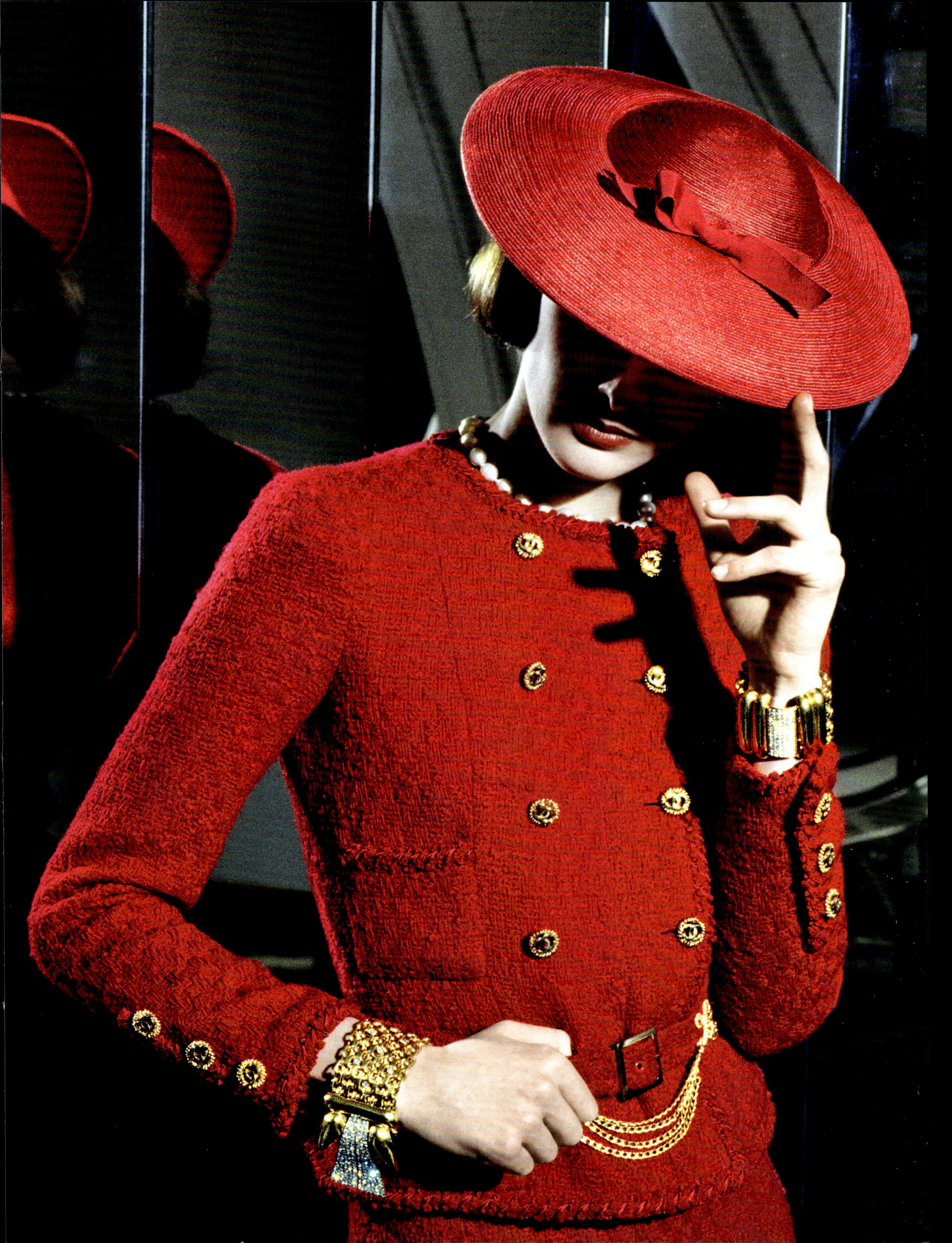

1983

> ❝ There would be no Chanel without the history of Chanel. I don't have to do it consciously. I do it unconsciously. ❞
>
> Karl Lagerfeld,
> interview with author, July 2017

54 EVENING SUIT, HAUTE COUTURE, SPRING 1983. Karl Lagerfeld deliberately looked not to Chanel's designs from the 1950s for his debut collection, but to her romantic work of the 1930s—especially her dreamy, drifting lace dresses, which the designer professed to especially admire. Here, he uses lace as an unconventional overlay on a traditionally shaped Chanel suit—wittily, the edge of the lace is used in lieu of braid trim, to delineate the jacket. The accessories—here, a black bow at the neck, elsewhere boater hats, chain belts, and brooches—were direct replicas of Chanel originals, tying past to present.

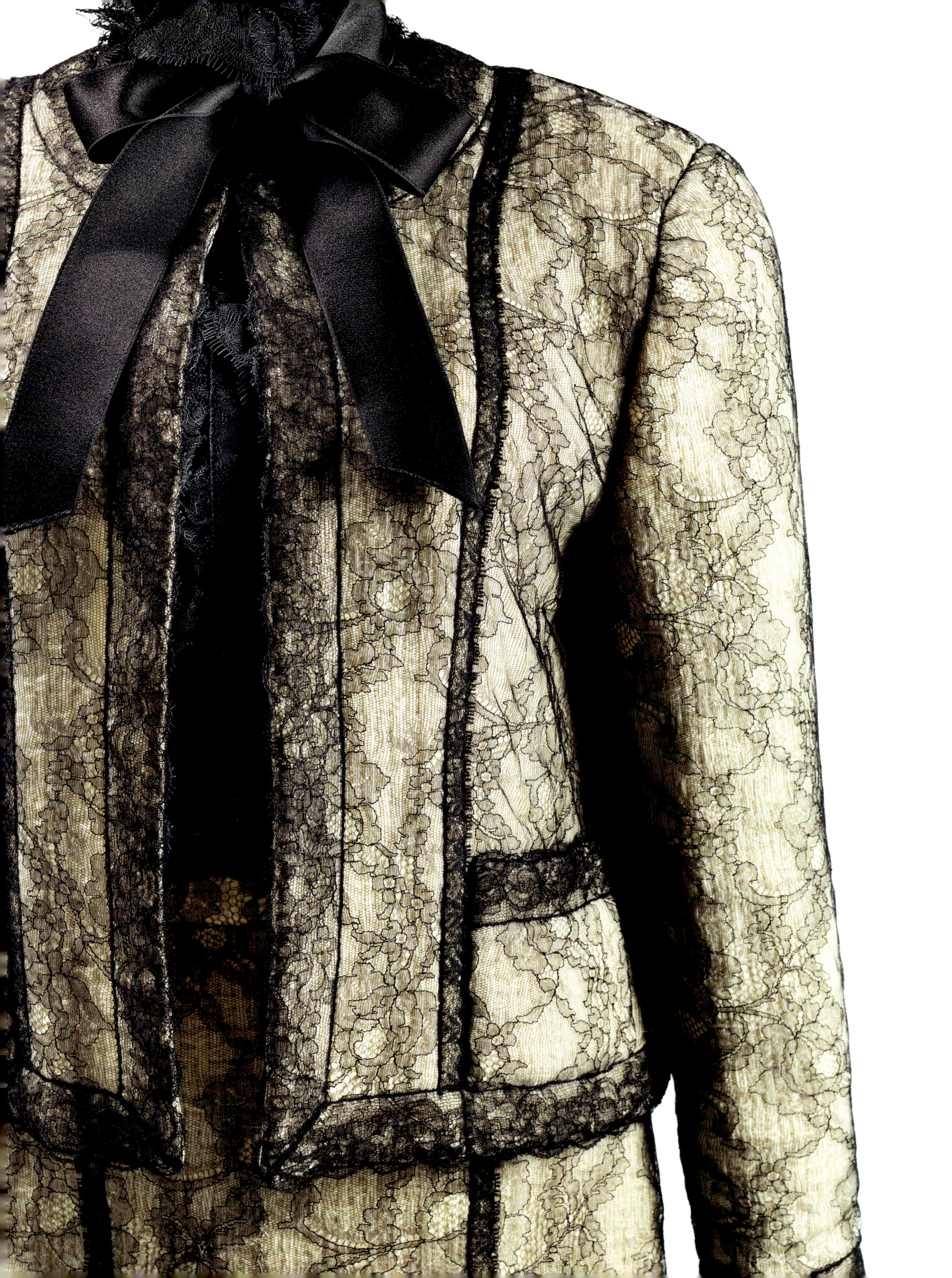

Model Inès de la Fressange wearing the dress, from *Vogue Paris*, March 1984.

1984

55 "CHANEL IMPERATRICE" COATDRESS, HAUTE COUTURE, SPRING 1984. By his third couture collection, Karl Lagerfeld had begun to challenge convention. In this outfit, the Chanel jacket is elongated to floor length, reflecting eighteenth-century styles, of which Lagerfeld was an admirer, and also the attenuated silhouettes of Chanel's 1930s fashions. The pure line of this coatdress is in the Chanel mold, as is the embellishment of faux pearls and chains. Echoing military decorations, these are a nod to the "empress" of the look's title, and underline the inspiration Chanel herself constantly took from the practical attire of infantry.

1984

> **" I'm like a computer who's plugged into the Chanel mode. "**
>
> Karl Lagerfeld,
> quoted by Christopher Petkanas, "Lagerfeld Tackles Couture,"
> *Women's Wear Daily*, January 19, 1983

56 EVENING SUIT, HAUTE COUTURE, SPRING 1984. Karl Lagerfeld began to loosen up the Chanel suit, easing the silhouette overall. This ensemble looks back to the evening clothes Chanel proposed in the 1920s (item 8, 1926), both in its surface decoration and in its languid, tubular silhouette. Lagerfeld was a fan of Art Deco, and had collected the style in his own apartment and revived its fashion look as designer of Chloé in 1969. This suit is worn by Inès de la Fressange, the first face of Chanel in the Lagerfeld era, who was presented as a contemporary counterpart to Mademoiselle in the house's shows and advertising campaigns.

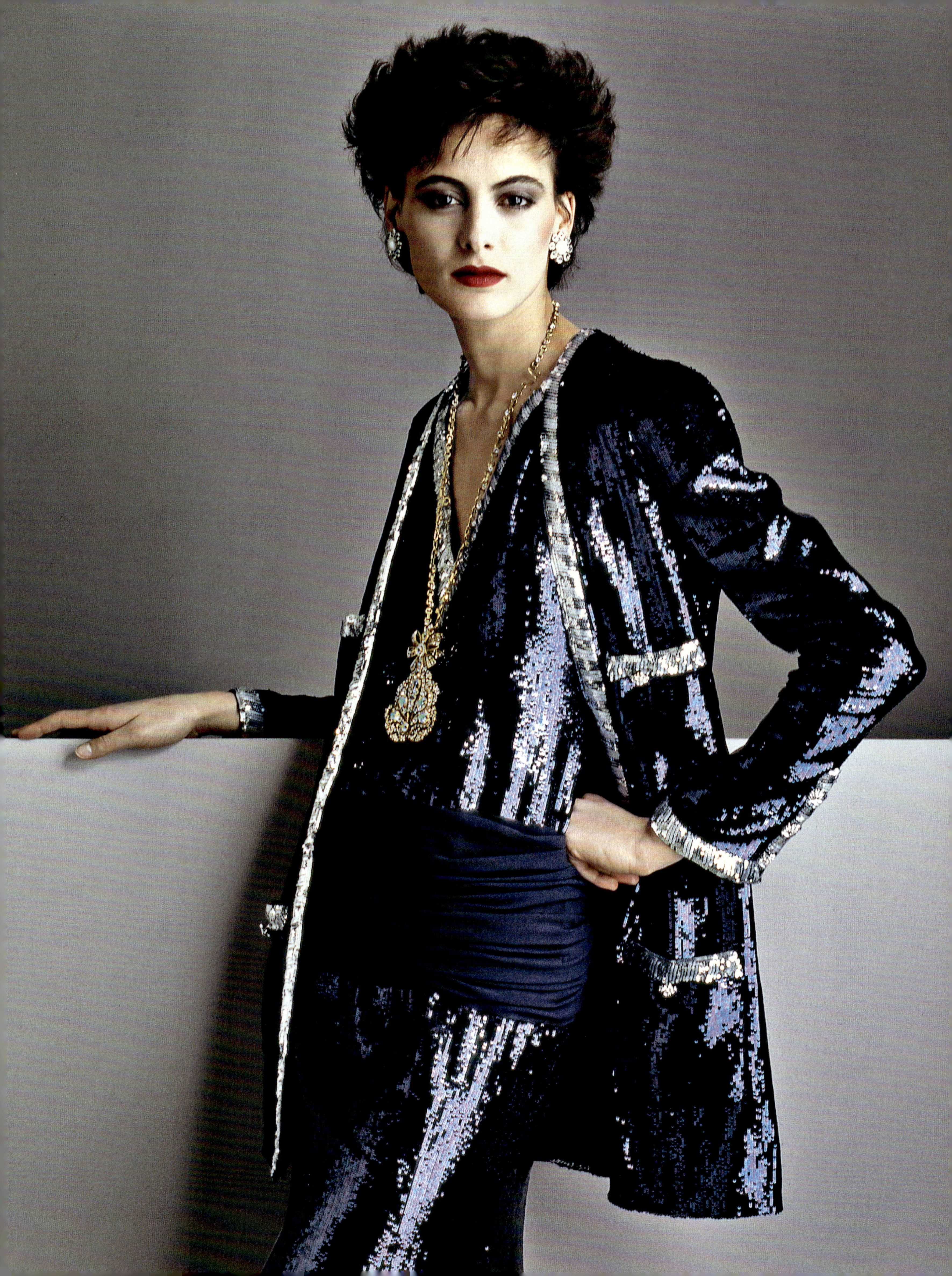

Actress Marilyn Monroe with a bottle of Chanel No. 5 perfume, photographed at the Ambassador Hotel in New York City, 1955. *Opposite:* Andy Warhol, *Chanel*, 1985, from the Ads portfolio, silk screen, edition of 190, 38 x 38 in.

1985

57 CHANEL NO. 5. Flagging sales of Chanel No. 5 was one of the reasons Karl Lagerfeld was chosen to resurrect and reinvent the fashion identity of Chanel. By the mid-1980s the perfume had regained its luster. So much so that in 1985 Andy Warhol chose an image of the bottle as part of a portfolio of ten advertising images, alongside the Paramount logo, Blackglama Furs featuring Judy Garland, and the nascent computer company Apple Macintosh. Melding commerce with art in his signature manner, this work places Chanel No. 5 on a par with Marilyn Monroe and Jacqueline Kennedy in terms of twentieth-century pop-culture iconography.

1986

58 EVENING SUIT, HAUTE COUTURE, SPRING 1986. Karl Lagerfeld took an irreverent Pop Art approach to his reworking of Chanel styles. This collection featured junk jewelry shaped like Chanel No. 5 bottles or the double-C logo. The gold buttons punctuating this black wool suit feature etched drawings of Chanel two-tone pumps, similar to Andy Warhol's early shoe ads. The shoulders are wide, the armholes dropped, and the hips emphasized by large satin bows. Although these elements seem almost an affront to the Chanel aesthetic, this suit references an archival style (item 44, late 1960s), demonstrating Lagerfeld's knowledge of Chanel history.

1986

59 EVENING SUIT, HAUTE COUTURE, AUTUMN 1986. Quilting, chains, the suit—Karl Lagerfeld pulls apart the building blocks of Chanel style and reassembles them in new and never-before-imagined ways. Here he riffs on the quilted Chanel bag he so successfully revived, reinventing it as a suit. The surface is decorated with sequins, harking back to Chanel designs of the 1930s (item 24, 1938), but crosshatched with quilting lines; the chain normally found on the inside becomes flashy sublimation of the traditional braid trimming, blown up in scale, becoming jewelry in itself.

Inès de la Fressange and Karl Lagerfeld photographed by Helmut Newton for *Paris Match*, February 1987.

1986

60 LITTLE BLACK DRESS, HAUTE COUTURE, AUTUMN 1986. In late-twentieth-century high fashion, leather occupied an odd position, redolent simultaneously of rebellion and expense. This dress uses the unconventional material to create a slender, elegant design with a touch of danger. Chanel herself used leather in garments—her Autumn 1965 collection featured a black-and-white dress with motorcycle belt and leather collar. This combination of leather and chain references the 2.55 handbag (as with the sequined, quilted suit from this collection, item 59), and also the trappings of bondage later employed by designers such as Gianni Versace.

1987

61 COCKTAIL DRESS, READY-TO-WEAR, AUTUMN 1987. Initially artistic director of haute couture, with two assistants handling ready-to-wear (due to a conflict with his contract at Chloé), Karl Lagerfeld oversaw both Chanel lines from 1984 onward. He brought a level of refinement that reflected his Chloé days, where he had invented a form of ready-to-wear equal to couture in terms of creativity and closer than ever before in quality. That ideology is reflected in this brief sequined cocktail dress of complex construction, in which lace underlays the bell-shaped skirt and overlays the neckline around a typically Chanel wide satin bow.

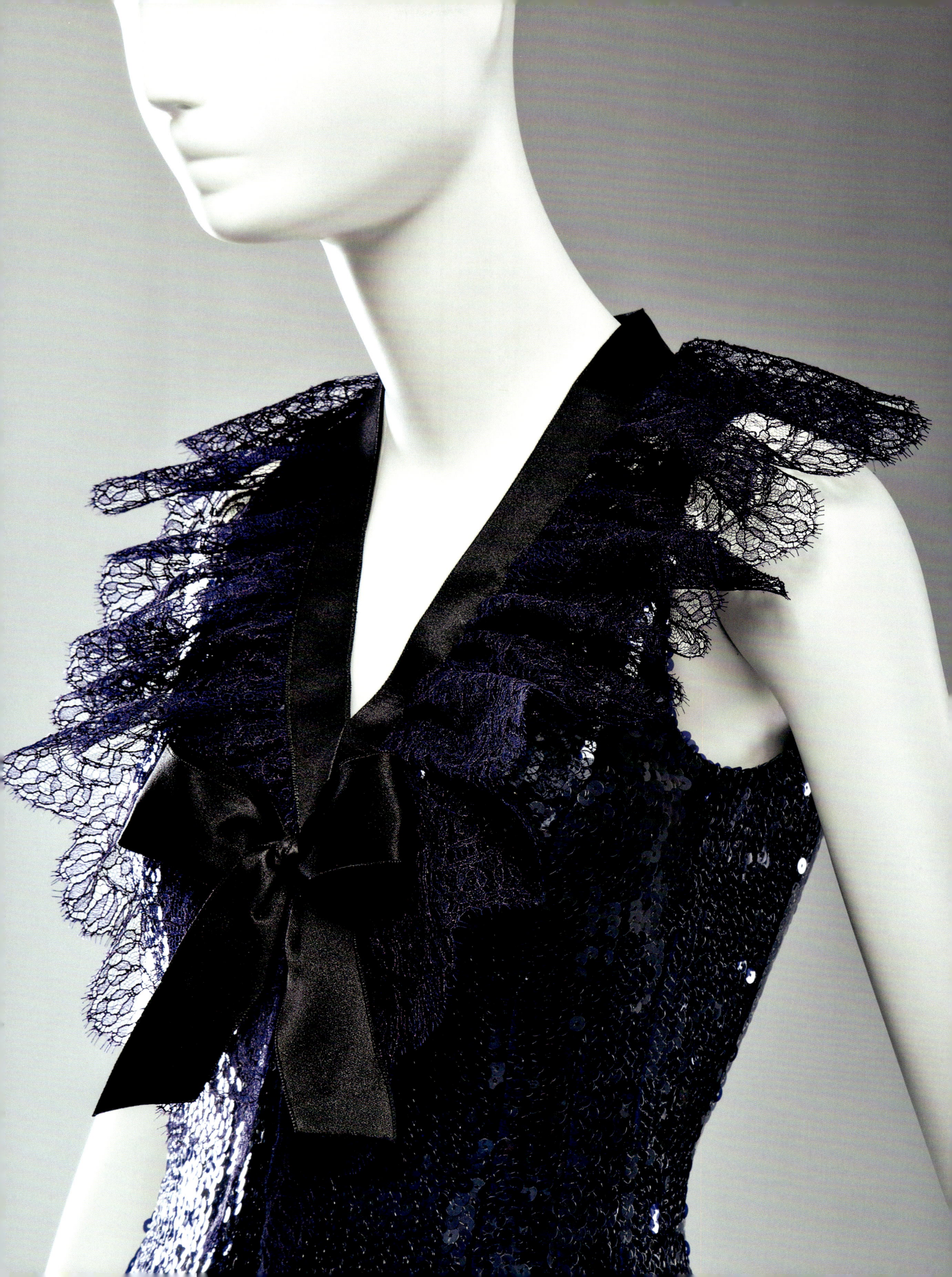

1987

> " I'm an intelligent opportunist.... I like the idea of doing things you're not supposed to do. "
>
> Karl Lagerfeld,
> quoted by Maureen Orth, "Kaiser Karl: Behind the Mask,"
> *Vanity Fair*, February 1992

62 DAY SUIT, HAUTE COUTURE, AUTUMN 1987. By now Karl Lagerfeld had turned Chanel upside down and inside out. The Autumn 1987 couture show introduced a new silhouette, dubbed "L'Oeuf," or the Egg, evincing a roundness seen elsewhere in fashion, notably in styles by Christian Lacroix and Vivienne Westwood, proponents of the "pouf" skirt that literally shaped fashion in the mid-1980s. Here, Lagerfeld slices the Chanel jacket high on the waist, emphasizing the wide shoulders and curving hips. The bicolored wool tweed was a feature of the collection, creating a new, arresting effect akin to Chanel's graphic two-tone shoes, across the whole body.

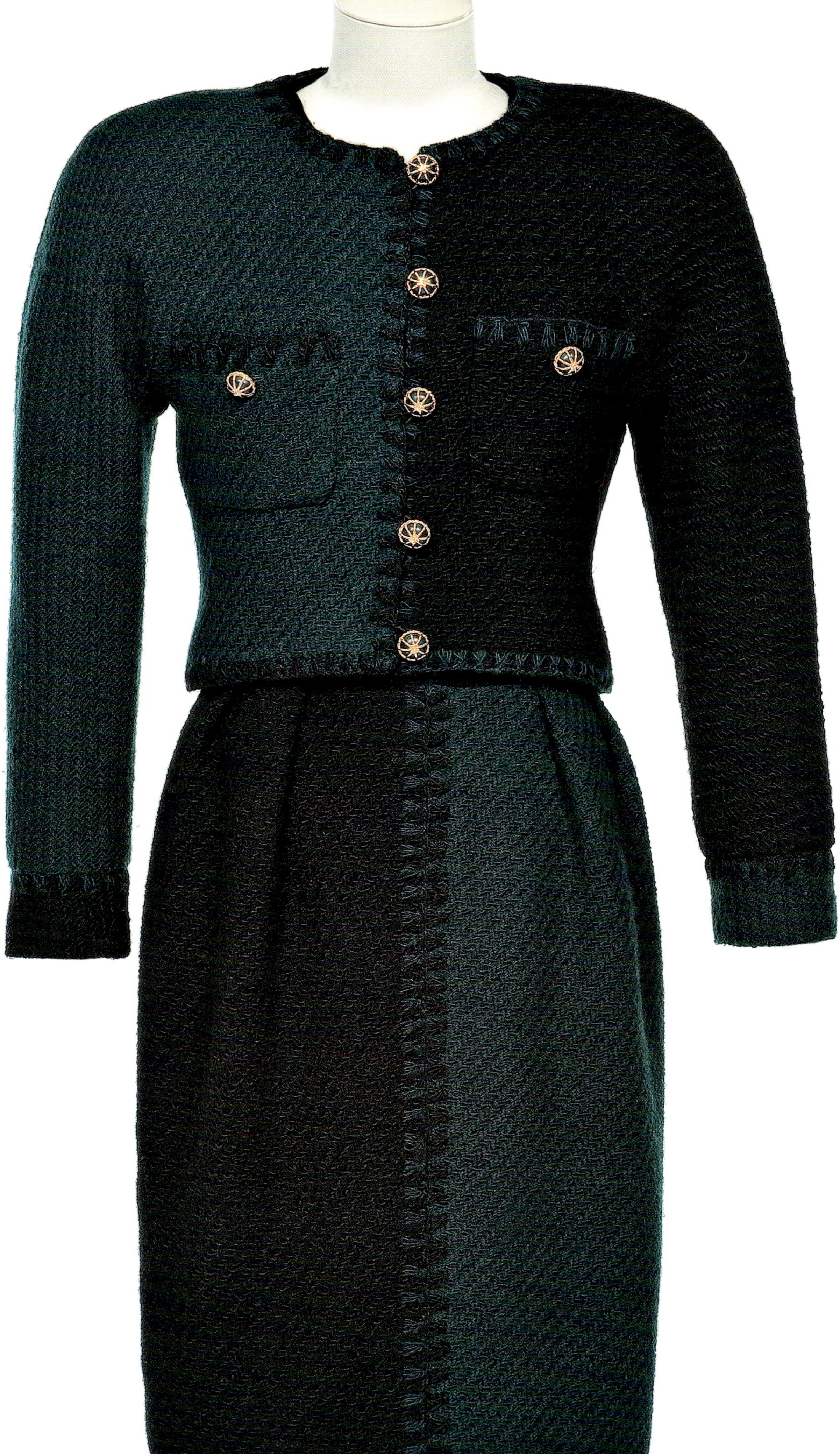

1987

63 EVENING ENSEMBLE, HAUTE COUTURE, AUTUMN 1987. Again influenced by Versailles, this ensemble—a lavishly embroidered jacket with pannier hips over beribboned breeches—draws on a costume devised for Louis XIV performing in Lully's *Ballet de la nuit* (1653). This design also shadows styles of Sèvres porcelain in its colors of rich gold and bleu de roi, and a cluster of white camellias at the neck. Despite its historicism, this outfit is very much of its time, reflecting the luxury and frivolity which dominated 1980s fashion before the stock market crash of October 1987—a style of which Lagerfeld was a leader.

1987

64 EVENING DRESS, HAUTE COUTURE, AUTUMN 1987. For this couture collection, Karl Lagerfeld drew inspiration from the seventeenth-century court of Versailles, specifically the costumes for the opera *Atys* by Jean-Baptiste Lully, staged in 1676 at the court of Louis XIV and revived at Versailles's Théâtre de la Reine in the spring of 1987 with all the pomp and ceremony of that earlier age. Even the stage itself was a source of decorative motifs, as seen in the theatrical drapes and swags embroidered by Lesage across a proscenium-like peplum. Uncharacteristically decorative for this couture *maison*, the base is a signature house shade of Chanel red.

1988

65 LITTLE BLACK DRESS, HAUTE COUTURE, SPRING 1988. Of course Lagerfeld tackled the Little Black Dress in his ticking-off of Chanel's iconography throughout his tenure, constantly reworked to the temperature of fashion then and there. In 1988, Lagerfeld's littlest of black dresses encapsulates the short, bouffant evening silhouette of the period as perfectly as did Chanel's flapper dresses of the 1920s. But there are also references to Chanel's past: The construction of this dress directly recalls mid-century Chanel creations (item 39, circa 1962) via horizontal "ribbons" of silk chiffon. Here, they are "knotted" into a make-believe bow.

1989

66 EVENING COAT, HAUTE COUTURE, AUTUMN 1989. About this collection, Lagerfeld quoted Goethe: "To make a better future, you must enlarge elements of the past." The inspiration for this came from a style Gabrielle Chanel created for herself in 1939: elongated, rounded over the hips, without padding. Here, Lagerfeld extends it to floor length in silk tulle embroidered with bouquets and ribbons, reminiscent of the eighteenth century. Lagerfeld amassed an important collection of rococo art, including paintings by Boucher and Fragonard; his mansion on rue de l'Université included a room by Jacques Verberckt, whose boiseries decorate Versailles.

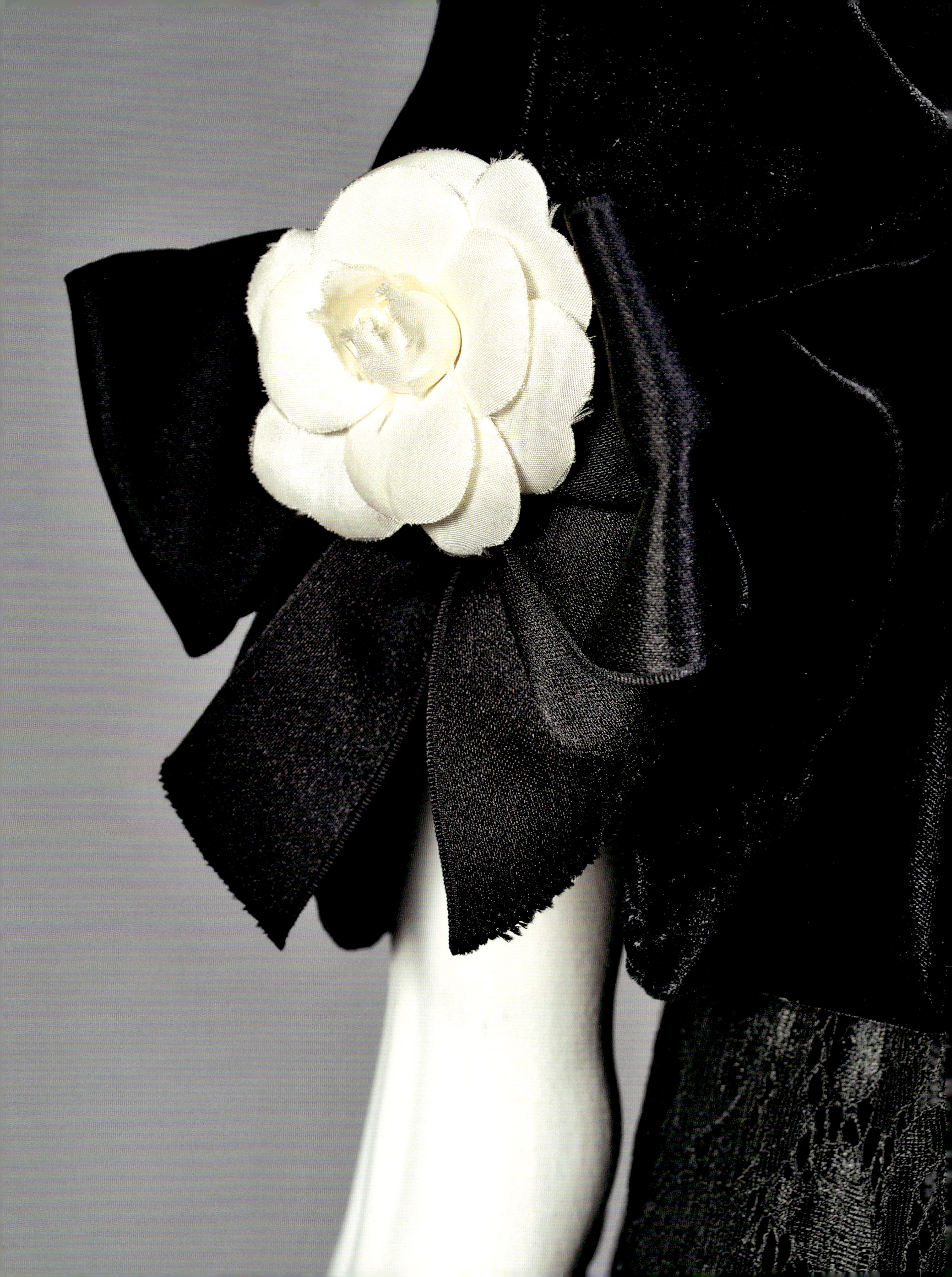

1989

67 EVENING DRESS, HAUTE COUTURE, AUTUMN 1989. Gabrielle Chanel's favored camellias became a token of house style with which Karl Lagerfeld often toyed, with both chic restraint and wild abandon. The latter is best summarized by his "strategic" placement of a tweed camellia on a pair of cotton jersey briefs in 1993; the former by this elegant evening ensemble, on which camellias clasp the neck and each bowed cuff. The outfit is a volte-face from Lagerfeld's highly structured couture of the late 1980s, instead comprising an easy velvet cardigan-jacket and long lace-and-organza skirt based on the simple lines of a petticoat.

1989

> **"My job is to make believe. There is no other way for a fashion house to survive."**
>
> Karl Lagerfeld,
> interview with author, July 2017

68 EVENING ENSEMBLE, READY-TO-WEAR, AUTUMN 1989. Lagerfeld's Chanel suits for this season consisted of jackets with ribbed tights or leggings rather than trousers, a conceit dubbed "the principal boy look" that influenced much of fashion in the late 1980s. At Chanel this is historically rooted in the idea of men's underwear as women's clothing. Lagerfeld's leggings were remarkably similar to men's thermal underwear, albeit elevated. This look is, therefore, quintessentially Chanel: jersey undergarments and collarless cardigan-jacket that technically combine to form a suit, yet appear anything but.

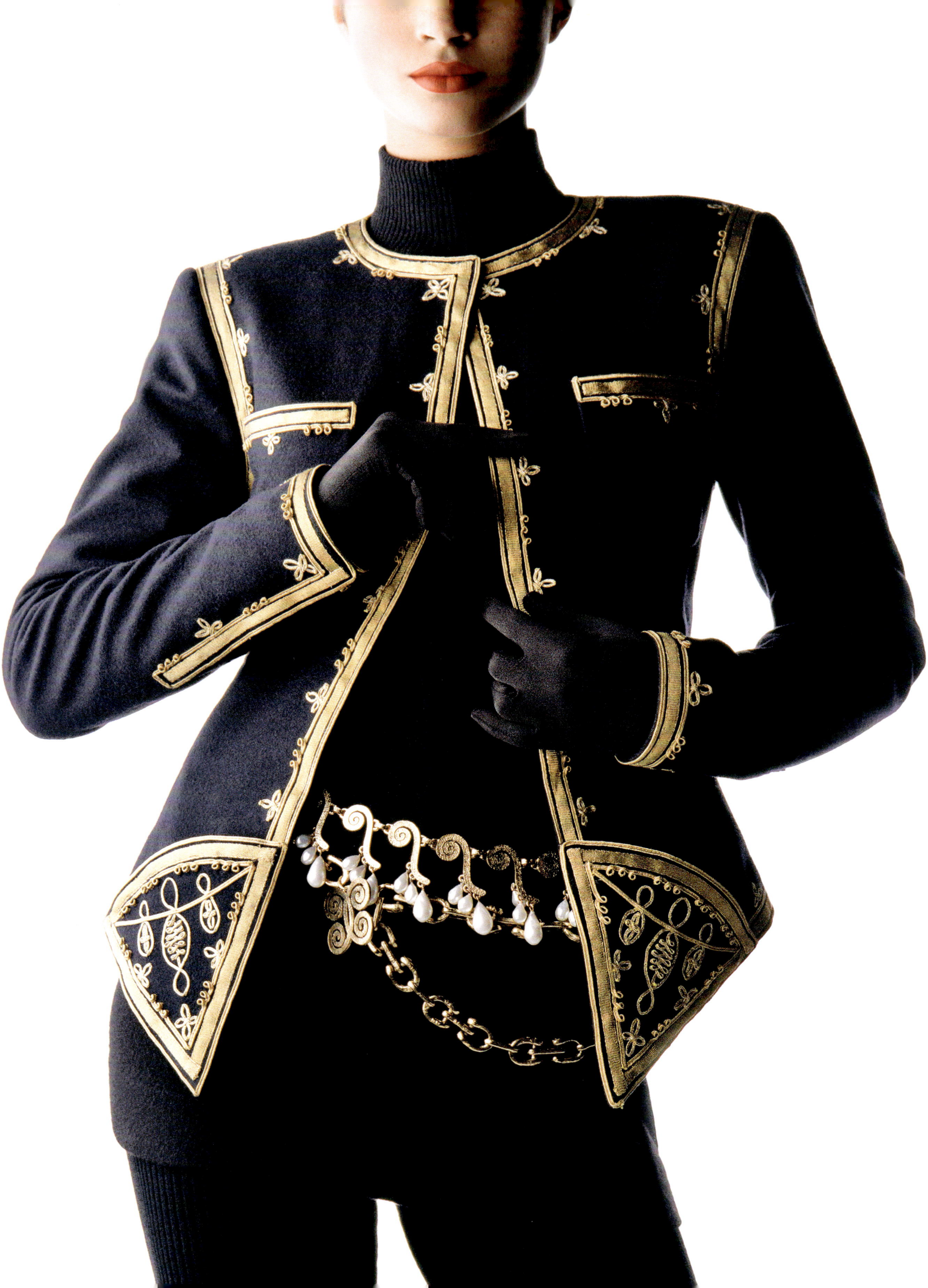

1990

69 EVENING DRESS, HAUTE COUTURE, AUTUMN 1990. At first, this richly embroidered gown with its wide-spreading skirt, compressed waist, and abundance of embroidery seems antithetical to Chanel's ideas. However, for this collection, evening dresses were cut like "bathrobes," according to Karl Lagerfeld, easily worn over short skirts. The high front slit mimics gowns of eighteenth-century court attire but also gives a modern freedom of movement and lightens the expanse of fabric. In the collection, this dress was worn over thigh-high boots—a wry nod from Lagerfeld to Gabrielle Chanel's self-declared reluctance to show her knees.

Model Christy Turlington wearing the dress, photographed by Irving Penn for "Rock 'n Royalty," *Vogue* US, October 1990.

1990

> " Chanel is Chanel wherever it is, in the shops, in the streets, in the salons. Chanel is Chanel. "
>
> Karl Lagerfeld,
> interview with author, July 2017

70 DAY SUIT, READY-TO-WEAR, AUTUMN 1990. By the 1990s, Lagerfeld's reworking of the Chanel suit had been pushed to extremes—this variation comes with matching gloves in braid-trimmed tweed. Here, the silhouette is significantly different from Gabrielle Chanel's, with a boxy jacket and fashionable micro-miniskirt. The proportions are emphasized by double-thick passementerie around the perimeter and along the sleeve seam, further delineating rounded shoulders; the pumped-up shape is almost a caricature of the original. By this period, the Chanel suit had become cemented once again as an aspirational status symbol.

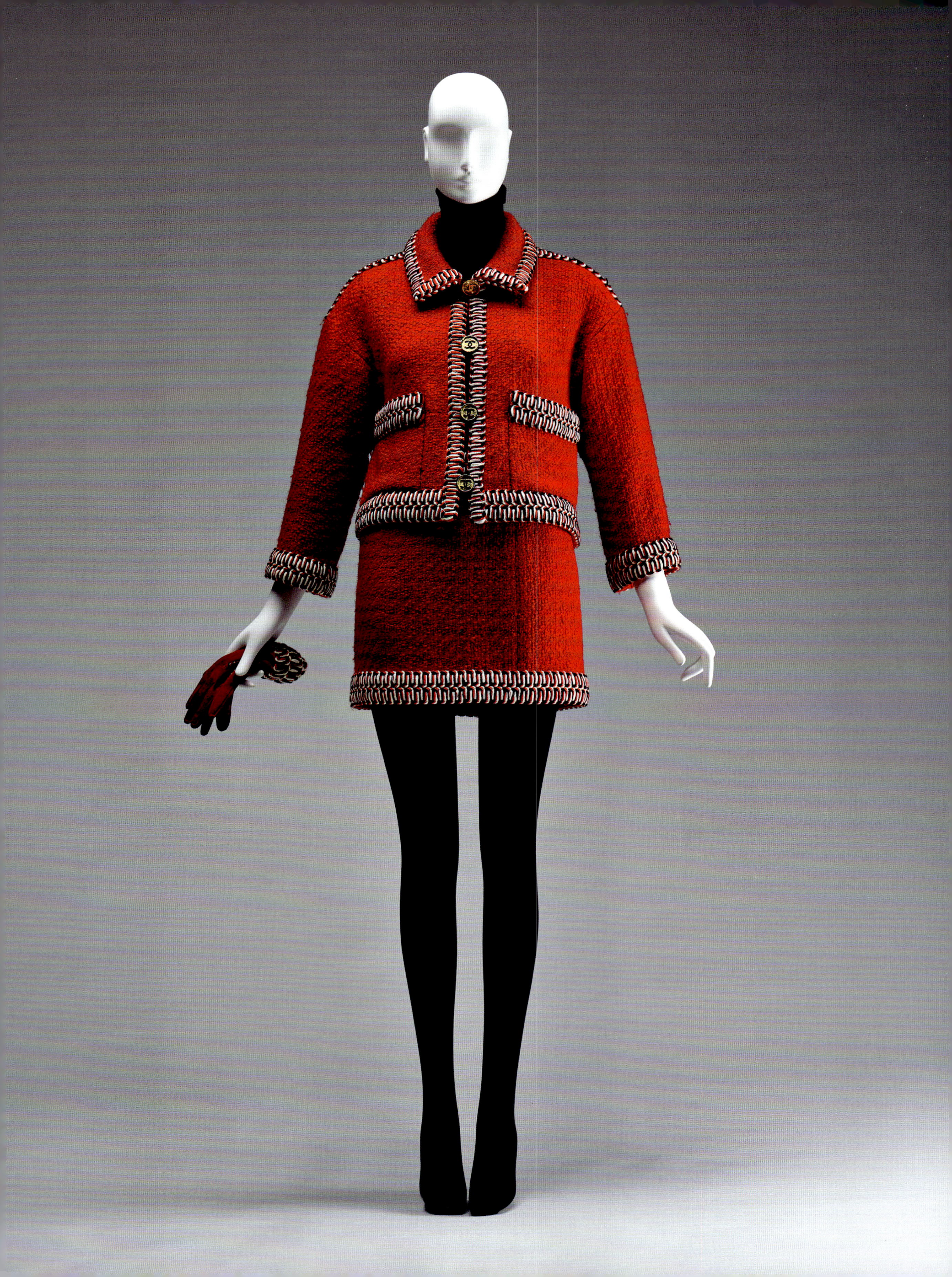

Chanel Spring 1990 haute couture evening gown with embroidered long-line bodice and pleated tulle skirt, painted by Ruben Alterio for *La Mode en Peinture*, issue no. 16, Spring 1990.

1990

71 EVENING DRESS, HAUTE COUTURE, SPRING 1990. Chanel's love of pearls was not restricted to jewelry with Karl Lagerfeld: In 1990 he challenged François Lesage to embroider an entire dress with them, resulting in this extraordinary creation, in which dress meets bijoux. It has an attenuated version of the Chanel suit jacket, fitted to the body, and the pearls are sewn to resemble the diamond quilting of Chanel's trademark handbag—a trick Lagerfeld had indulged before (item 59, 1986) but never seemed to tire of. Here, the hips are spanned by a belt executed by Gripoix in *pâte de verre*, resembling a precious antique necklace.

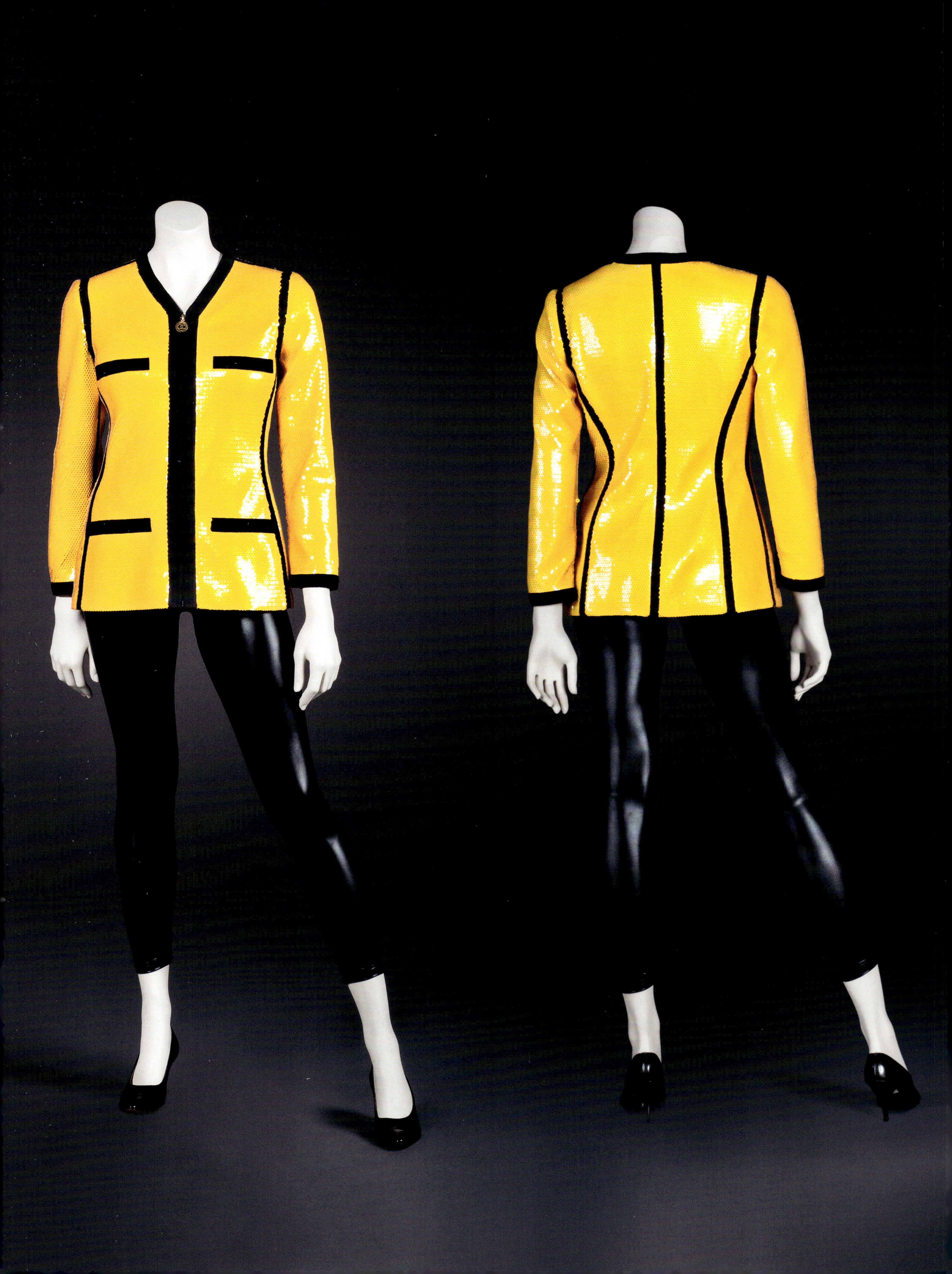

1991

> **To say that there is no fashion anymore is ridiculous. The fashion of no-fashion is still fashion. And fashion is a train that waits for nobody. Get on it, or it's gone.**
>
> Karl Lagerfeld,
> quoted in "King Karl," *Women's Wear Daily,* November 20, 1991

72 TROUSER SUIT, READY-TO-WEAR, SPRING 1991. Karl Lagerfeld proved adept at simultaneously revering and reinventing Gabrielle Chanel's trademarks. The influence of sportswear, evident in Chanel's creations from the outset, is here inverted—rather than giving haute couture the ease of sportswear, Lagerfeld seizes upon sportswear items and gives them the glossy finesse of fashion. A wetsuit is transmogrified into a Chanel suit, the banding for insulating seams used as a decorative device. It is coated in glistening sequins both to elaborate its surface and as a witty nod to the fad of wet-look fabrics.

Supermodels Helena Christensen, Stephanie Seymour, Karen Mulder, Naomi Campbell, Claudia Schiffer, and Cindy Crawford, photographed by Peter Lindbergh for "Wild at Heart," *Vogue*, September 1991.

1991

73 EVENING ENSEMBLES, READY-TO-WEAR, AUTUMN 1991. By the 1990s, Karl Lagerfeld had expanded the universe of Chanel to such a degree that the merest signifiers were enough to lasso wild ideas to the house's legacy. He was especially adept at toying with these conventions in his ready-to-wear, taking a wide swing at a larger audience than that for haute couture, and they seized on his parodies and pastiches of Chanel's designs with joy. Here, Lagerfeld juxtaposes pastel taffeta ball skirts hung with chains and biker leather hatched with Chanel quilting. "Chanel herself did more daring things than this," he said.

Model Kristen McMenamy on the runway in the Chanel Spring 1993 ready-to-wear show.

1992

74 EVENING ENSEMBLE, READY-TO-WEAR, SPRING 1992. While seeming utterly contemporary, this outfit riffs on multiple historic codes of the house. The bouffant full skirt, recalling Chanel styles of the late 1950s, is accessorized with a chain belt and topped by a *marcel*, a French undershirt (in actuality, a bodysuit), that cleverly references the source of Gabrielle Chanel's trademark jersey. The logo-emblazoned design is inspired, in part, by counterfeit Chanel goods Lagerfeld saw in the Far East—source material which, like men's undergarments in the past, caused a frisson of shock in 1990s fashion.

Model wearing the Matelassé Perles cuff, photographed by Tiziano Magni for a Chanel Jewelry press release.

1993

75 MATELASSÉ PERLES CUFF. The elemental components of the Chanel look are strong enough to cross-pollinate various mediums. Just as Lagerfeld took inspiration from jewelry to embellish fashion (item 51, 1983), so Chanel fashion fed into jewelry designs. In 1993, Chanel launched fine jewelry—the antecedent being Gabrielle Chanel's own collection of diamonds (item 18, 1932), treated with irreverence and extraordinary invention. The same is true here: A cuff in 18-karat gold, diamonds, and cultured pearls is arranged in a quilted effect mimicking the 2.55 handbag, while the shape is similar to Chanel's signature cuffs (item 15, 1930).

1994

> " Making the timeless
> exist in the immediate and
> allowing the fleeting
> to be perpetually reborn:
> These are the deep secrets
> of the Chanel style. "
>
> Karl Lagerfeld,
> *Chanel* exhibition catalog, Metropolitan Museum of Art, 2005

76 DAY SUIT, READY-TO-WEAR, SPRING 1994. A decade into his tenure at Chanel, Karl Lagerfeld seemed able to endlessly rework the Chanel suit. If Chanel cemented her clothing styles, Lagerfeld made them emblematic of the ever-changing winds of fashion—for Spring 1994 it was shrunken, with a miniskirt and abbreviated jacket over a waist-cincher in matching tweed. Chanel herself created dresses with boned bodices, so this is not as radical a departure as may be first assumed. It is a testimony to the power of the style that, even reconfigured drastically, this look is still recognizably Chanel, while also a witness of its time.

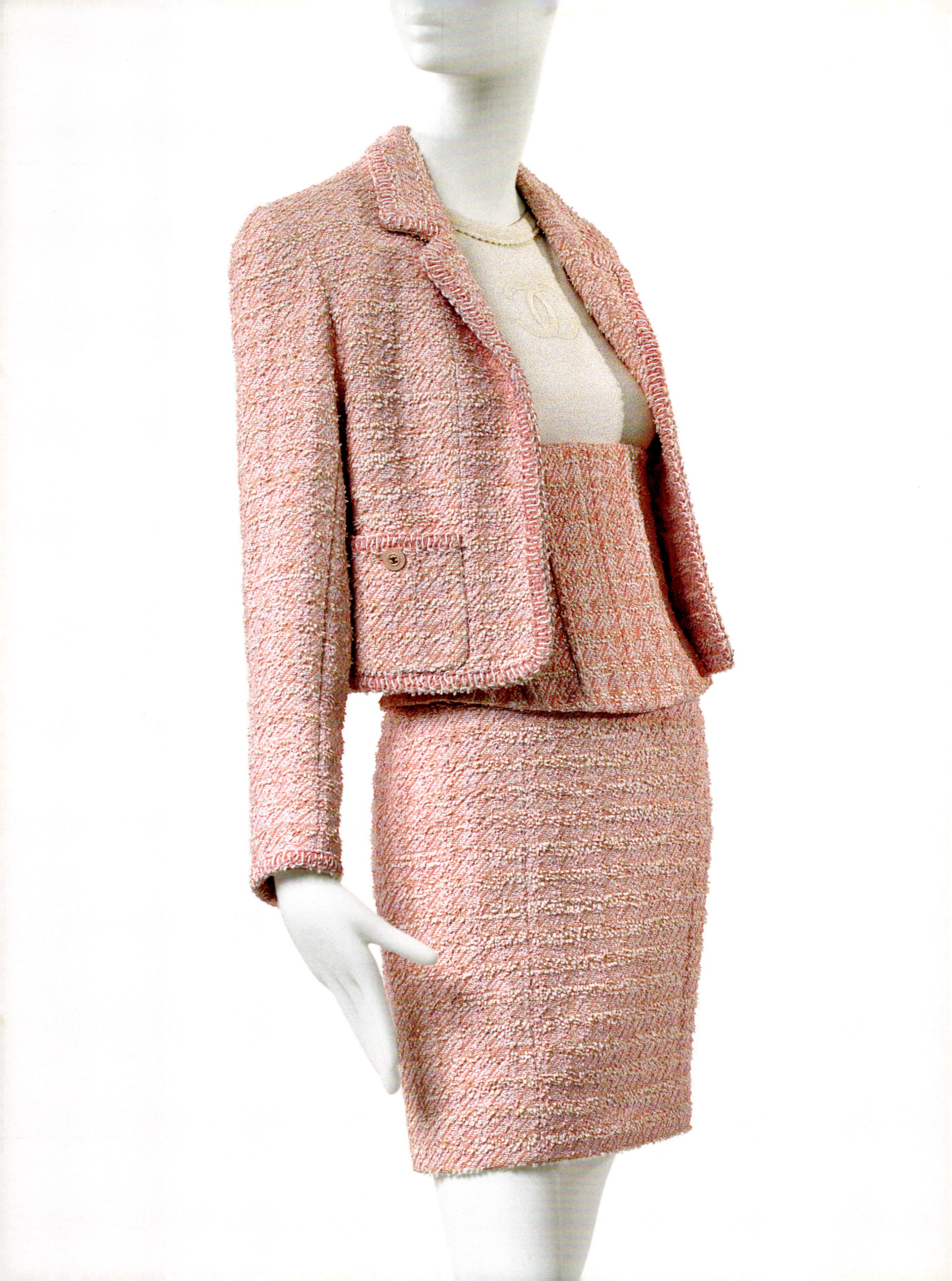

1996

77 "COROMANDEL" EVENING DRESS, HAUTE COUTURE, SPRING 1996. This was the first Chanel collection presented in Paris's Hôtel Ritz—where Gabrielle Chanel slept each night, despite keeping a luxurious apartment above her salons on the rue Cambon. This dress is one of the most painstaking and expensive ever produced by the house—embroidered by Lesage with gold thread, in a lattice design inspired by Chanel's Coromandel screens. The embroidery alone required 1,200 hours of handwork, but the simplicity of silhouette recalls both Chanel's 1930s creations and sportswear-influenced ready-to-wear of the 1990s.

Model Shalom Harlow wearing the dress, photographed by Irving Penn for *Vogue*, April 1996.

1996

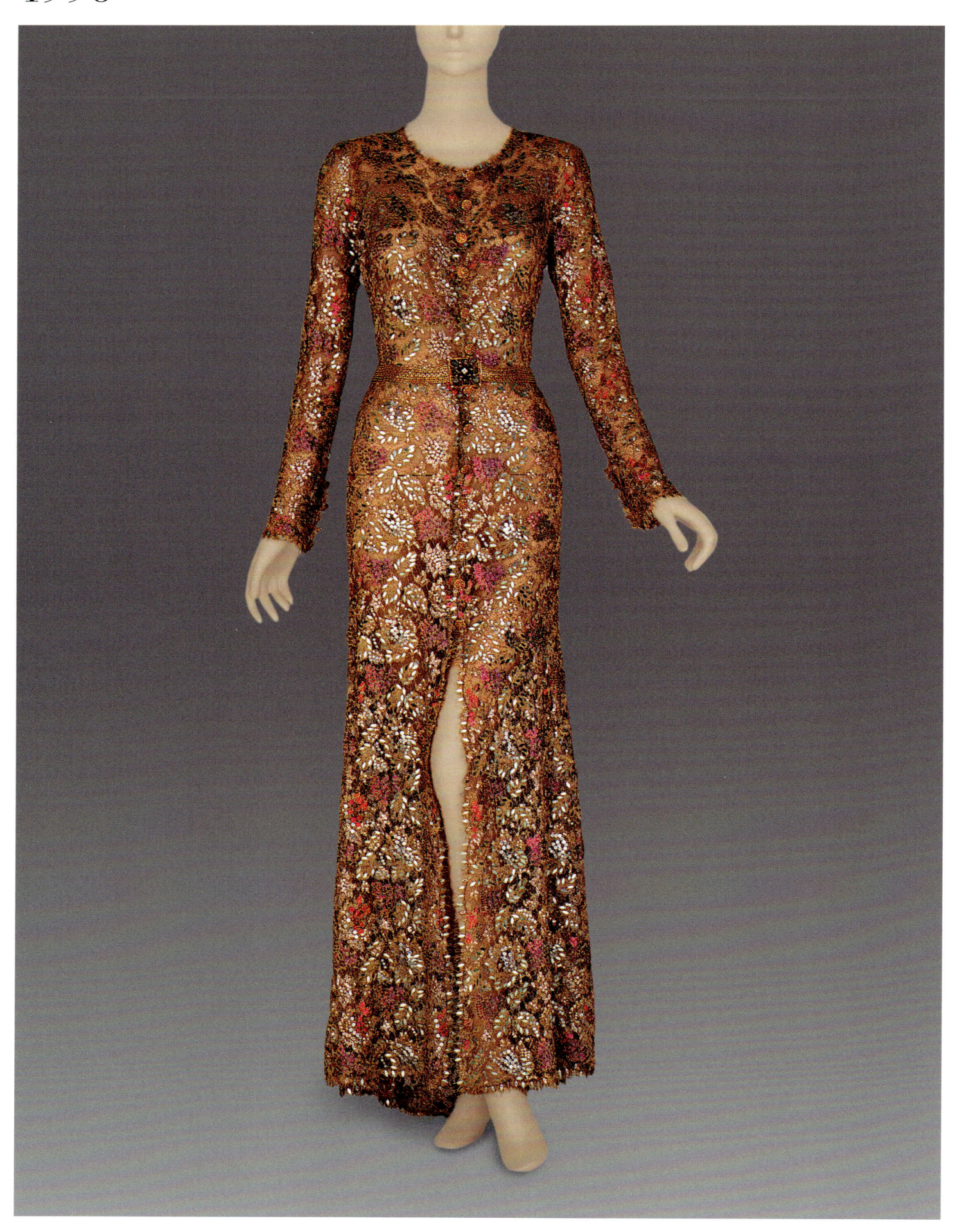

78 EVENING DRESS, HAUTE COUTURE, SPRING 1996. This show marked twenty-five years since Gabrielle Chanel's death, so Karl Lagerfeld returned to the opulent suites where she lived during World War II, and where she passed away in 1971, to resurrect her ghost. Embroidered with sequins and clasped with metal, this lace gown is almost a direct facsimile of a gown from Chanel's Autumn 1937 collection, in which the *couturière* was photographed by Cecil Beaton for *Vogue* (*opposite*). This dress, in the collection of the socialite Mouna Ayoub, shows the remarkable modernity of Chanel's style in that it still felt contemporary almost sixty years later.

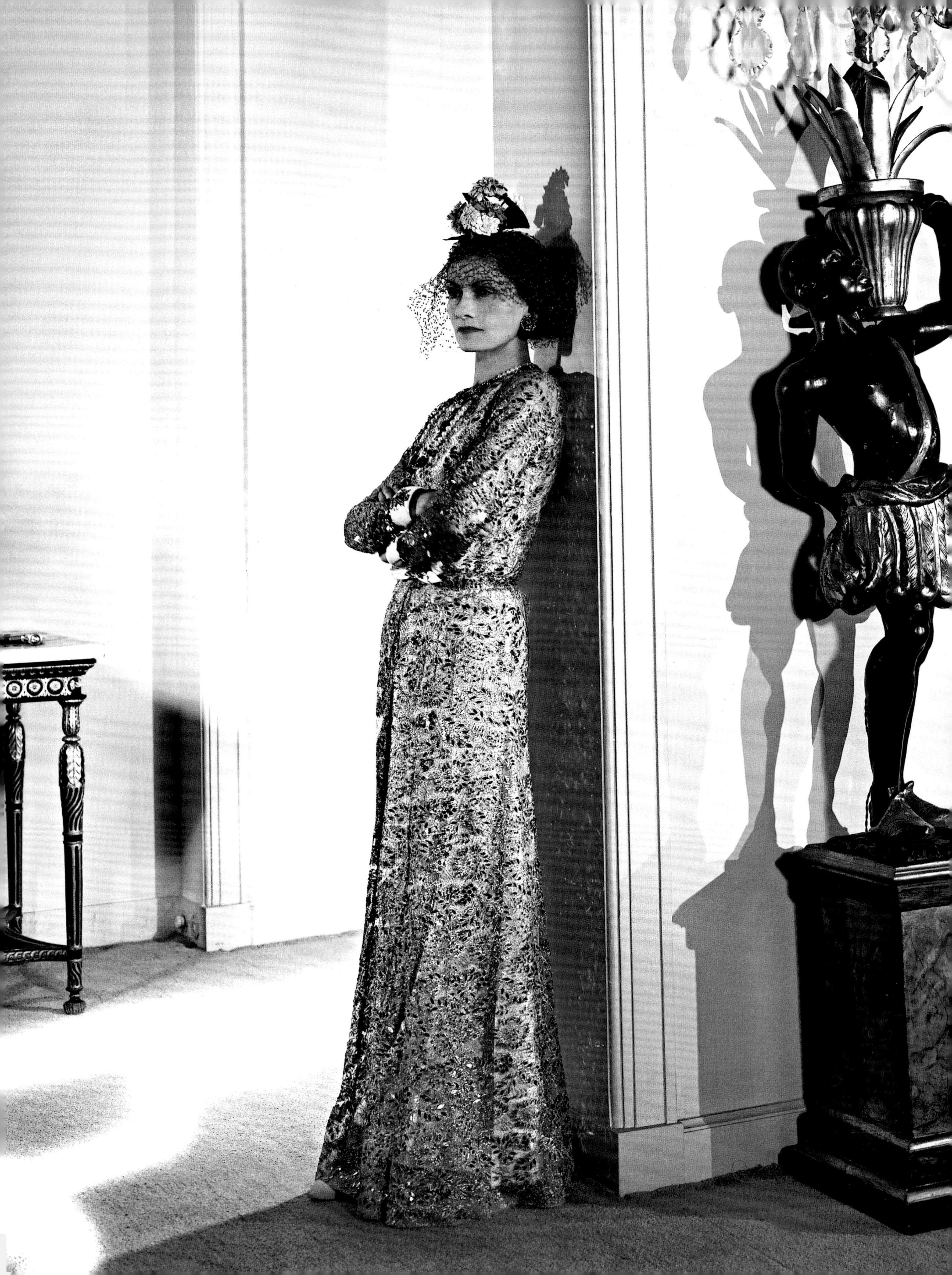

Model Stella Tennant wearing the ensemble, from *L'Officiel de la Mode*, no. 807, August 1996.

1996

79 EVENING ENSEMBLE, READY-TO-WEAR, AUTUMN 1996. Directly echoing Gabrielle Chanel's 1960s evening designs (item 35, 1960), Karl Lagerfeld used rich figured lamé and jeweled buttons to create arresting cocktail ensembles of otherwise simple, even utilitarian cut and shape. Influenced by the military shoulders of his Spring 1996 couture collection, Lagerfeld riffed on an army theme, which had also inspired many of Chanel's fashion innovations. As if to demonstrate his knowledge, he wittily underlined them here—such as a lining that extends onto the revers, drawn from uniforms.

1996

80 EVENING DRESS, HAUTE COUTURE, AUTUMN 1996. Wheat is considered a symbol of prosperity and renewal—perfect for fashion—and for the superstitious Gabrielle Chanel it was a good-luck talisman. It was present in each room of her apartment, as gilded ormolu and decorative brass ornaments, and even a 1947 painting by Salvador Dalí. Both Chanel and Lagerfeld featured it in their collections for the *maison*. The first example was for Spring 1960, a white lace dress embroidered with wheat; Lagerfeld later used the motif a number of times, for Spring 1988 couture, Spring 2010 ready-to-wear, and here for Autumn 1996 couture.

1996

81 EVENING COAT, HAUTE COUTURE, AUTUMN 1996. For the second in a trio of couture collections shown at the Ritz, Karl Lagerfeld once again riffed on iconography drawn from Chanel's apartments across the rue Cambon, and reinterpreted her beloved Coromandel lacquer screens in a different way: A series of styles Lagerfeld dubbed "endless suits" saw Chinese-inspired Chanel jackets elongated into mid-thigh-, knee-, or ankle-length coats, worn over slender leggings. The coats were richly embroidered by Lesage with seed beads and paillettes in Orientalist designs that directly mirrored the inlaid decorations of the originals.

1998

> **❝ If I would be pretentious, I would say that I reinvent tradition. ❞**
>
> Karl Lagerfeld,
> interview with author, July 2017

82 EVENING DRESS, HAUTE COUTURE, SPRING 1998. In 1997, Lagerfeld shuttered his eponymous label and eschewed his role at Chloé to focus on his designs for Chanel. What followed was a series of pre-millennium collections that dug to the root of Chanel's identity, reexamining styles and motifs from the 1920s. This collection was the first staged in the salons of 31 rue Cambon since Lagerfeld's debut fifteen years earlier. Models descended the mirrored staircase in styles that could have come from the hand of Chanel herself—including this sheath embroidered with tonal abstract camellias, and veiled headdress reminiscent of a cloche.

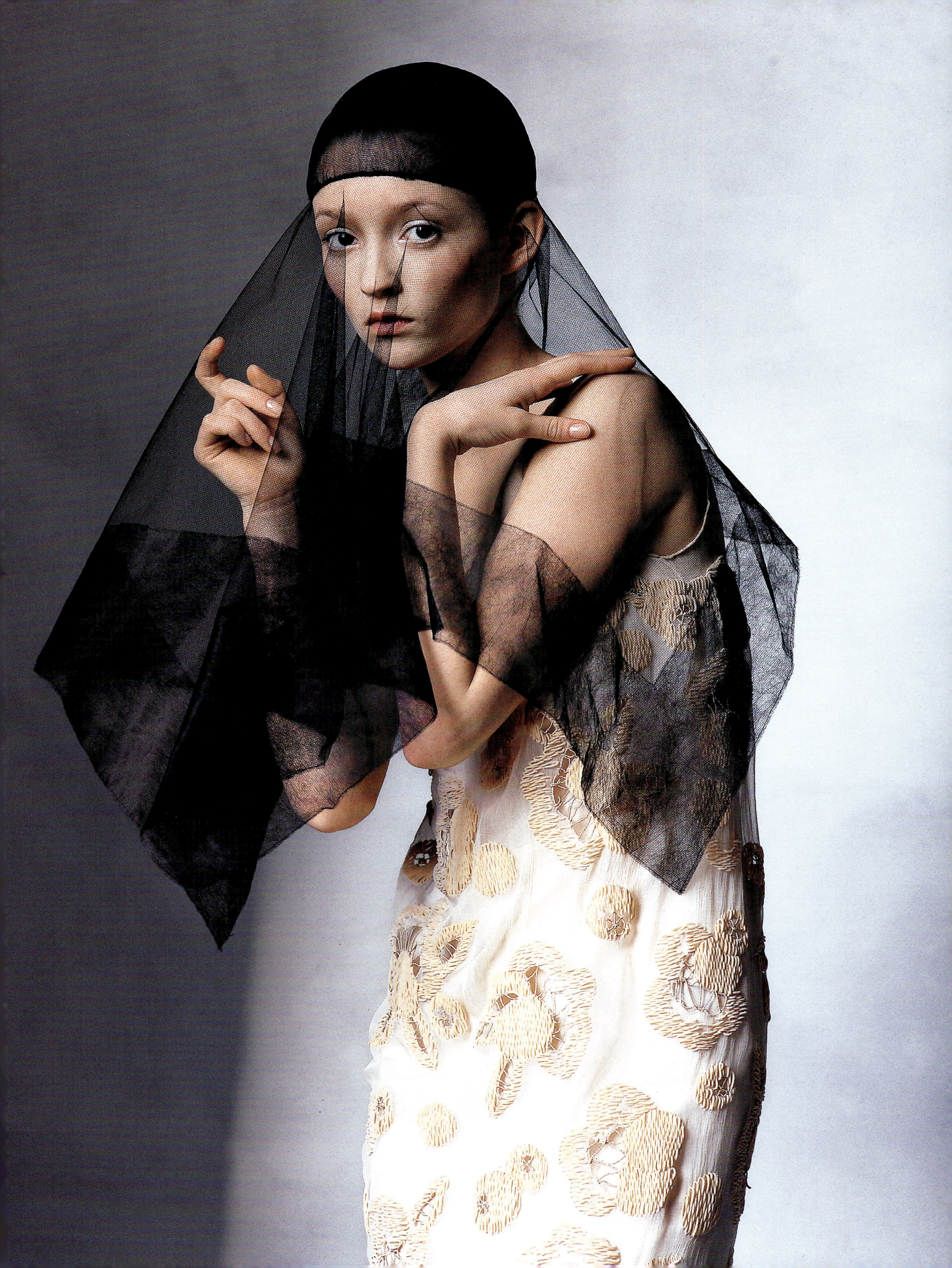

2002

> **I had to go from what Chanel was to what it should be, could be, what it had been to something else.**
>
> Karl Lagerfeld

83 DAY SUIT, HAUTE COUTURE, AUTUMN 2002. This suit combines sobriety with extravagance: A faultlessly tailored wool jacket, whose matte surface appears molded and almost seamless, sits over a kicked-out skirt, flaring over seven layers of tulle, the edges embroidered with metal paillettes. The narrow sleeves and shoulders underscore Chanel's own obsession with fit, specifically on these areas of the body, but there is also a new reflection of Karl Lagerfeld himself—in 2001, the designer shed 42 kilograms, and the tautly tailored jackets and stovepipe collars of his new personal wardrobe were mirrored in this collection's day clothing.

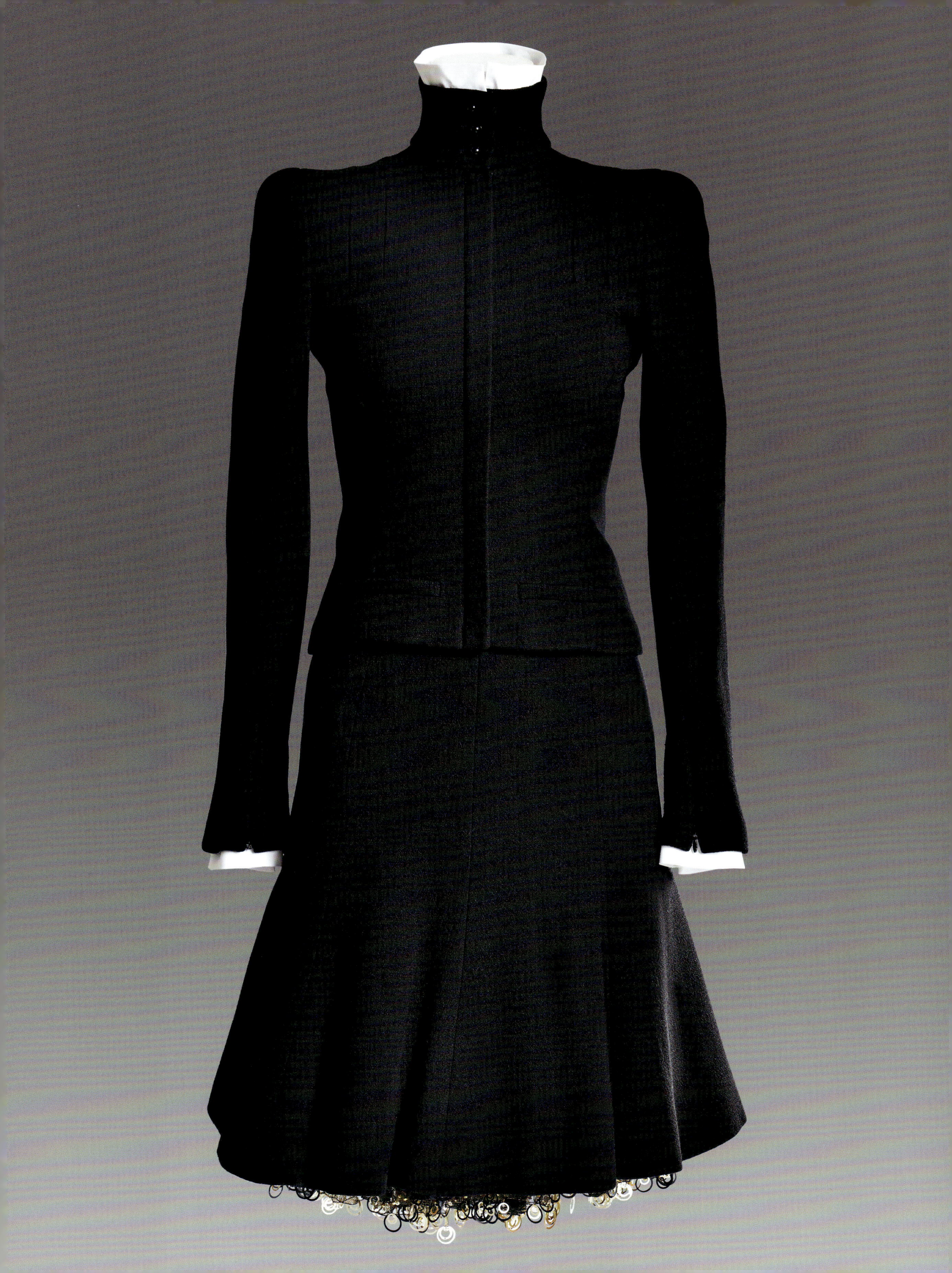

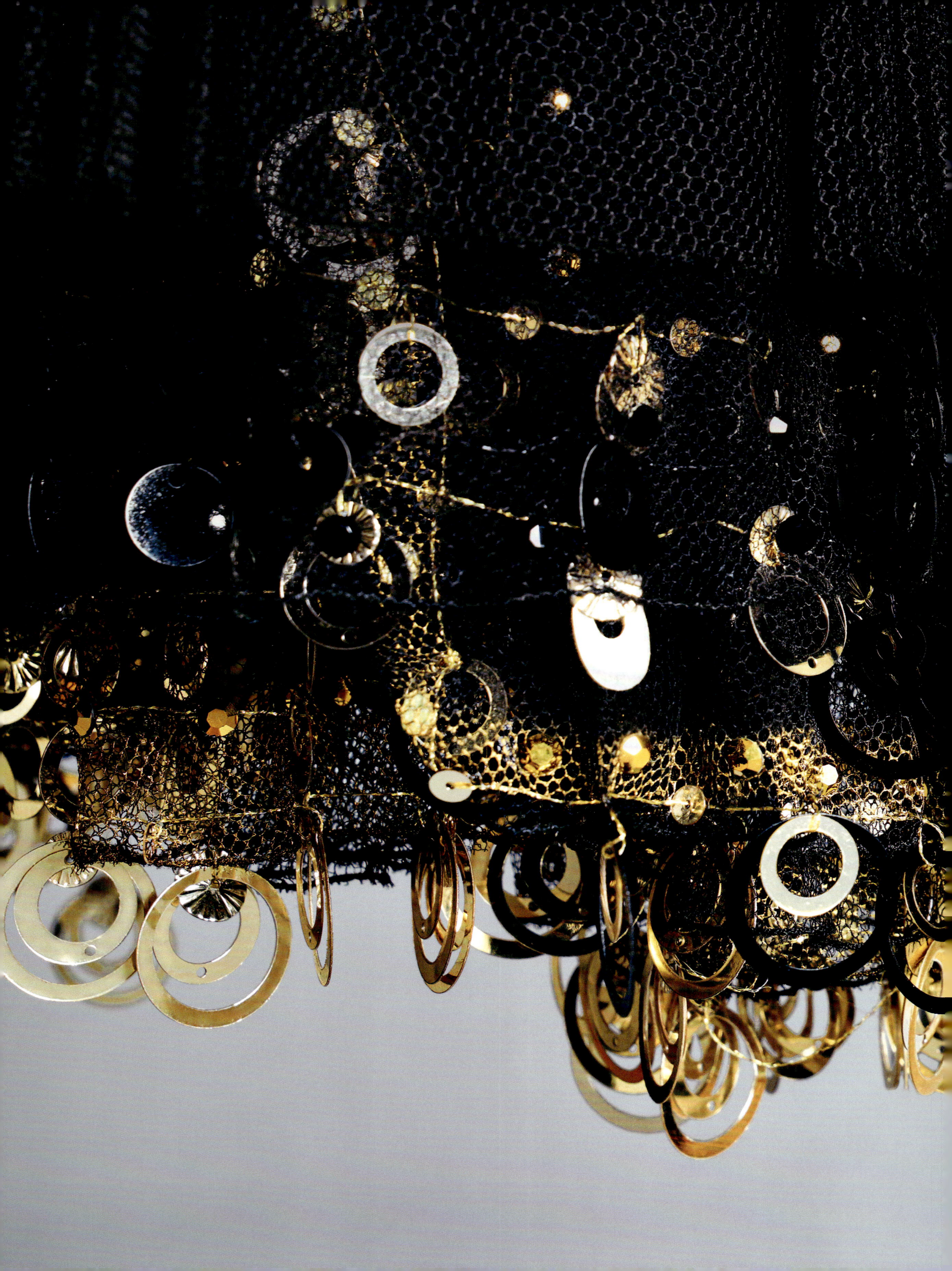

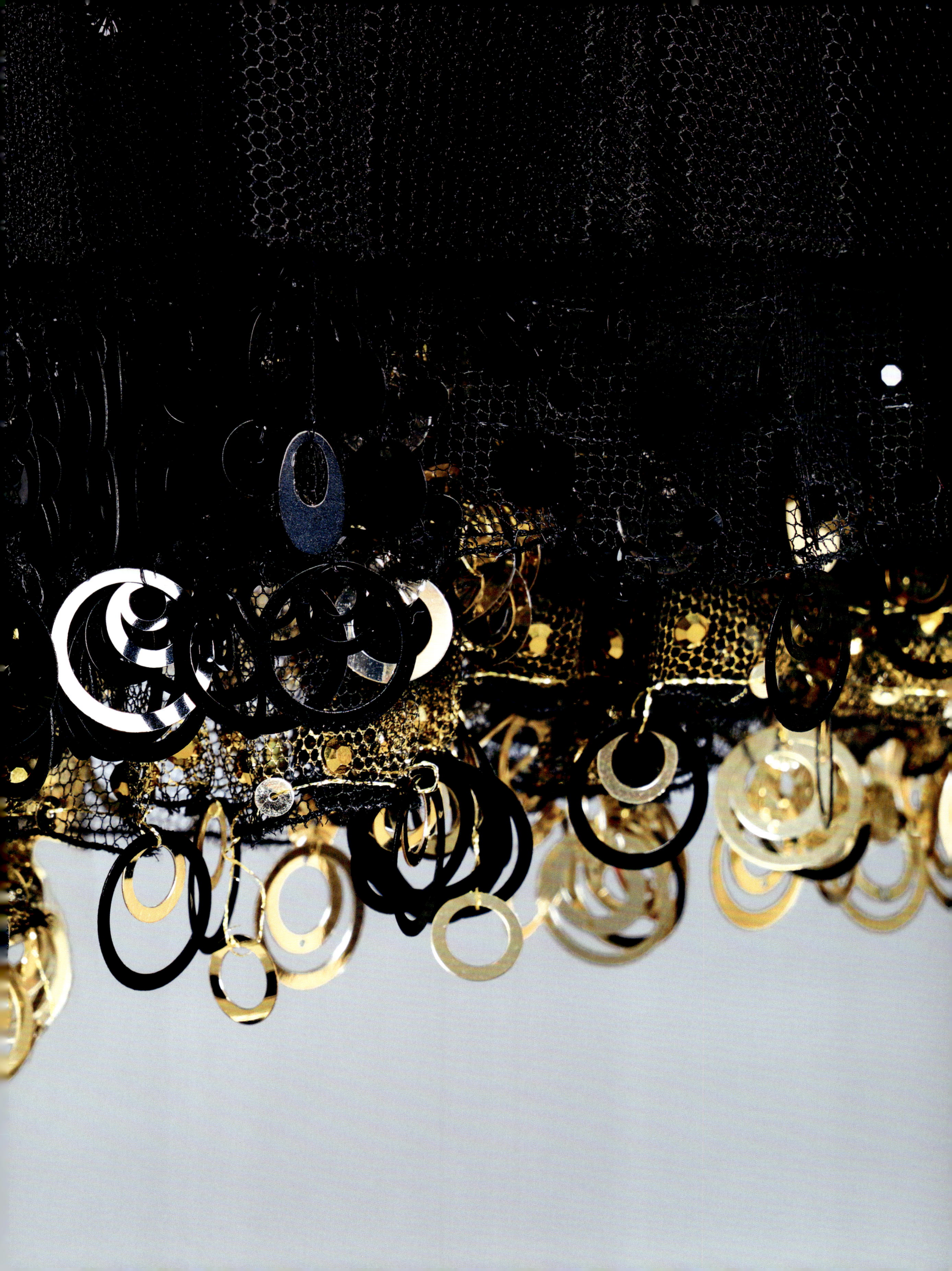

2002

> " Luxury is the ease of a T-shirt in a very expensive dress. "
>
> Karl Lagerfeld

84 EVENING DRESS, HAUTE COUTURE, AUTUMN 2002. Embellished with thousands of hand-sewn sequins, this dress seems a wearable version of the famous mirrored staircase at rue Cambon. While the collection's tailoring was reminiscent of Chanel's Edwardian-era origins, the dress borrows its silhouette from the Jazz Age, the dancing rows of dagger-point hems recalling Chanel's tiers of fringe, and Lagerfeld's toying with deconstruction and destruction. The juxtaposition of strikingly simplistic silhouette—sleeveless and round-necked, like a man's undershirt—with intricate detail is one of the house's enduring hallmarks.

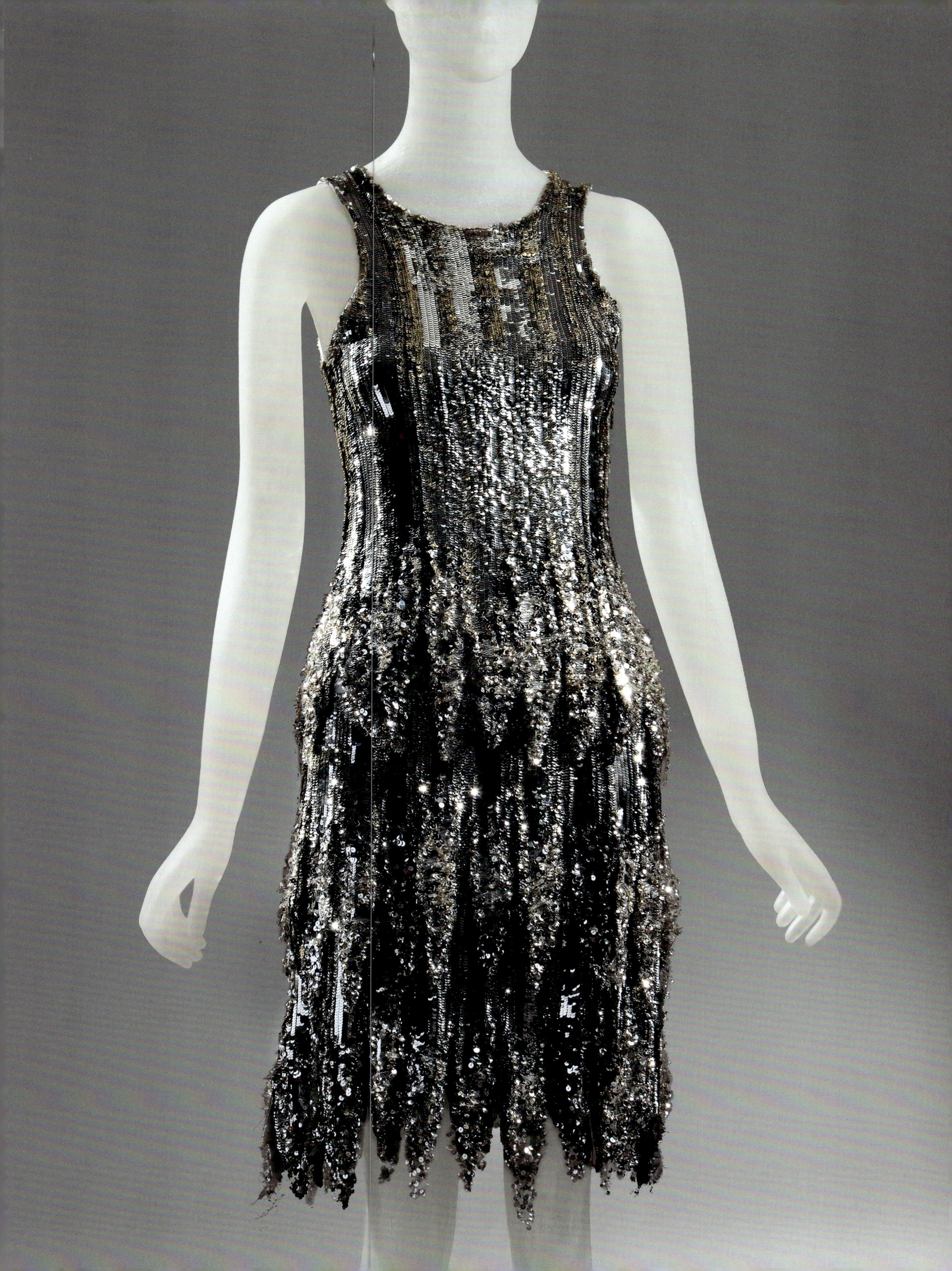

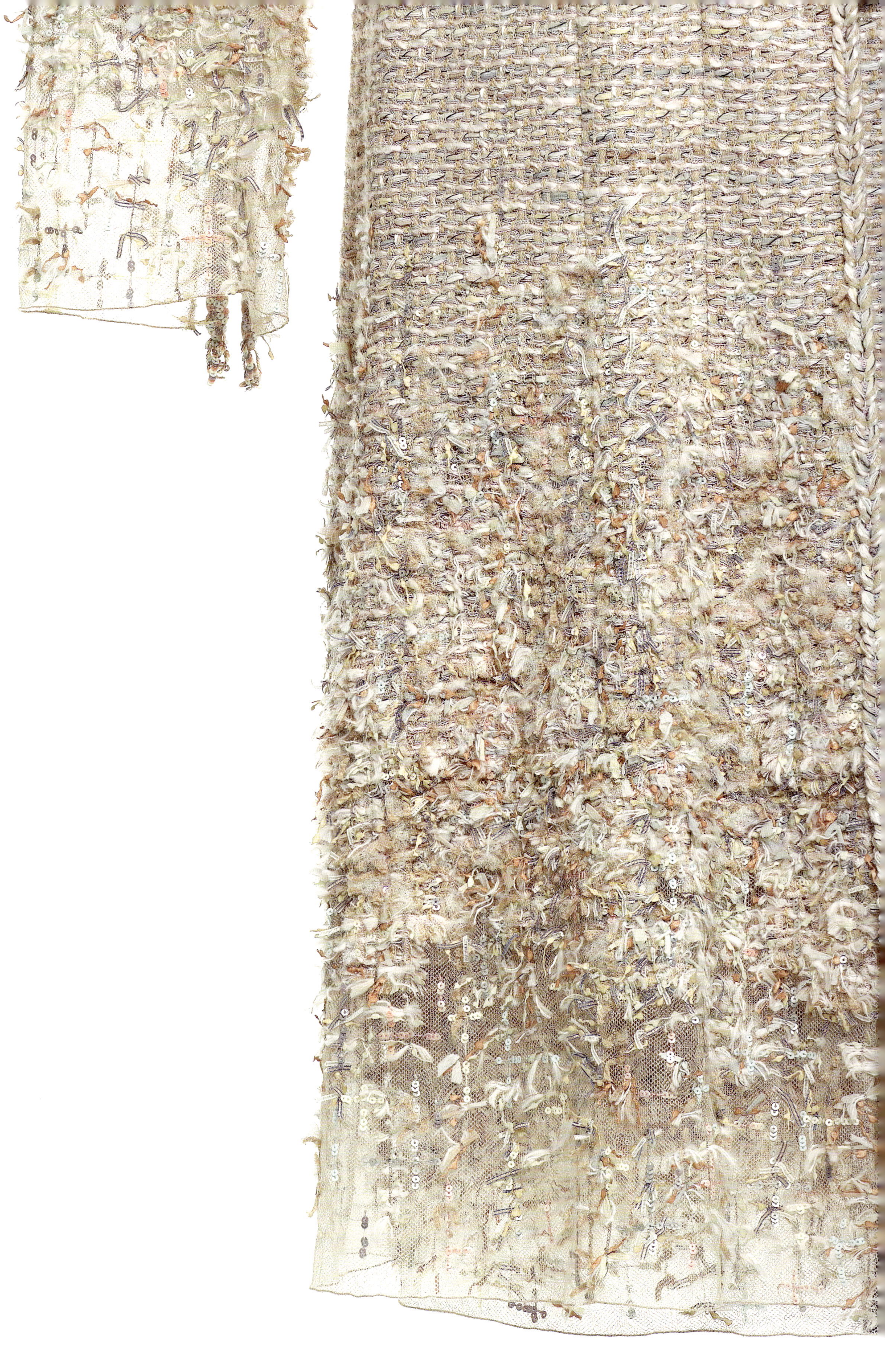

2003

85 DAY SUIT, HAUTE COUTURE, SPRING 2003. Inspired by various influences—including Gabrielle Chanel's self-professed disdain for fine fabrics, and Chanel suits from the 1950s with frayed edges, or yarns of the tweed unraveled and woven into their contrasting braid—Karl Lagerfeld pulled the Chanel suit apart. Instead of rage, however, this was executed with poetic beauty, unraveling the wool tweed threads and embroidering them with sequins and beads on silk tulle. This was a painstaking technique executed by Atelier Montex, one of a stable of Parisian specialists to which Chanel turns to supply its haute couture ateliers.

2003

86 DAY SUIT, HAUTE COUTURE, SPRING 2003. Marking the start of his third decade at Chanel, Karl Lagerfeld was inspired by the idea of lightness—a fixation of Gabrielle Chanel herself, who softened her tailoring to such a degree it was necessary to weight the hem. This example plays with Chanel silhouettes of the 1950s, particularly the tiered lace evening dresses, here transposed into a raw-edged tulle skirt. The wool jacket is tightly fitted and trimmed in velvet, recalling historical styles, and the ruff at the neck is reminiscent of Chanel's Watteau costume (item 25, 1939). Despite these references, this suit feels modern and new.

2003

87 COATDRESS, HAUTE COUTURE, AUTUMN 2003. Of the house's founder, Lagerfeld said: "There is no designer who gave her fashion an image of her person as Chanel." Yet in the new millennium—following his own image reinvention—Lagerfeld began to marry his own persona with that of Coco. Increasingly, his trademark high collars, monochrome palette, heavy jewelry, and starched white shirts would appear—all of which, of course, also link back to Gabrielle Chanel. This collection focused on attenuated slenderness, and this style, with its Draculean collar and silk jabot, is a feminine counterpart to Lagerfeld's attire.

2004

> **"Nothing is granted in fashion, and this is what I love about fashion."**
>
> Karl Lagerfeld,
> quoted by Marc Karimzadeh, *Women's Wear Daily,* January 9, 2013

88 EVENING ENSEMBLE, HAUTE COUTURE, SPRING 2004. Lagerfeld titled this collection "The Duality of Contrasts," juxtaposing severity and extravagance, fragility with strength. In this ensemble, the duality of male and female dress is expressed via a precisely tailored jacket over a delicate chiffon skirt embroidered with ostrich fronds. The tiered skirt recalls numerous Chanel styles (item 12, 1930; item 20, 1937), while the jacket is seemingly influenced by Lagerfeld's own wardrobe. The overarching masculine-feminine contrast and the tiniest detail of a black satin ribbon at the neck are equally and unmistakably Chanel.

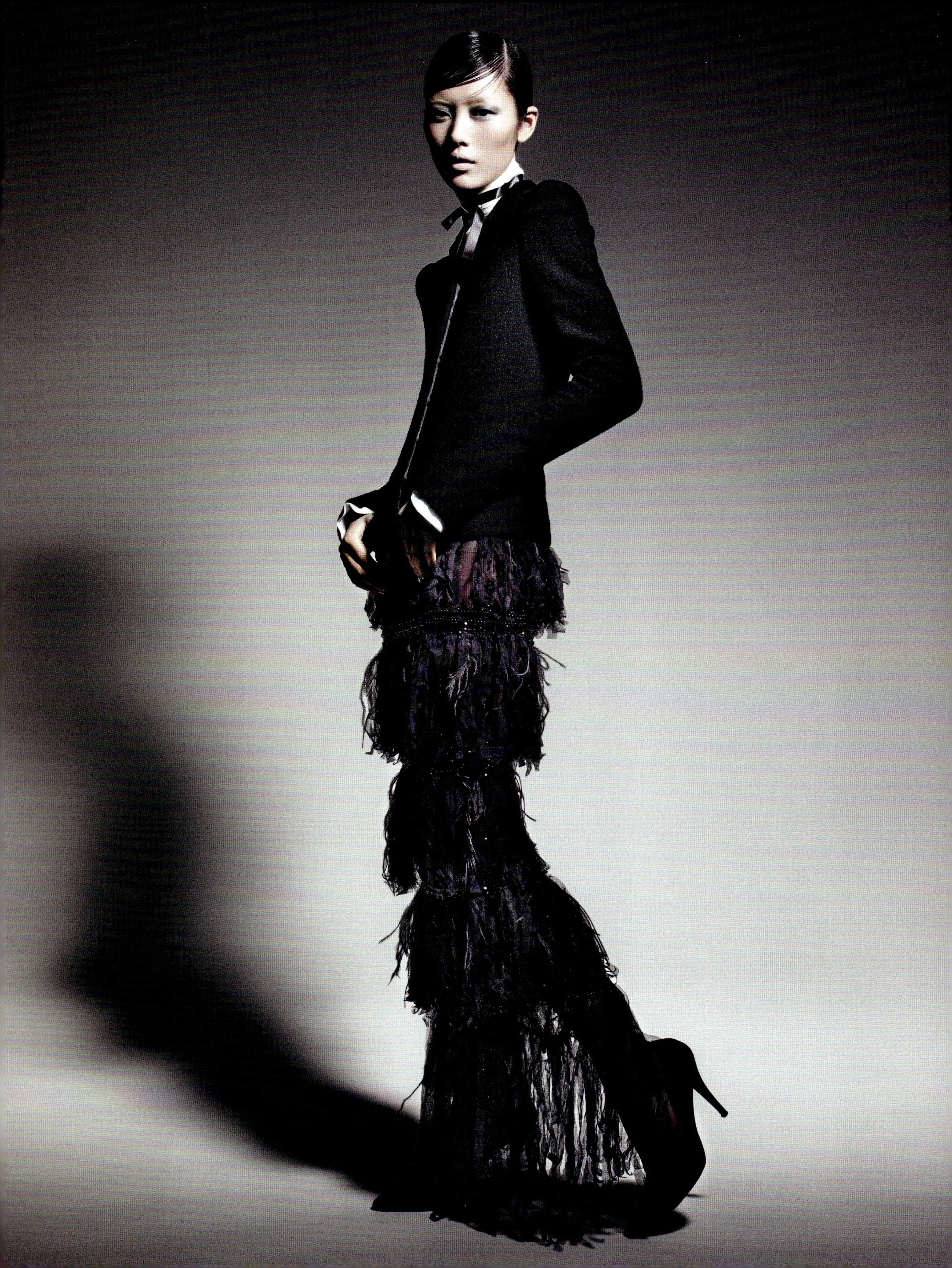

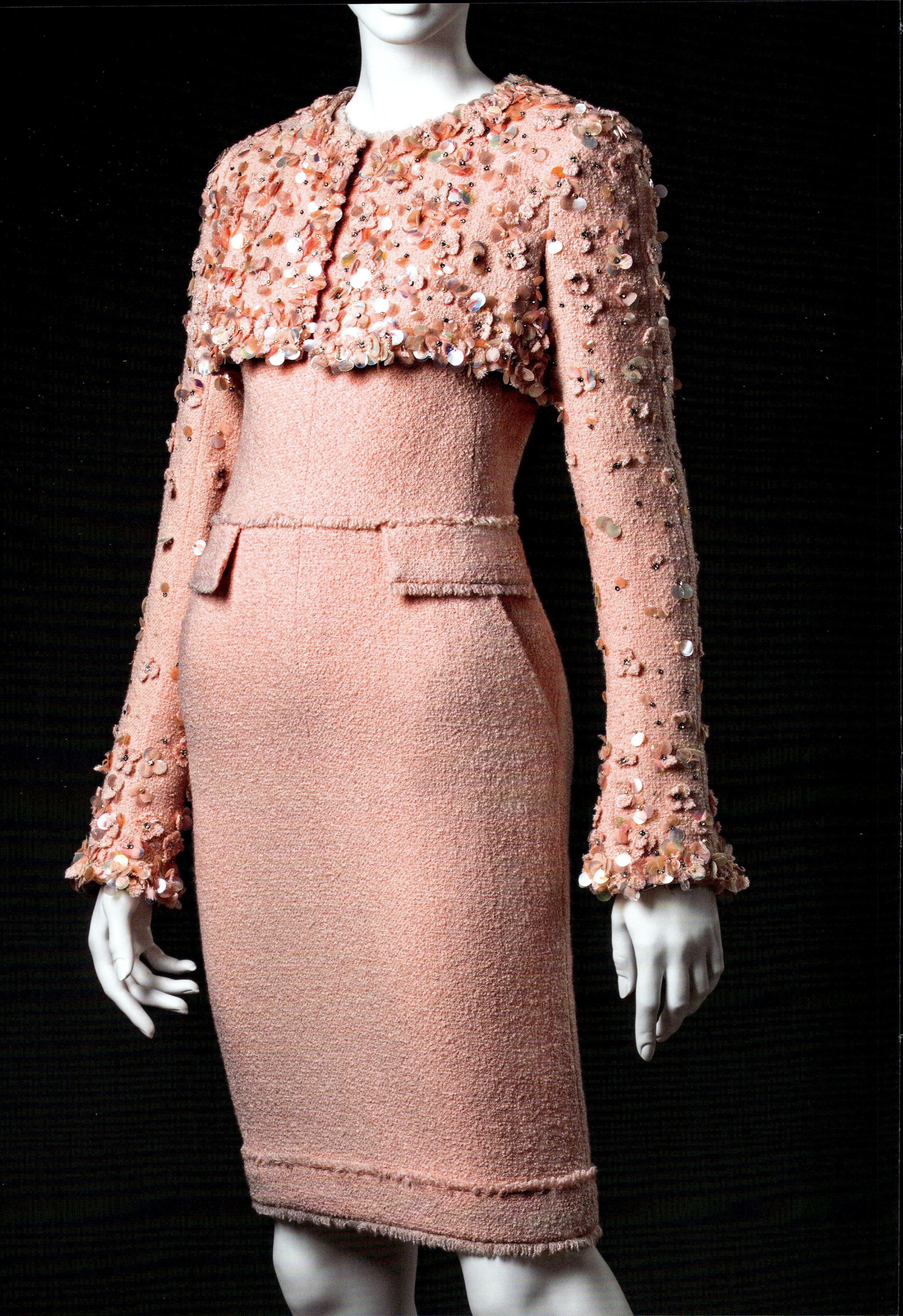

2004

89 DAY ENSEMBLE, HAUTE COUTURE, SPRING 2004. Pale shades of pink, from rose-beige to candy, are as much a part of the Chanel canon as black, suggestive of femininity and even nudity. Here, Karl Lagerfeld uses the color for a Chanel suit that defies conventions: The jacket is shortened to a brief bolero over a sleeveless sheath dress, the former richly embellished with embroidery that blurs the line between day and evening. For the show the dress was belted, but was adapted for the client, the editor in chief of American *Vogue*, Anna Wintour.

2005

90 WEDDING DRESS, HAUTE COUTURE, AUTUMN 2005. Well into his third decade at the house, Lagerfeld continued to toy with recognizable markers of Chanel—here, the fabric flowers that Gabrielle Chanel used as decoration on her suits and evening dresses from the 1920s onward. This wedding dress is created from 2,500 camellias, all handmade by Lemarié, which supplies about 40,000 fabric flowers to Chanel annually. Each individual camellia, varying from buds to full blossoms, took ninety minutes to create, then was further embroidered with sequins and ostrich feathers. Lagerfeld compared the dress to a bridal bouquet.

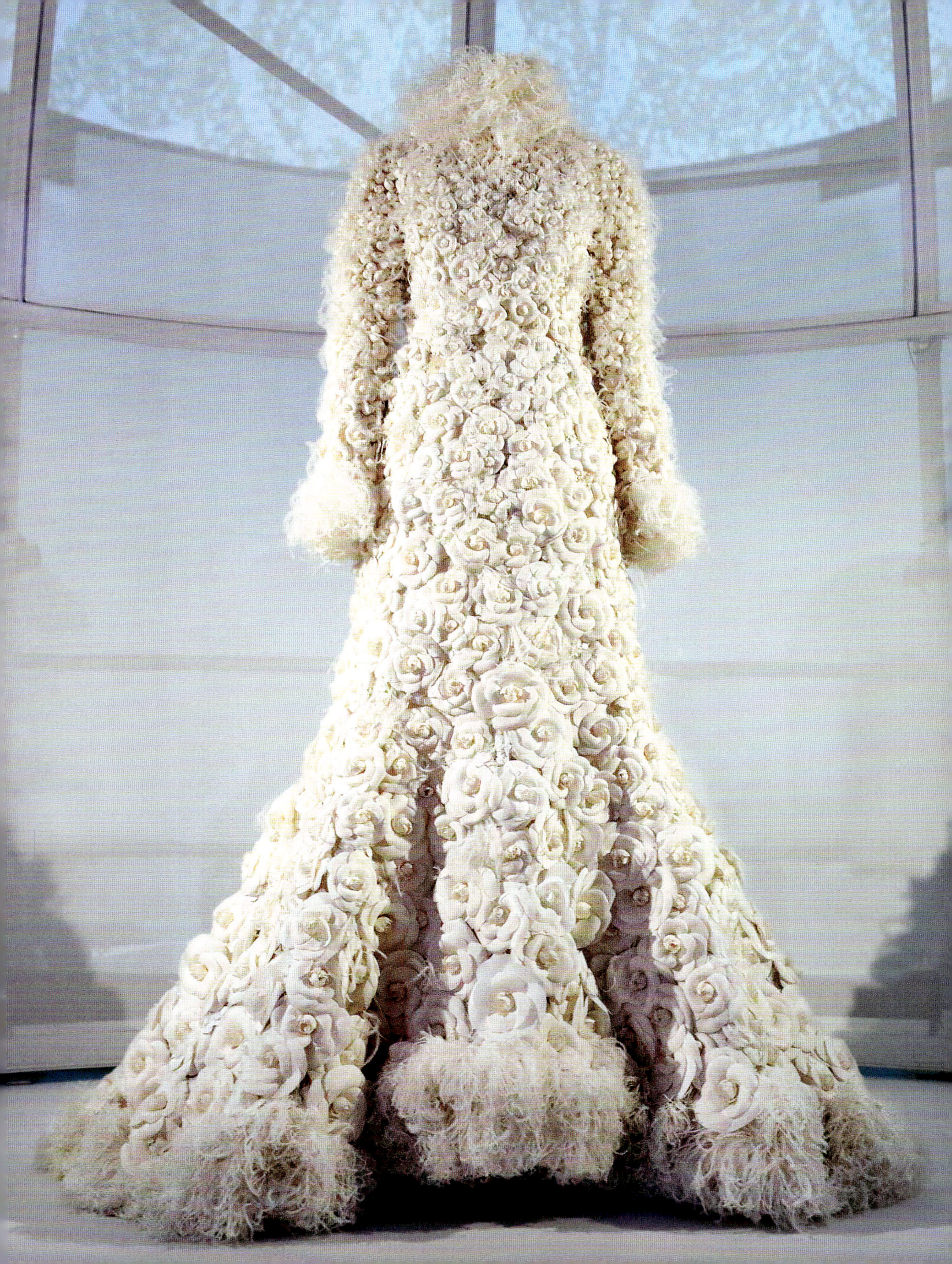

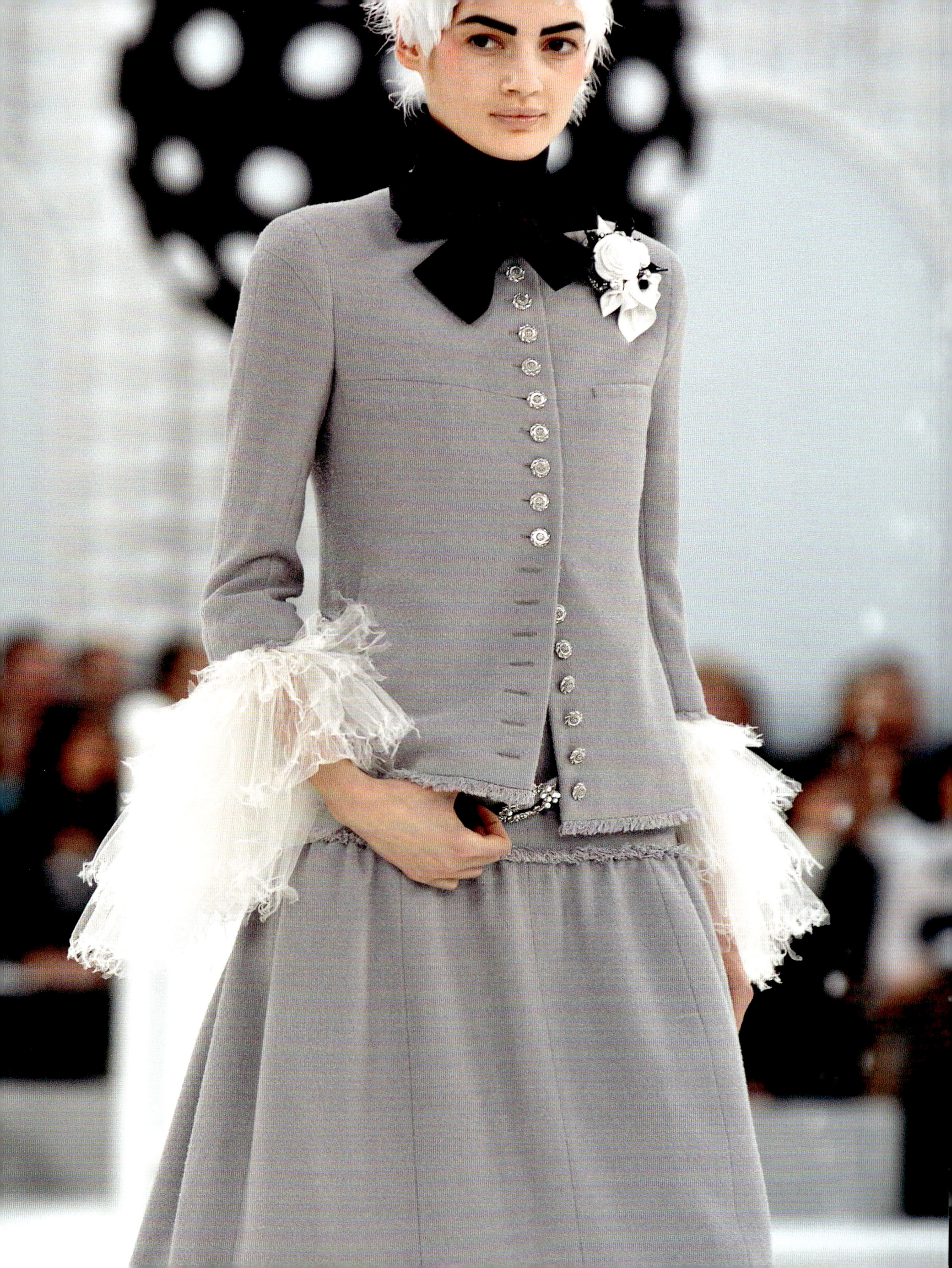

2005

91 COAT, HAUTE COUTURE, SPRING 2005. This piece is derived from Look 13 in the Spring 2005 couture collection (*opposite*), originally a suit in dove gray wool with organdy ruffles, reworked as a black coat. It is a privilege of couture clients to redesign outfits, sometimes significantly, in collaboration with the ateliers. Here the client—the artist Daphne Guinness—pulls the piece closer to the styles of Gabrielle Chanel herself in its monochrome simplicity. The ruffled sleeves resemble *engageantes*—the sleeve ruffles of eighteenth-century women's costume—and the dandyish style also references the men's court clothing of that period.

2006

92 EVENING JACKET, HAUTE COUTURE, SPRING 2006. Known for flower and feather work, the skills of atelier Lemarié are voluble here, in a remarkable embroidered evening jacket that dissolves at the cuffs and the shoulder—usually the most structured component of a jacket—into a froth of feathers. The piece resembles one of Karl Lagerfeld's dynamic sketches, often executed with makeup, which lends this garment a palette of porcelain and blush. Unlike Gabrielle Chanel, Lagerfeld operated in the traditional couture manner, making sketches that seemed artistic but were actually precise technical drawings to be interpreted by the ateliers.

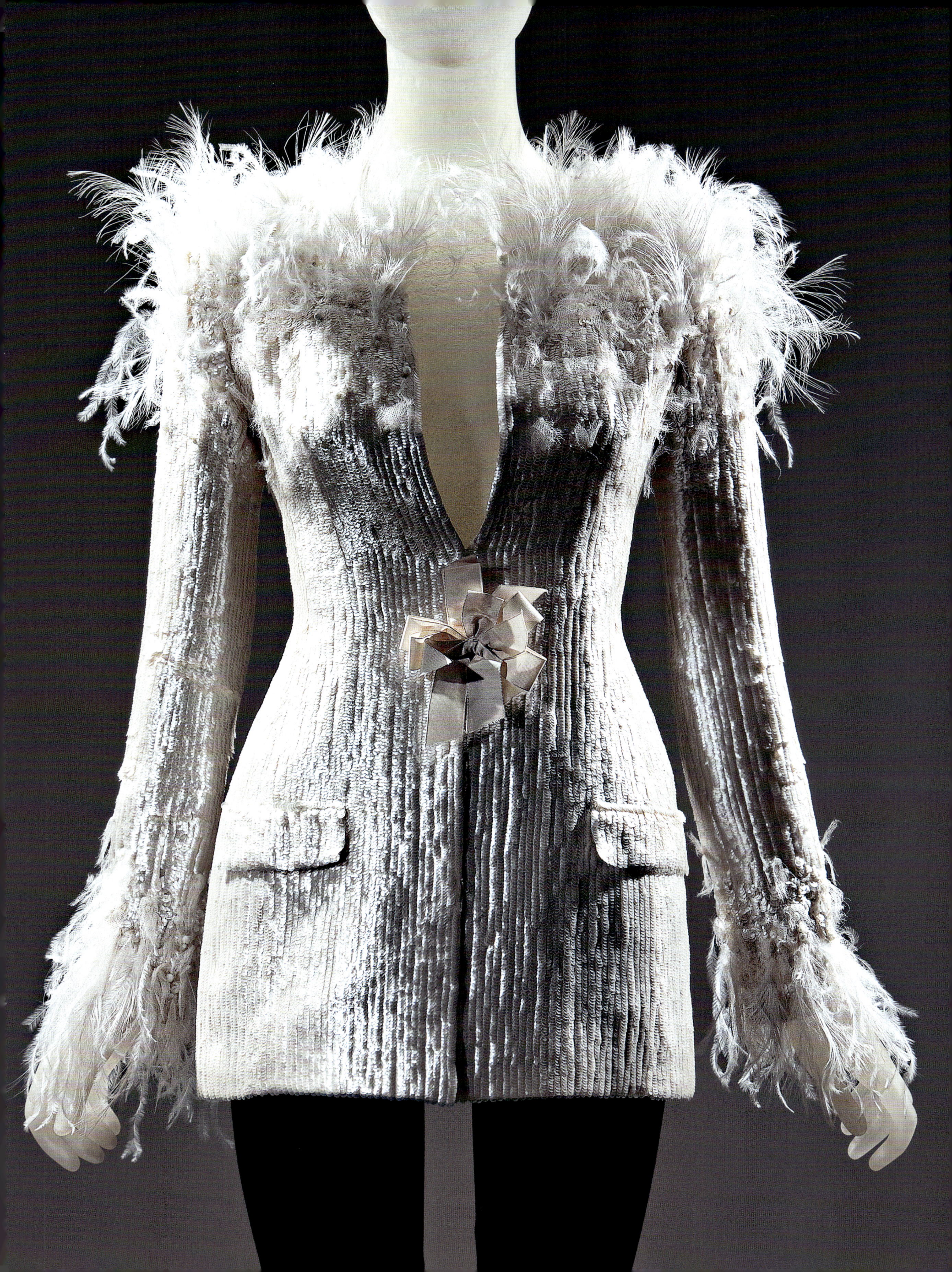

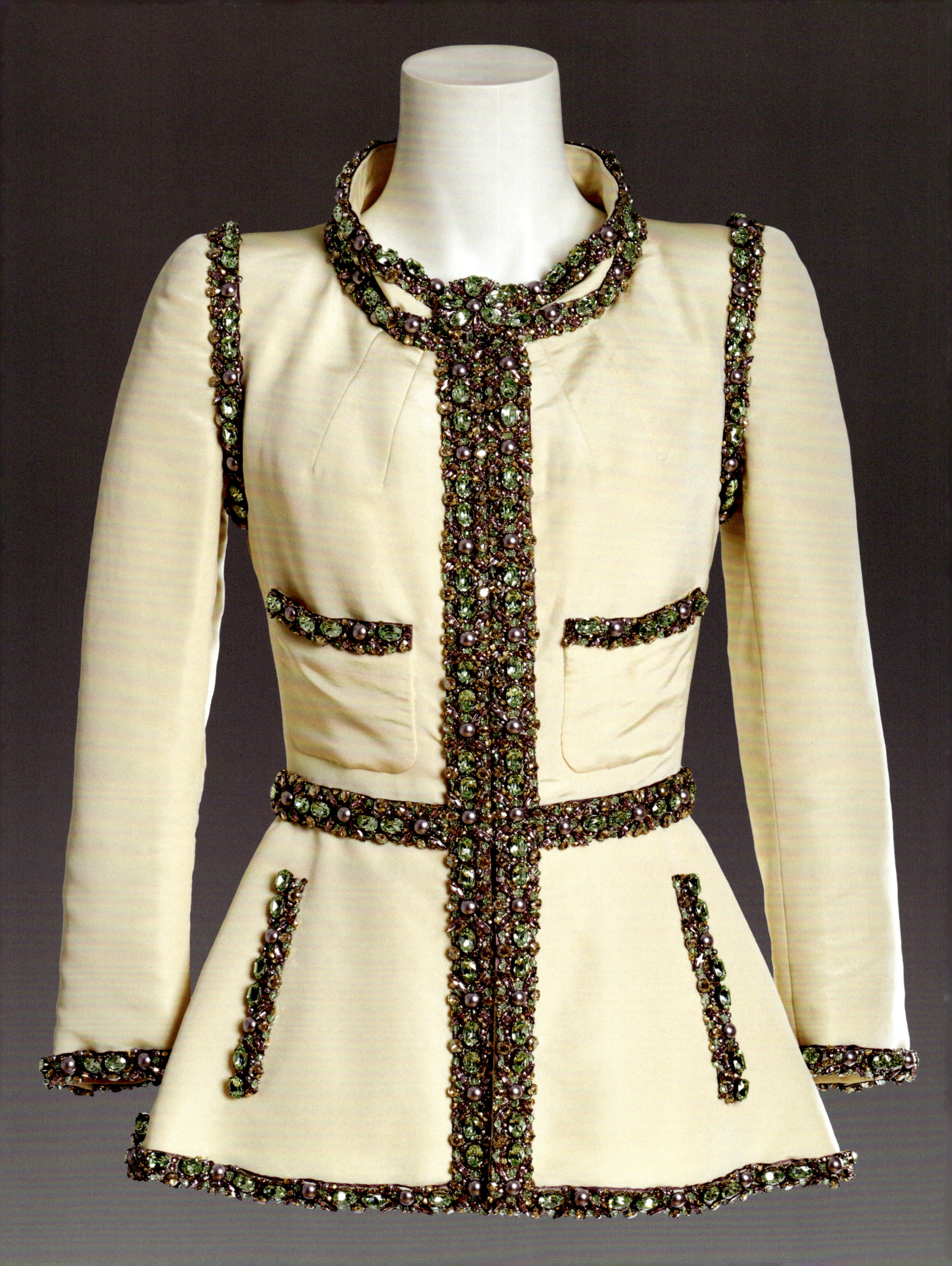

2007

> **"I design like I breathe. You don't ask to breathe. It just happens."**
>
> Karl Lagerfeld,
> quoted in "Karl Lagerfeld: The Banker's Holiday,"
> *Women's Wear Daily,* April 1983

93 EVENING JACKET, HAUTE COUTURE, AUTUMN 2007. Inspired by the idea of seeing a woman from the side—the usual mode of audience observation at a fashion show—Lagerfeld created this collection, titled "High Profile," with details only visible in profile. Here, a Chanel jacket is cut with a flared, almost two-dimensional peplum, its hems, pockets, front, and major seams outlined with graphic embroideries of strass, pearls, and semiprecious stones, designed to imitate traditional Chanel *gallon* braid. The stand-away neckline can be seen on a number of Chanel's designs from the 1960s (item 46, 1966).

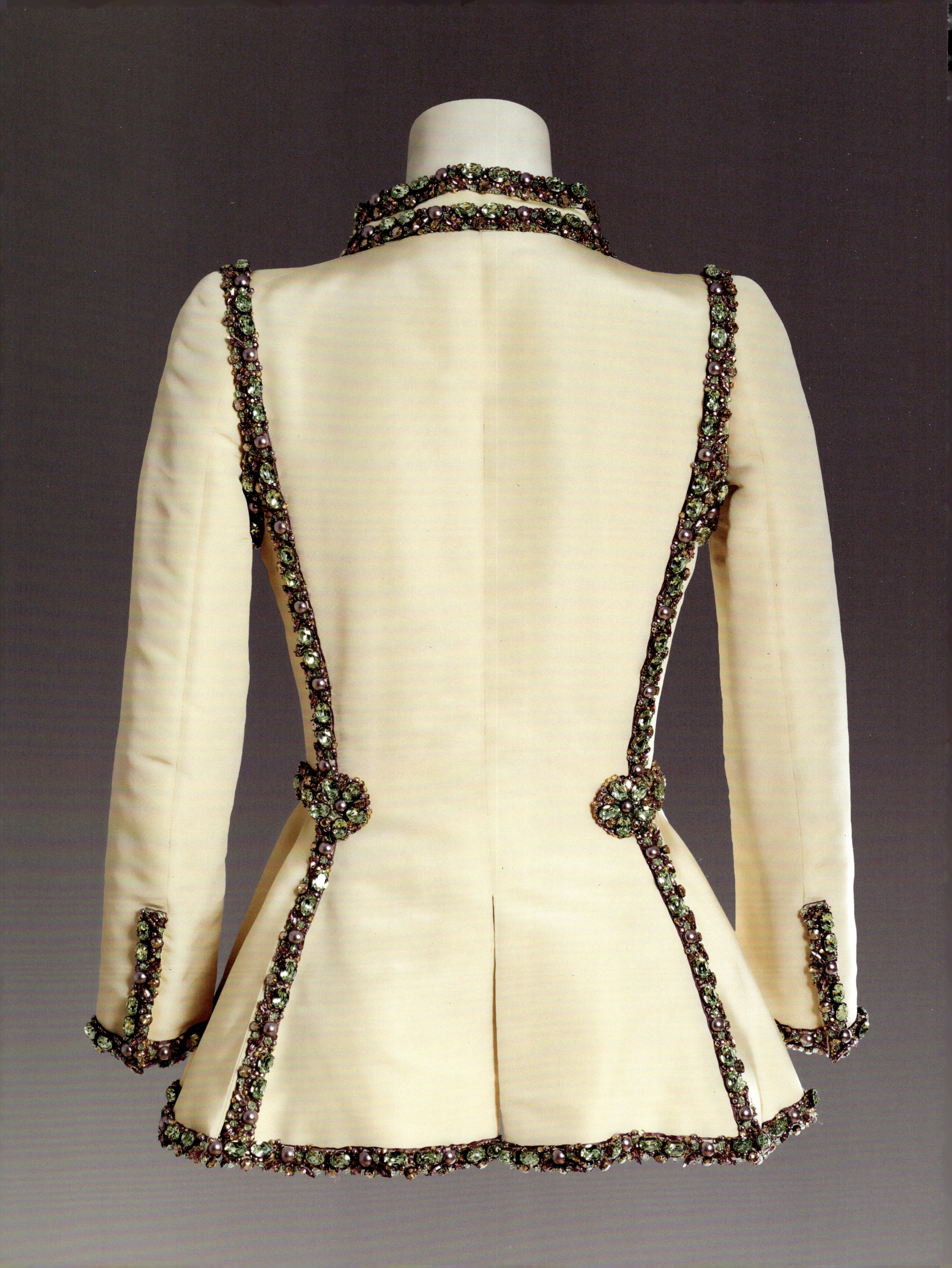

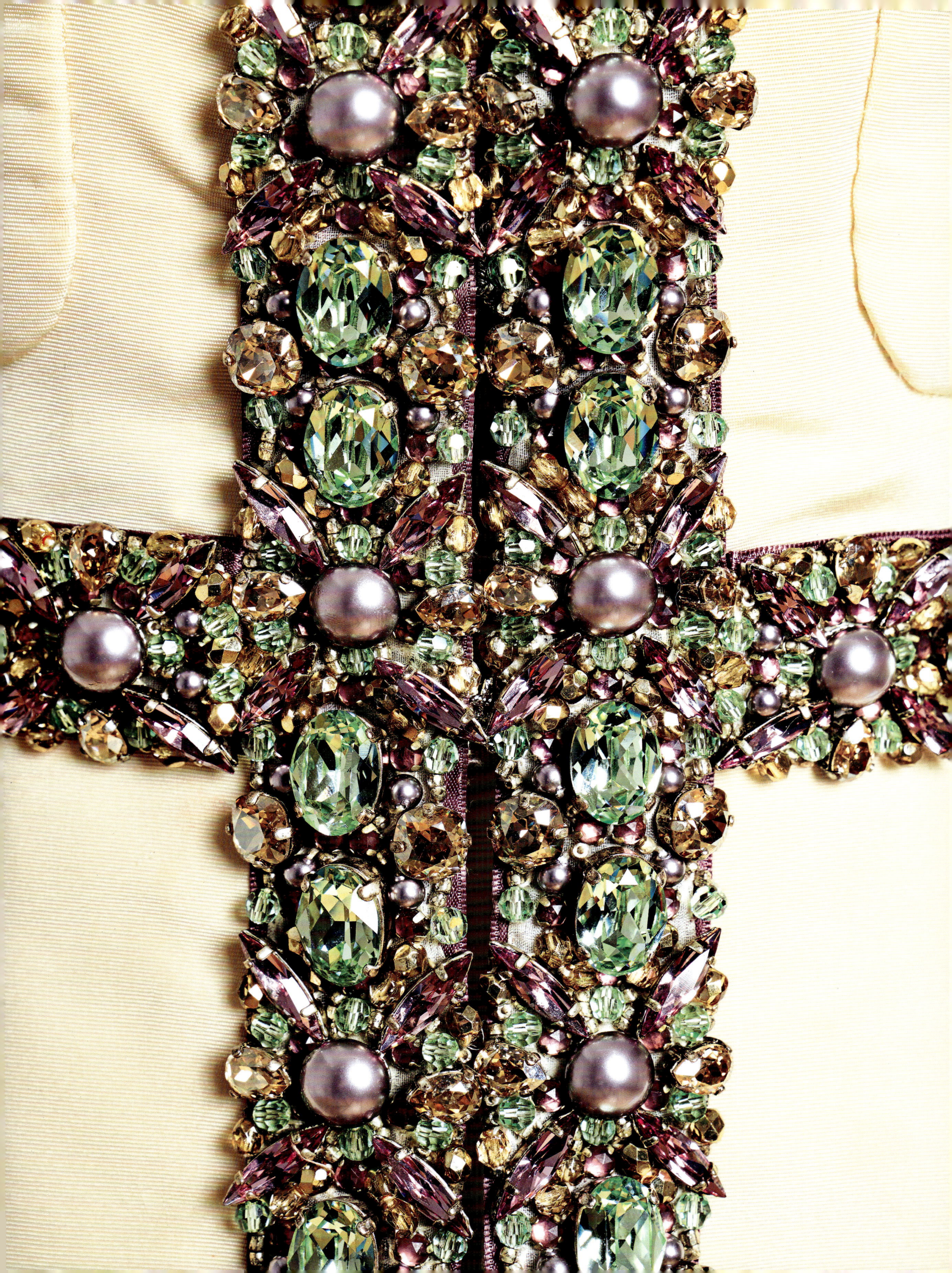

The Chanel Spring 2008 haute couture show presented in the Grand Palais featured a sixty-six-foot-tall replica of the classic tweed suit jacket, from which the parade of models emerged.

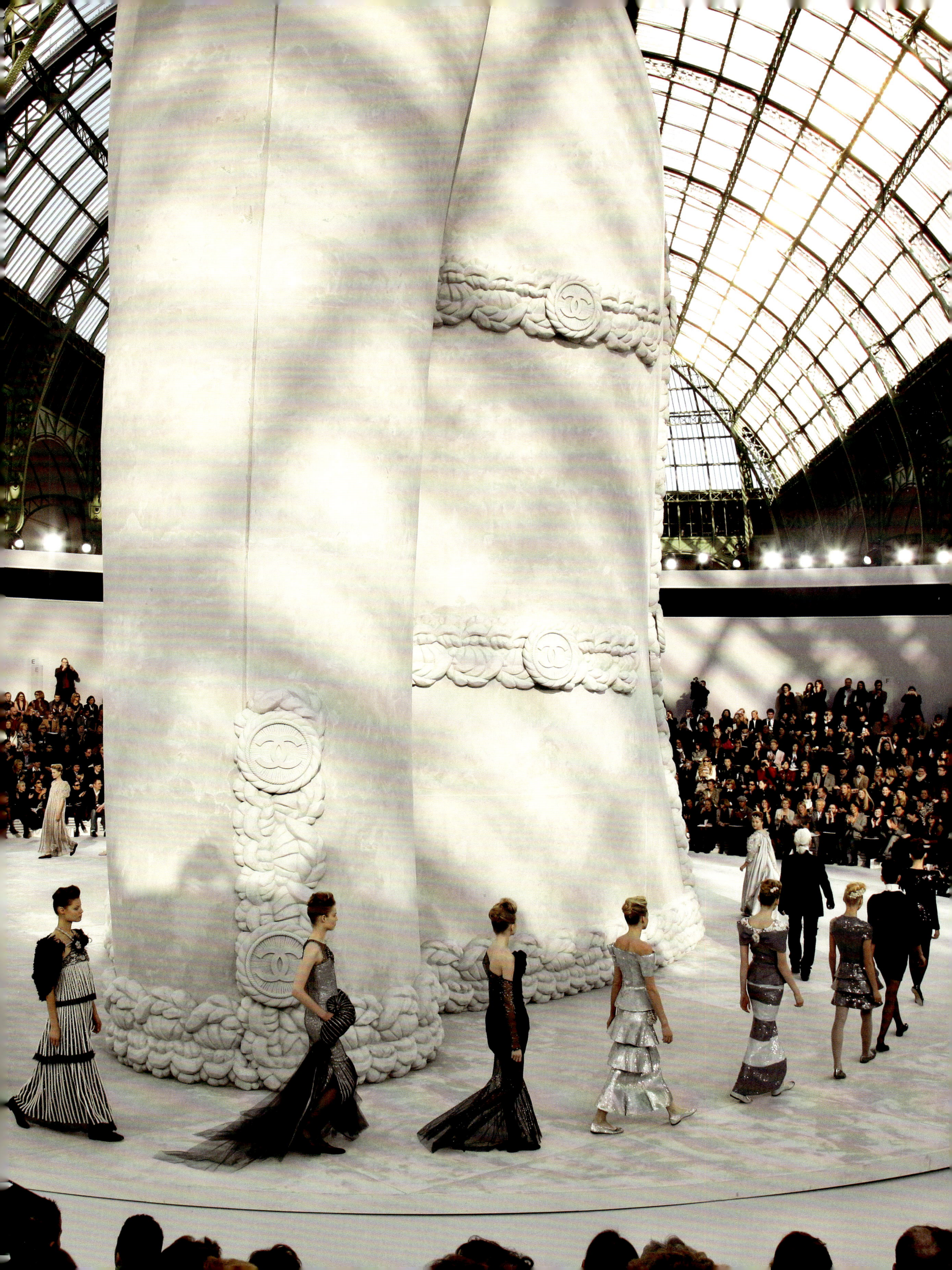

2009

94 EVENING DRESS, HAUTE COUTURE, SPRING 2009. Karl Lagerfeld's January 2009 couture show was inspired by paper, apparently one of his favorite things. The entire collection was monochrome, with a large portion solely in white tones, an idea with roots in Chanel iconography—pearls on pearls, camellia petals, and lace, all of which are present in this short evening dress (*far right*). The austerity is tied to Chanel's aesthetics but also reflects the mood of the time: The collection was shown in the aftermath of the collapse of Lehman Brothers in September 2008, during a global financial crisis comparable to the Great Depression of the 1930s.

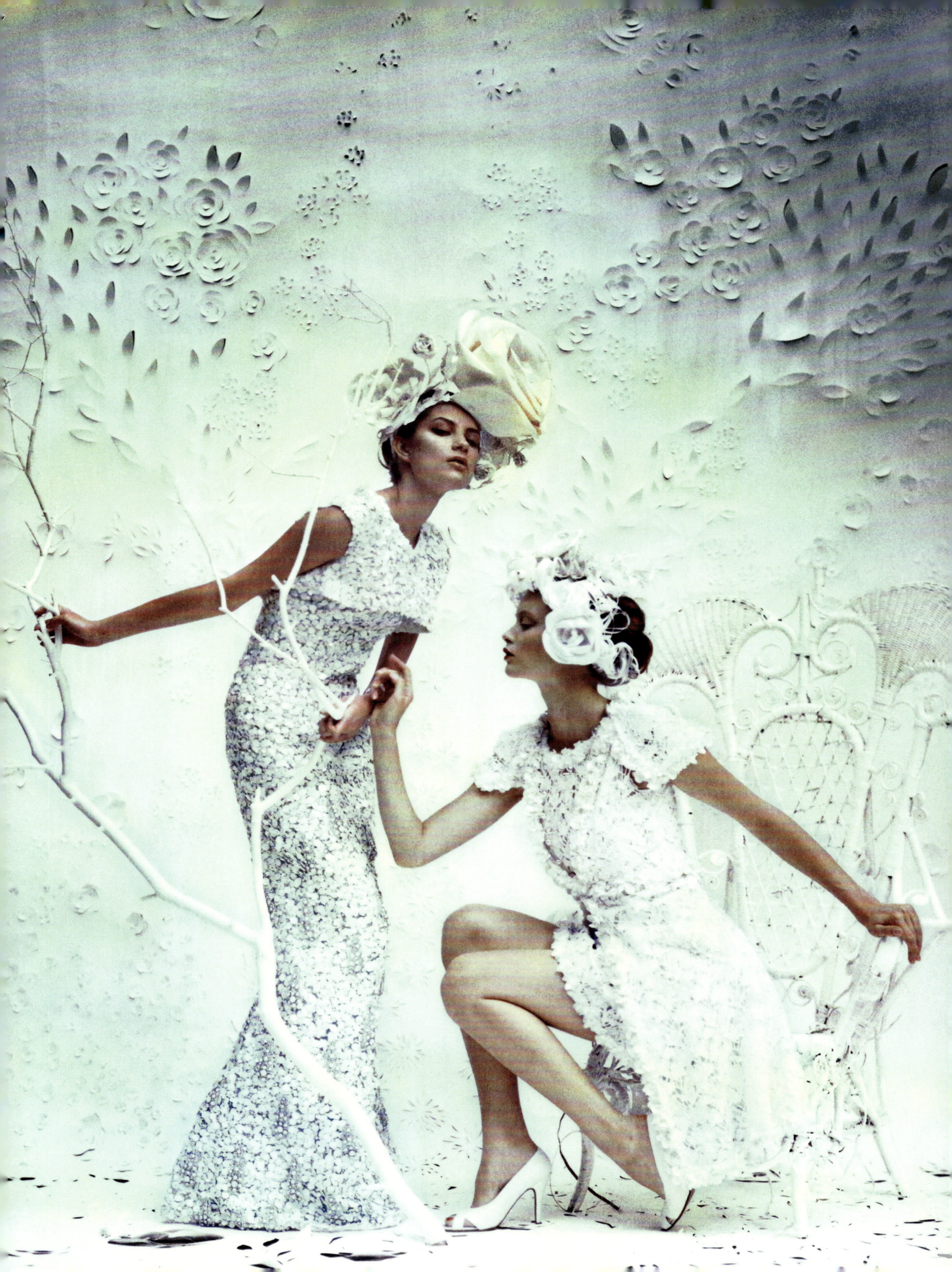

2011

> **" I don't reinterpret the past. I'm pretentious enough to say that we invent something for today that people can identify as Chanel, even if she never did it. "**
>
> Karl Lagerfeld,
> interview with author, July 2017

95 DAY SUIT, READY-TO-WEAR, SPRING 2011. Chanel's style was often described—both positively and pejoratively—as *genre pauvre*, the "poor look." The idea here is taken to an extreme in an otherwise staidly classic Chanel tweed suit "decorated" with great rifts torn in the fabric. They recall moth holes, 1970s punk, and 1980s slashed jeans—as well as a dress of printed and appliquéd shredded "flesh" proposed in 1938 by Chanel's archrival, Elsa Schiaparelli. Although appearing raw, this garment is actually refined—each hole is painstakingly finished, lined with transparent tulle to support the garment and prevent unintentional fraying.

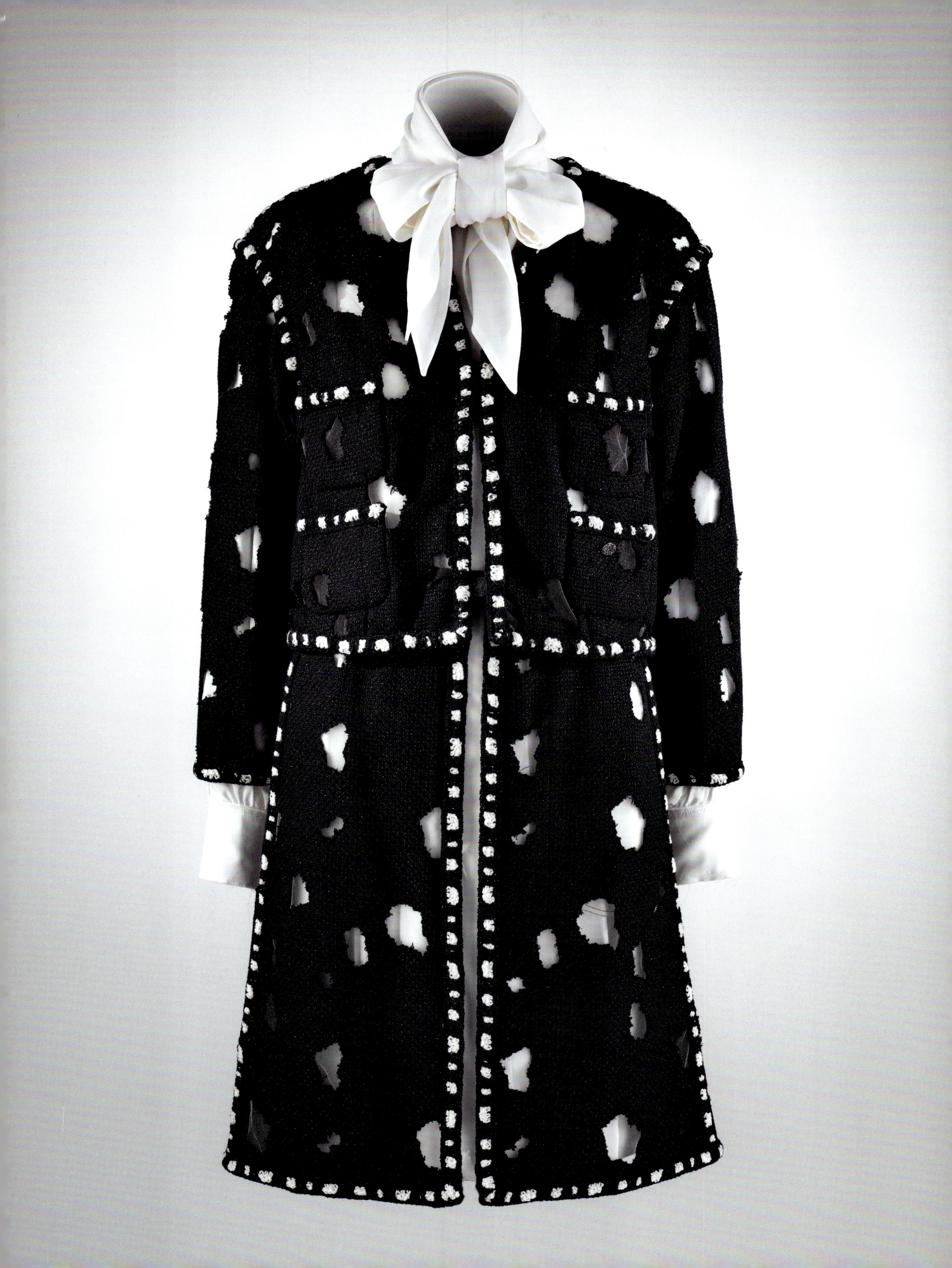

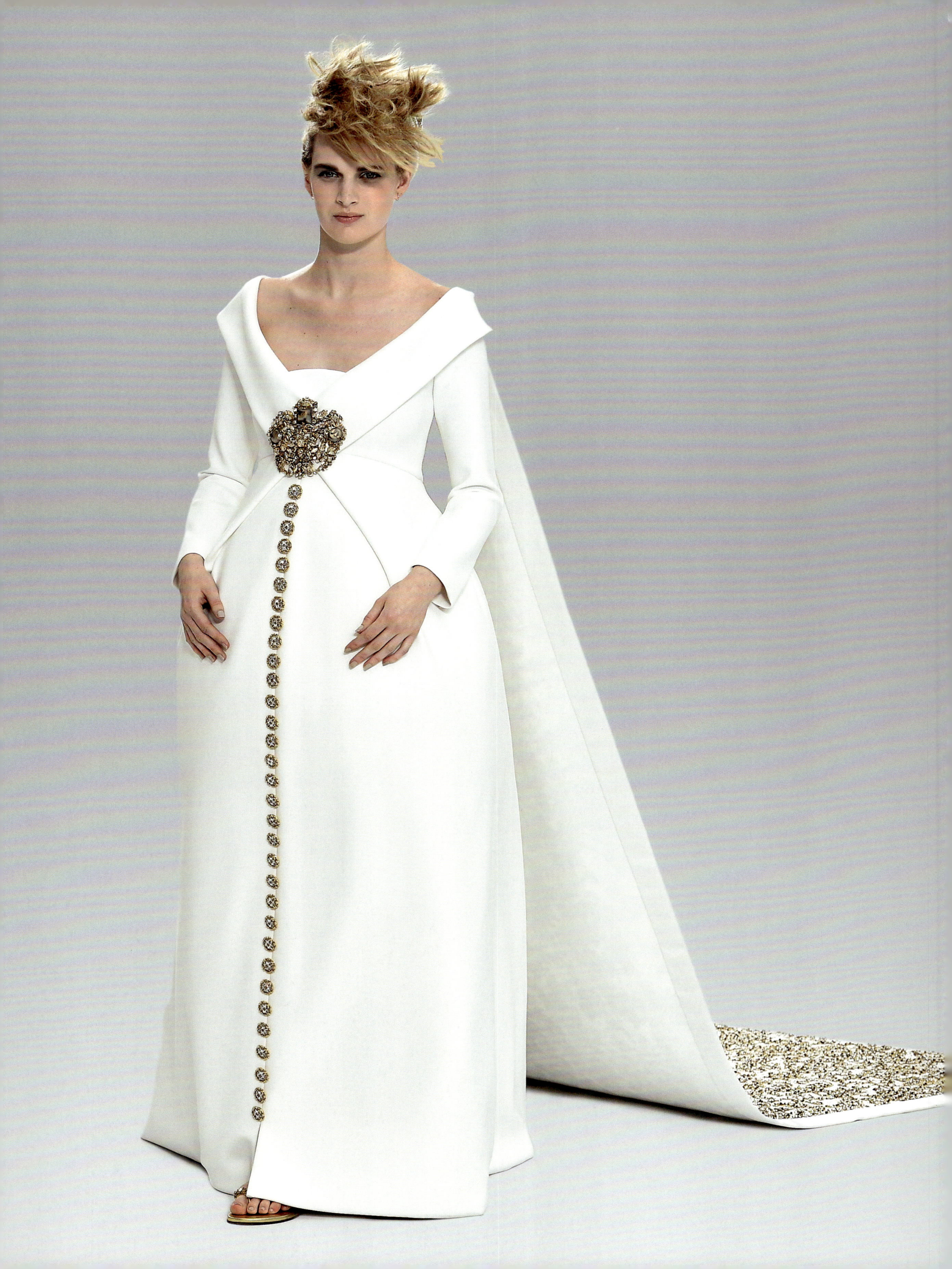

> **"Fashion is also an attempt to make certain invisible aspects of the reality of the moment visible."**
>
> Karl Lagerfeld,
> *Chanel* exhibition catalog, Metropolitan Museum of Art, 2005

96 WEDDING DRESS, HAUTE COUTURE, AUTUMN 2014. In a collection that married Louis XIV's Versailles with Le Corbusier, Lagerfeld explored contrasting notions in the iconography of Chanel. How to reconcile her luxurious apartment with her Little Black Dresses? Her eschewing of decoration in the 1920s, and embracing of frills and flounces a decade later? Lagerfeld broaches it by meshing opposites, particularly in this bridal gown. The long train features a rococo-inspired design hand-embroidered onto the Angelskin neoprene, a knit scuba fabric that was molded to the shape of the body with minimal seaming.

The gown on display for the exhibition *Manus x Machina: Fashion in an Age of Technology* at the Metropolitan Museum of Art Costume Institute in New York, 2016.

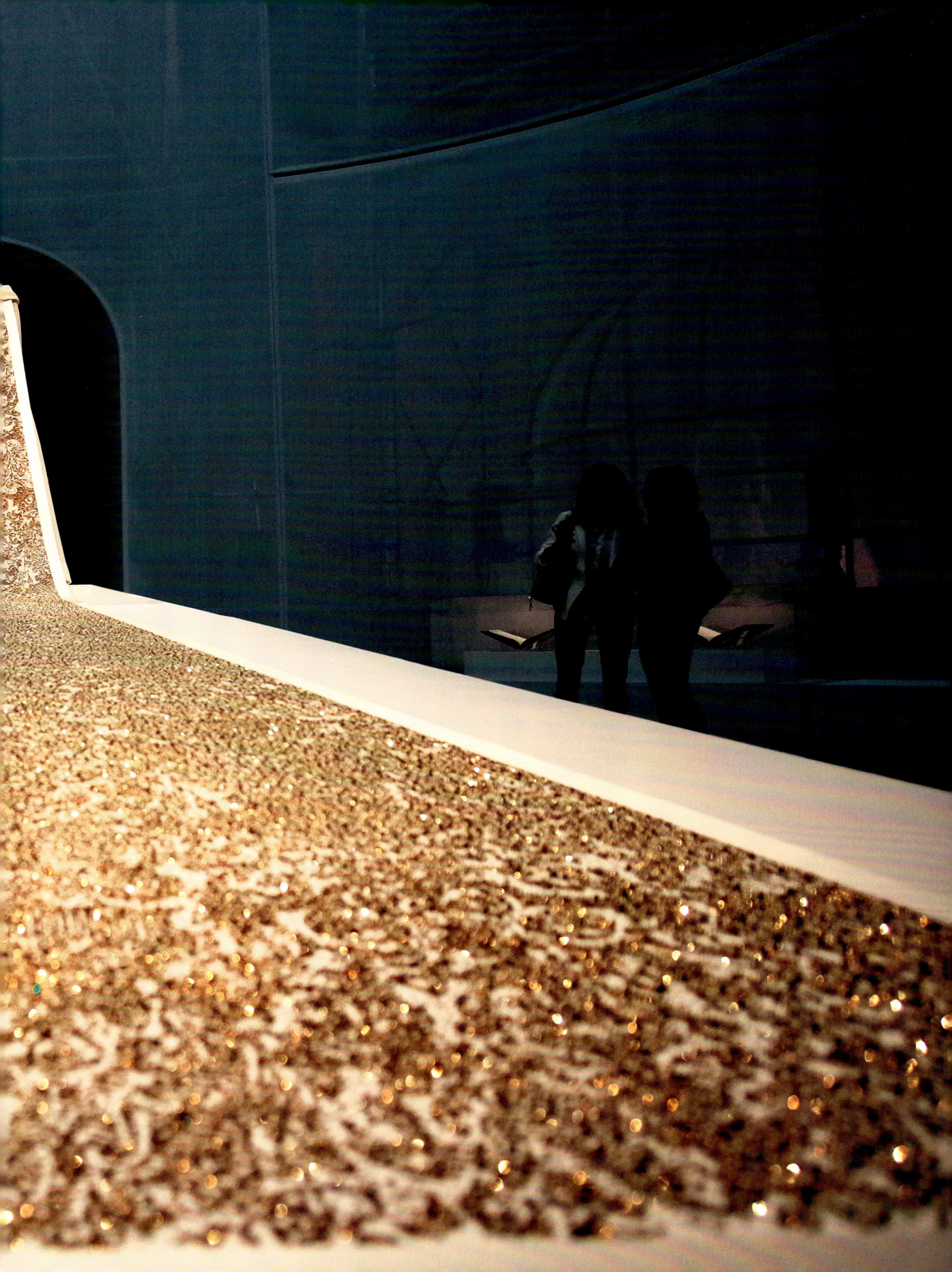

2015

97 DAY SUIT, HAUTE COUTURE, AUTUMN 2015. This collection was titled "Chanel 3-D," underscored by suits using 3-D printing to create a new iteration of the timeless quilted Chanel ensemble. The industrial technique, normally used for prototyping, was used here to blast powder into a mesh with a bubbly, geodesic look. Despite the futuristic technique, the rest of the suit was constructed entirely by hand—the cage of fabric embroidered with braid and lined in silk. This suit was created without using any traditional tailoring techniques—ironically, akin to Chanel's original softly quilted cardigan-jackets.

2015

98 ENSEMBLE, READY-TO-WEAR, AUTUMN 2015. This collection was presented in a facsimile of a French brasserie. The visual language of those establishments—bentwood chairs, marble-topped tables, brass, and mirrors—has become shorthand for the quintessentially Parisian. Today, the same has happened to the style of Chanel. When Lagerfeld presented this outfit—a transmogrification of French waiters' attire—we see the sketched-out codes of the house: monochrome palette, masculinity translated to the feminine, white frills, and black bows. To the seasoned observer, all spell Chanel.

2017

99 EVENING DRESS, HAUTE COUTURE, SPRING 2017. Inspired in part by the white, mirrored interiors proposed by designer Syrie Maugham, as well as Chanel's own mirrored staircase, this collection contrasted subdued, sculptured suiting with extravagant evening clothes featuring mirror-inspired Lesage embroideries. This dress, the final look, worn by Lily-Rose Depp, harked back to Chanel's evening frocks of the early 1930s, the ruffled volumes alluding to the grandeur of the Second Empire. A riff on the formal couture wedding gown finale, this look is in fact an exaggerated variant of the humble shirtdress, featuring the rounded Claudine collars Gabrielle Chanel favored.

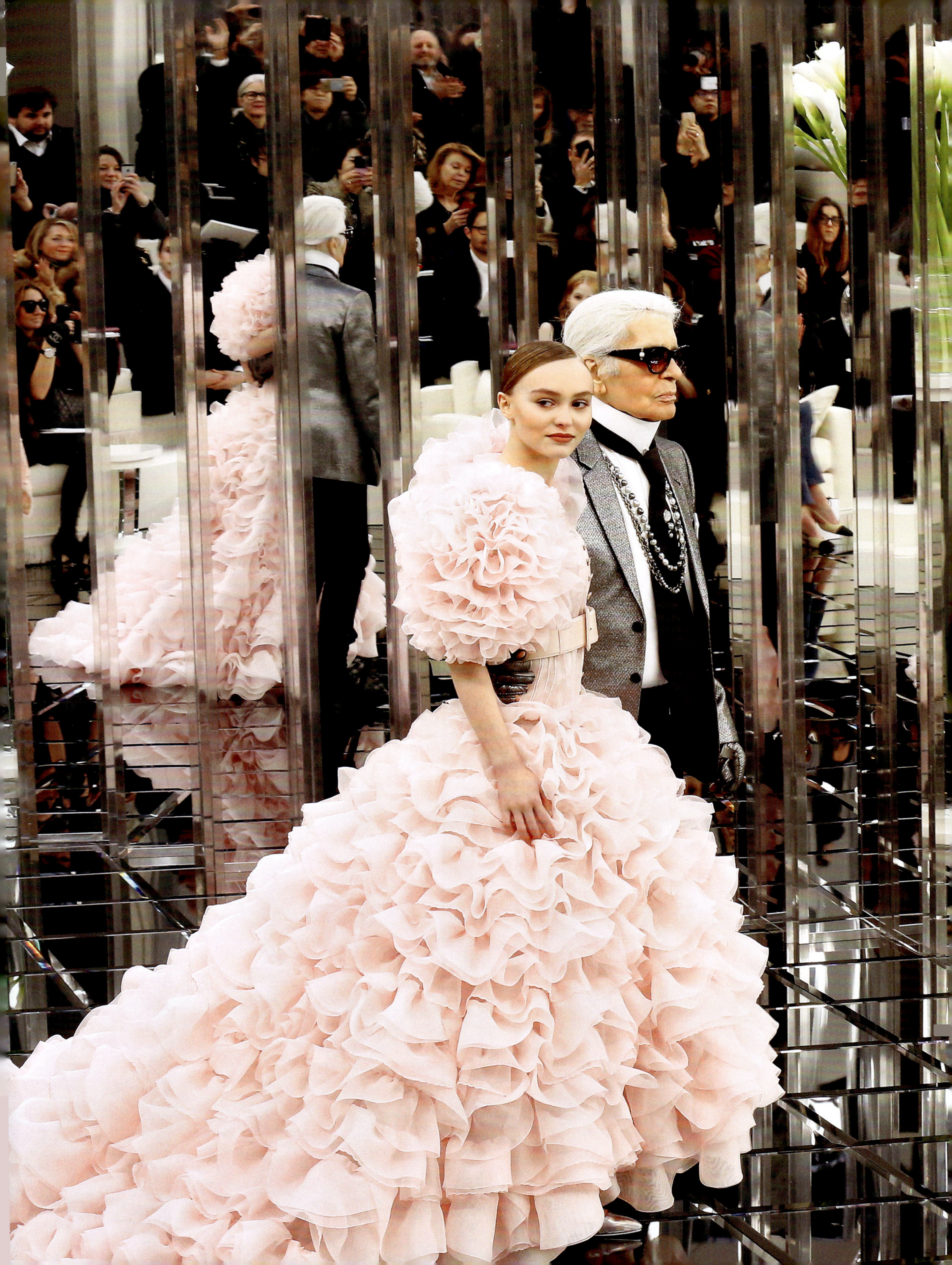

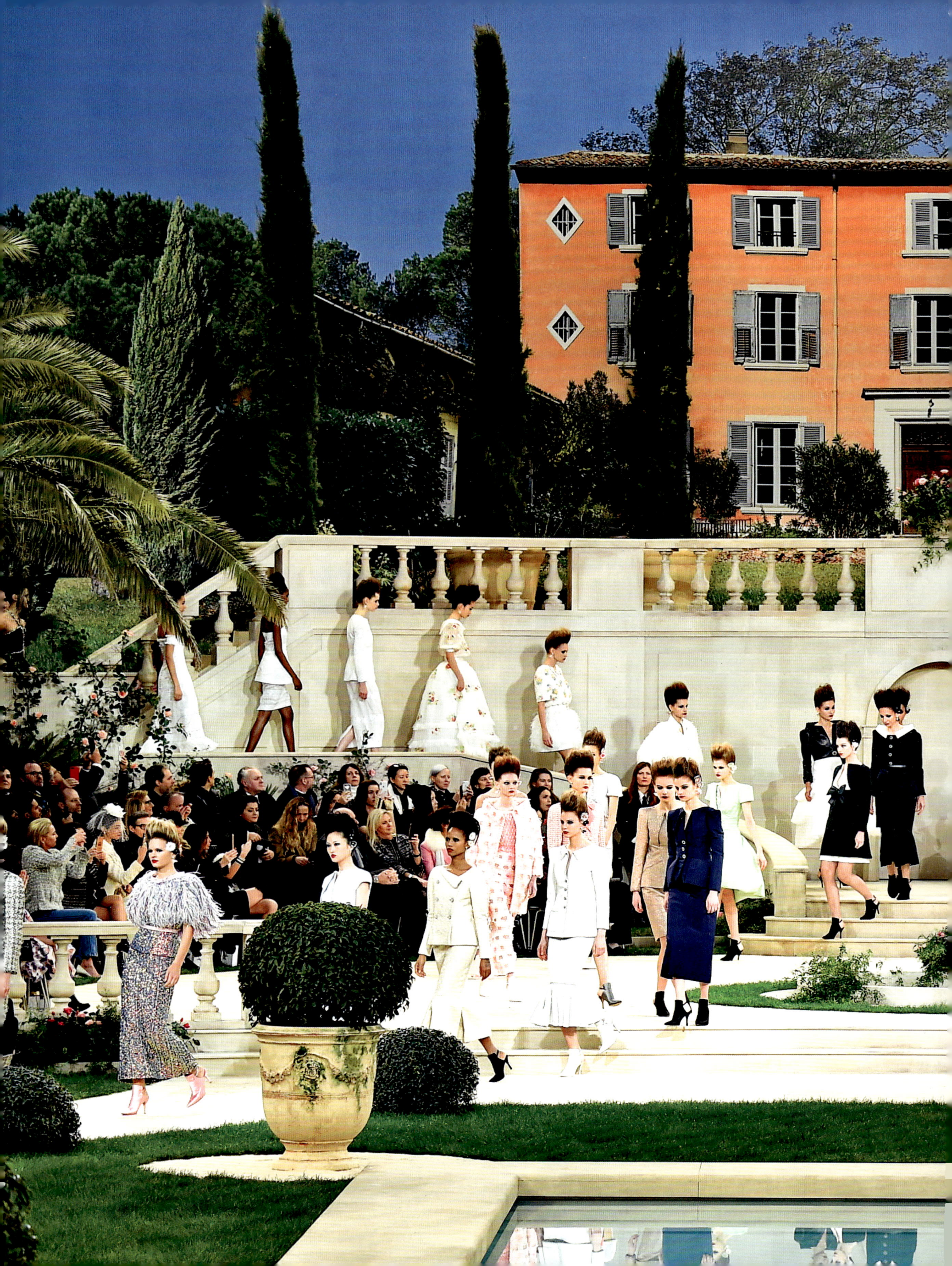

The Chanel Spring 2019 haute couture show, presented in the Grand Palais, transported the audience to an Italianate villa.

2019

100 EVENING DRESS, HAUTE COUTURE, SPRING 2019. Remembrance of things past: Karl Lagerfeld offered decor of an Italianate villa, reminiscent of Chanel's house La Pausa, near Monte Carlo. The past also inspired the clothes—namely Chanel's designs of the 1930s, romantic and often elaborate. This dress with defined waist, blouson bodice, and gently spreading skirt is hand-embroidered with floral sprigs executed in feathers by Lemarié. It echoes styles worn by Chanel herself, as well as fashions Lagerfeld, born in 1933, may have remembered from his childhood. This was the final collection shown before Lagerfeld's death on February 19, 2019.

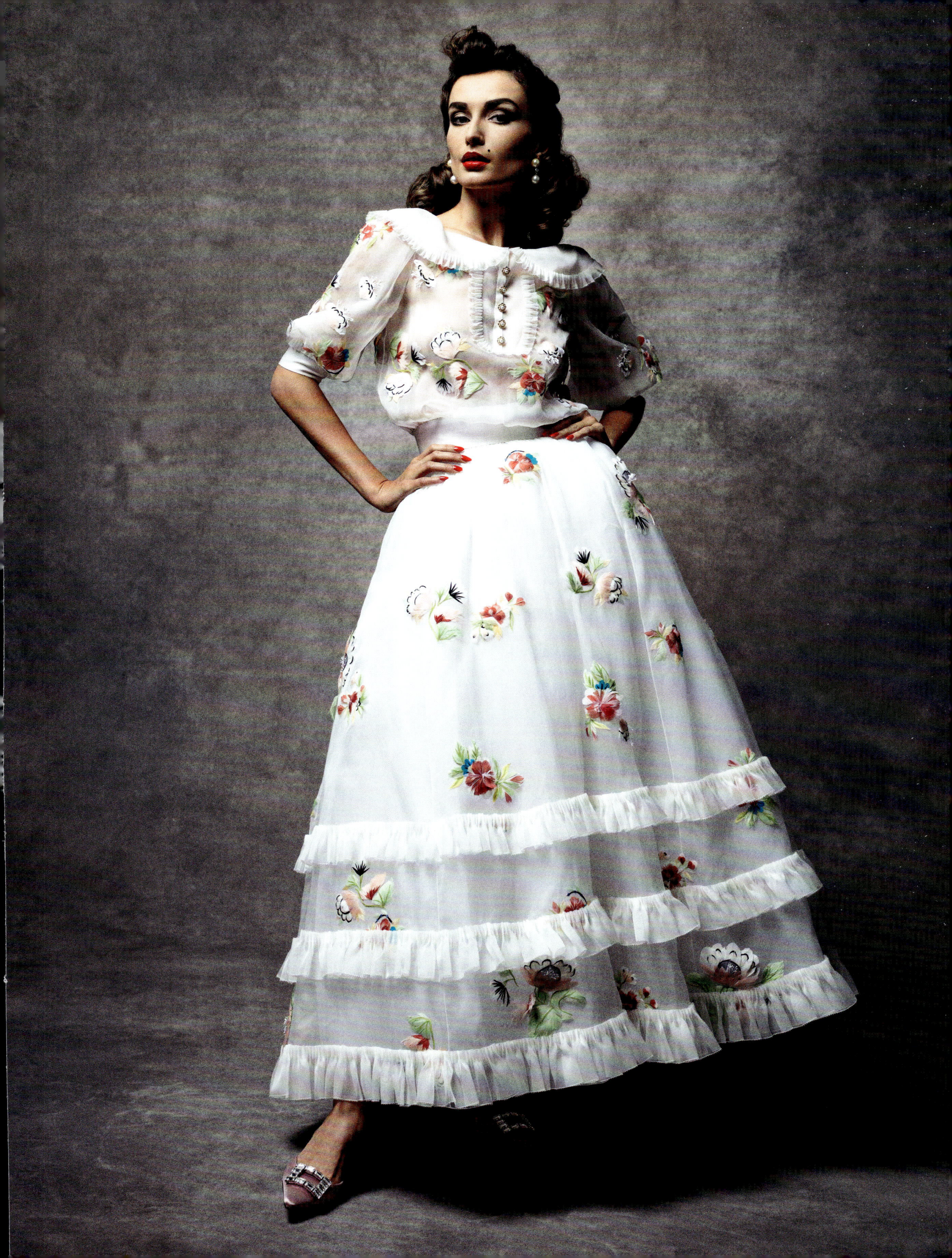

> "I've always known that I was made to live this way, that I would be this sort of legend."
>
> Karl Lagerfeld,
> *The World According to Karl*

Karl Lagerfeld photographed by Helmut Newton, 1976.

NOTES

1. Interview with author, May 2014.
2. Janet Flanner, "31 Rue Cambon," *The New Yorker*, March 14, 1931.
3. Justine Picardie, *Coco Chanel: The Legend and the Life*, HarperCollins, 2010.
4. Cecil Beaton, *The Glass of Fashion*, 1954.
5. Paul Morand, *The Allure of Chanel*, Pushkin Press, 2008.
6. Ibid.
7. Picardie, op. cit.
8. Morand, op. cit.
9. Ilya Parkins, *Poiret, Dior and Schiaparelli: Fashion, Femininity and Modernity*, Berg, 2012.
10. Morand, op. cit.
11. Interview with author, July 2017.
12. Interview with author, July 2017.
13. Alicia Drake, *The Beautiful Fall: Fashion, Genius and Glorious Excess in 1970s Paris*, Bloomsbury, 2012.
14. Georgina Howell, *Sultans of Style*, Ebury Press, 1990.
15. Interview with author, July 2017.
16. June Weir, "The Designer Who Destroys the Past," *The New York Times*, August 15, 1982.
17. Morand, op. cit.
18. Christopher Petkanas, "Lagerfeld Tackles Couture," *Women's Wear Daily*, January 19, 1983.
19. Petkanas, op. cit.
20. Interview with author, May 2014.
21. Susannah Frankel, "My Year With Karl," *AnOther Magazine*, Spring/Summer 2016.

ABOUT THE AUTHOR

Alexander Fury is a fashion journalist, author, and critic. He is Fashion Features Director of *AnOther Magazine* and Men's Critic for *Financial Times*. From 2016 to 2018 he was the first Chief Fashion Correspondent at *T: The New York Times Style Magazine*, and from 2013 to 2016 he was fashion editor of *The Independent*, *i*, and *The Independent on Sunday* newspapers. In 2018, Fury received the Honorary Doctorate of Humane Letters from the Academy of Art University, San Francisco. His previous books include *Dior by Gianfranco Ferré* (Assouline, 2018); *Dior: Catwalk* (Thames and Hudson, 2017); and *Catwalking: Photographs by Chris Moore* (Laurence King, 2017).

ACKNOWLEDGMENTS

Thank you to Martine and Prosper Assouline, Esther Kremer, Amy Slingerland, Elizabeth Eames, Charlotte Sivrière, and the entire team at Assouline for their unfailing patience and tenacity. A huge thank-you to Daphne Guinness for the loan of several key archive pieces, and to Hamish Bowles for his assistance. Thanks to Justine Picardie for her sound advice and to Amanda Harlech for her endless font of wisdom. An enormous thank-you to Susannah Frankel for her skills in editing, her always salient suggestions, and her constant support. And a special thank-you to Joseph Larkowsky for being a sounding board, proofreader, opinion-giver, general right arm, and wonderful.

Alexander Fury

Assouline would like to especially thank the great collectors Daphne Guinness, Mouna Ayoub, and Barbara Berger for their precious help in the creation of this book.

Thank you also to the collections of Fashion & Lace Museum, Brussels; FIDM Museum at the Fashion Institute of Design & Merchandising, Los Angeles; Kent State University Museum, Ohio; Kyoto Costume Institute; The Metropolitan Museum of Art, New York; Musée des Arts Decoratifs, Paris; The Museum at FIT, New York; Museo del Traje, Madrid; Palais Galliera, Musée de la Mode de la Ville de Paris; The Philadelphia Museum of Art; Savannah College of Art and Design; University of Melbourne; Museum of Fine Arts, Boston.

And to the photographers, models, and agencies who made this beautiful project possible: Escarlen Baque, Trunk Archive; Jennifer Belt, Ken Johnston, Art Resource; Gilles Bensimon; Caroline Berton, Laure Fournis, Condé Nast France; Quentin Bertoux; Naomi Campbell; Flore Campestrini, Musée des Arts Decoratifs; Faith Cooper, FIT; Cindy Crawford; Pablo Esteva; Nick D'Emilio; Andreea Diaconu; Carole Dumoulin, Condé Nast UK; Caroline Esgain, Fashion and Lace Museum, Brussels; Jeff Goldstein, Caroline Packer, Verdura; Lorraine Goonan, Mark Antman, Image Works; Inès de la Fressange; Hideki Fukushima, Kyoto Costume Institute; Starr Hackwelder, Alamy; Thomas Haggerty, Bridgeman; Laziz Hamani; Francis Hammond; Meghan Grossman Hansen, FIDM Museum; Shalom Harlow; Erin Harris, Avedon Foundation; Dominique Hascoet-Brunet, Chloé Chaudsaygues, Studiocanal; Crystal Henry, Redux Images; Andy Howick, MPTV Images; Houlux, Paris; Sara Hume, Sarah J. Rogers, Kent State University Museum; Nathalie Ifrah, Jalou Media Group; Jennifer Jeffrey, Jamie Owen, AKG Images; Lauren Kelly, August Images; Benjamin Lindbergh; Audrey Marnay; Wayne Maser; M. Fernanda Meza, Artists Rights Society; Brigitte Moral; Miranda Muscente, Condé Nast; Cathleen Naundorf; Emma Nichols, Sotheby's; Robert Pritchard, Maconochie Film & Photography Ltd.; Donald Robertson; Didier Roy; Thibaut de Saint Chamas; Stella Tennant; Teri Toeun; Christy Turlington; Addie Elliott Vassie, Laetitia Braquenié Viot, Willy Rizzo Estate; Brian Stehlin, Getty Images; Claartje van Dijk, International Center of Photography; Ashley Williams, Summer Orndorff, Savannah College of Art and Design.

CREDITS

p. 4: PVDE/Bridgeman Images; pp. 5, 10: Bibliothèque Nationale de France; p. 7: © 2024 Artists Rights Society (ARS), New York; p. 13 (clockwise from top left): Photo © Ministère de la Culture – Médiathèque de l'architecture et du patrimoine, Dist. RMN-Grand Palais/André Kertész; © All Rights Reserved/Photo V.H. Grandpierre; © ARS/Comité Cocteau, Paris/ADAGP, Paris 2024; Photo by Jean Moral © Brigitte Moral. Paris; Pictorial Press Ltd/Alamy Stock Photo; © 2024 Artists Rights Society (ARS), New York, Photo Christian Bérard, *Vogue* © Condé Nast; Photo © Ministère de la Culture–Médiathèque de l'architecture et du patrimoine, Dist. RMN–Grand Palais/François Kollar; pp. 16-17: Lebrecht Music Arts/Bridgeman Images; p. 20: © Francis Hammond; pp. 21, 52: Cecil Beaton Archive © Condé Nast; pp. 24-25: © Giancarlo Botti/Gamma-Rapho/Getty Images; p. 29: Photograph by Richard Avedon, Copyright © The Richard Avedon Foundation; pp. 32-33, 37: © Jean-Claude Sauer/Paris Match/Getty Images; pp. 34, 42, 100, 141: © Laziz Hamani; p. 38 (clockwise from top left): © Dominique Charriau/WireImage/Getty Images; © Serge Benhamou/Gamma-Rapho/Getty Images; © Angela Weiss/AFP/Getty Images; © Stephane Cardinale/Corbis/Getty Images; © SBM/Realis/Getty Images; p. 41: Jacket and dress belonging to Rose Grainger, 1920, image courtesy Grainger Museum, The University of Melbourne; pp. 43, 181: © Didier Roy; p. 44: Purchase, Irene Lewisohn Bequest, 1975 (1975.7), image © The Metropolitan Museum of Art, image source Art Resource, NY; p. 45: Private Collection/Archives Charmet/Bridgeman Images; p. 46: Gift of Gytha M. Rupp, 1994 (1994.474a, b), image © The Metropolitan Museum of Art, image source Art Resource, NY; pp. 47, 59: © Edward Steichen/Condé Nast/Shutterstock; p. 49: The Museum at FIT (P83.39.8); p. 50: Pictorial Press Ltd/Alamy Stock Photo; p. 51: Hideoki; p. 53: Purchase, The New-York Historical Society, by Exchange Fund, 1984 (1984.28a-c), image © The Metropolitan Museum of Art, image source Art Resource, NY; p. 55: Gift of Mrs. Georges Gudefin, in memory of Mrs. Clarence Herter, 1965 (C.I.65.47.2a, b), image © The Metropolitan Museum of Art, image source Art Resource, NY; p. 57: Private Collection/Photo © Christie's Images/Bridgeman Images; pp. 60, 61: Isabel Shults Fund, 1984 (1984.31a-c), image © The Metropolitan Museum of Art, image source Art Resource, NY; p. 62: Isabel Shults Fund, 2004 (2004.447a, b), image © The Metropolitan Museum of Art, image source Art Resource, NY; p. 63: ©The Kyoto Costume Institute, photo by Takashi Hatakeyama (AC4479 83-11-15); p. 65: Brooklyn Museum Costume Collection at The Metropolitan Museum of Art, Gift of the Brooklyn Museum, 2009; Gift of the Smithsonian Institution, 1984 (2009.300.8101), image © The Metropolitan Museum of Art, image source Art Resource, NY; p. 66: © Lipnitzki/Roger Violet/Getty Images; p. 67: Courtesy of Verdura; pp. 68, 89: All Rights Reserved; p. 69: © Fashion & Lace Museum, Brussels, photo J.M. Byl (C. 83.14.03); pp. 70,71: Silverman/Rodgers Collection, courtesy The Kent State University Museum (1983.001.1891); p. 73: © Ullstein Bild/Getty Images; pp. 74-75: Photo by André Kertesz for *Vogue Paris*; p. 76: Gift of Hugh L. Bulkley, in memory of his mother, Margaret Ludlum Bulkley, 1977 (1977.325a, b), image © The Metropolitan Museum of Art, image source Art Resource, NY; p. 77: Gift of Yann Weymouth, 1981 (1981.348.2a, b), image © The Metropolitan Museum of Art, image source Art Resource, NY; p. 79: Gift of Diana Vreeland, 1954 (C.I.54.16.2a, b), image © The Metropolitan Museum of Art, image source Art Resource, NY; p. 80: Gift of Mlle. Chanel, 1955 (C.I.55.61.2a, b), image © The Metropolitan Museum of Art, image source Art Resource, NY; pp. 81, 88: © 2024 Artists Rights Society (ARS), New York, Photo Christian Bérard, *Vogue* © Condé Nast; p. 83: Donation of Mr. and Mrs. Viguier's heirs (GAL1968.55.23 A, B et C) © Eric Emo/Galliera/Roger-Violett/The Image Works; p. 85: David Seidner, Moments de Mode: Chanel, ca.1986. © David Seidner Archive/International Center of Photography; p. 86: Rue des Archives/Granger, All rights reserved; p. 87: Gift of Diana Vreeland, 1954 (C.I.54.16.1a, b), image © The Metropolitan Museum of Art, image source Art Resource, NY; p. 91: Silverman/Rodgers Collection, courtesy The Kent State University Museum (1983.1.1252a, b); p. 92: Courtesy of Houlux, Paris; p. 93: © AFP/Getty Images; p. 95: Photo by Frances McLaughlin for *Vogue Paris*; p. 97: © Scoop/Elle, photo J.F. Clair; p. 99: © Willy Rizzo, Photograph permanently exhibited at Studio Willy Rizzo; p. 101: Gift of Bradford Dillman, 2004 (2004.333.2a, b), image © The Metropolitan Museum of Art, image source Art Resource, NY; p. 102: © Henry Clarke/Condé Nast/Shutterstock; p. 103: courtesy Barbara Berger, photo Pablo Esteva; p. 104: The Museum at FIT (69.161.26); p. 105: The Museum at FIT (76.185.3); p. 106: © Bennett Raglin/WireImage/Getty Images; p. 107: The Museum at FIT Collection (89.160.1), image © The Metropolitan Museum of Art, image source Art Resource, NY; pp. 108-109: © Astor Pictures/Photofest; p. 111: Glasshouse Images/Alamy Stock Photo; p. 112: L'Officiel, 1961, Georges Saad; p. 113: © Gilles Trillard/Éditions Assouline; pp. 114-115: ScreenProd/Photononstop/Alamy Stock Photo; pp. 116-117: © Mark Shaw/mptvimages.com; p. 119: © Bridgeman Images; p. 121: © Walter Carone/Paris Match/Getty Images; p. 122: Gift of Mrs. Murray Graham, 1973 (1973.297.2a, b), image © The Metropolitan Museum of Art, image source Art Resource, NY; p. 123: Gift of Joanne T. Cummings, 1976 (1976.360.10a-c), image © The Metropolitan Museum of Art, image source Art Resource, NY; p. 124: © Photo 12/Getty Images; p. 125: Brooklyn Museum Costume Collection at The Metropolitan Museum of Art, Gift of the Brooklyn Museum, 1977; Gift of Jane Holzer, 1977 (2009.300.524a, b), image © The Metropolitan Museum of Art, image source Art Resource, NY; p. 126: © The Museum at FIT (78.179.4); p. 127: Donation of Chanel, UFAC, 1976 (UF 76-29-20 AB), © Les Arts Décoratifs, Paris/Jean Tholance/akg-images; p. 128: © Gianni Penati/Condé Nast/Getty Images; p. 131: Legacy transmitted by Mr. Georges, in memory of the late HRH the Duchess of Windsor, 1986 © Les Arts Décoratifs, Paris/Jean Tholance/akg-images (56961.A); p. 132: Philadelphia Museum of Art, Gift of Mrs. Stuart A. Prosser (1979-123-3a-c); pp. 133, 136: Copyright © by Fairchild Publishing, LLC. All Rights Reserved. Used by Permission; p. 135: © Donald Robertson; pp. 137, 140, 154-155, 236-237: © Helmut Newton Foundation/Trunk Archive; p. 138: Donation by François Lesage, 2001 (2001.144.44), © Les Arts Décoratifs, Paris/Jean Tholance/akg-images; p. 139: Gift of Chanel, in honor of Harold Koda, 2016 (2016.632), image © The Metropolitan Museum of Art, image source Art Resource, NY; pp. 142-143: © Jean-Pierre Couderc/Roger-Viollet/The Image Works; p. 145: © Julien Vidal/Galliera/Roger-Viollet/The Image Works; pp. 146, 149: Photo by Daniel Jouanneau for *Vogue Paris*; p. 147: Gift of Anne E. Reed, 1988 (1988.172a-d), image © The Metropolitan Museum of Art, image source Art Resource, NY; p. 150: © Ed Feingersh/Michael Ochs Archives/Getty Images; p. 151: Andy Warhol, *Chanel*, 1985, from the *Ads* portfolio, screenprint on Lenox Museum board, 38 x 38 inches, Courtesy Ronald Feldman Gallery, New York, © The Andy Warhol Foundation for the Visual Arts/Artists Rights Society (ARS), New York/Ronald Feldman Gallery, New York; p. 152: Gift from The Estate of Tina Chow © The Museum at FIT (91.255.3); p. 153: Arthur Elgort, *Vogue*, © Condé Nast; pp. 156, 157: Chicago History Museum/Getty Images; p. 159: Donation by Hélène David-Weill, 2008 (2008.38.20.2), © Les Arts Décoratifs, Paris/Jean Tholance; p. 160: Patrick Demarchelier/Trunk Archive; p. 161: © Wayne Maser/Trunk Archive; p. 162: Donation by Hélène David-Weill, 2004 (2004.12.3), © Les Arts Décoratifs, Paris/Jean Tholance/akg-images; p. 163: Gift of Mrs. Charles Wrightsman, 1993 (1993.157.7a, b), image © The Metropolitan Museum of Art, image source Art Resource, NY; pp. 164, 165: Silverman/Rodgers Collection, courtesy The Kent State University Museum (1999.049.0012 a-g); p. 167: © Gilles Bensimon/Trunk Archive; p. 168: Gift of Mouna Ayoub, 1996 (1996.129a-i), image © The Metropolitan Museum of Art, image source Art Resource, NY; p. 169: © Irving Penn/Condé Nast/Shutterstock; p. 171: ©The Kyoto Costume Institute, photo Takashi Hatakeyama (AC10462 2001-13-3AD); p. 172: © Ruben Alterio; p. 173: © Keiichi Tahara; p. 174: Gift of Steven & Linda Plochocki, courtesy the FIDM Museum at the Fashion Institute of Design & Merchandising, Los Angeles, CA (2009.899.2); pp. 176-177: © Peter Lindbergh/Courtesy of Peter Lindbergh Foundation, Paris; p. 178: © Victor Virgile/Gamma-Rapho/Getty Images; p. 179: Gift of Chanel, 1993 (1993.104.2a-j), image © The Metropolitan Museum of Art, image source Art Resource, NY; p. 180: Assouline/Photograhy by Tiziano Magni; p. 183: Gift of Chanel Inc. © The Museum at FIT (94.80.1); p. 184: Donation by Mouna Ayoub, 2014 (2014.47.1.1-4), © Les Arts Décoratifs, Paris/Jean Tholance/akg-images; pp. 185, 193: Irving Penn, *Vogue*, © Condé Nast; p. 186: © Thibaut de Saint Chamas; p. 187: © Condé Nast Ltd - Cecil Beaton/Trunk Archive; p. 188: © L'Officiel, 1996, Francesco Scavullo; p. 189: Gift of Julia Anderson Frankel (2008.322.1-3), photograph © 2019 Museum of Fine Arts, Boston; pp. 190, 205: Victor Demarchelier/AUGUST; p. 191: © Quentin Bertoux; pp. 195, 196-197, 214, 216, 217: Courtesy Daphne Guinness/Photography Nick D'Emilio; p. 199, 211, 213: © The Museum at FIT (Collection of Daphne Guinness); pp. 200, 201: Donation by Alain Pompidou, 2008 (2008.39.1.1), © Les Arts Décoratifs, Paris/Jean Tholance; p. 202: Donation by Lucía Ybarra Zubiaga. Colección del Museo del Traje. Centro de Investigación del Patrimonio Etnológico; p. 203: Gift of Mrs. William McCormick Blair Jr., 2016 (2016.757.1a-d), image © The Metropolitan Museum of Art, image source Art Resource, NY; p. 206: Courtesy of SCAD; p. 209: © Nancy Kaszerman/ZUMA Wire/Alamy Live News; p. 210: © Camera Press Ltd/Alamy Stock Photo; pp. 218, 219: © Stéphane Cardinale/Corbis/Getty Images; p. 221: © Cathleen Naundorf; p. 223: Gift of Chanel, 2013 (2013.157.1a-h), image © The Metropolitan Museum of Art, image source Art Resource, NY; p. 224: Pascal Le Segretain/Getty Images; pp. 226-227: Jewel Samad/AFP/Getty Images; p. 228: Gift of Chanel, 2016 (2016.379a-c), image © The Metropolitan Museum of Art, image source Art Resource, NY; p. 229: Gift of Chanel, image courtesy Eileen Costa/© The Museum at FIT (2015.64.1); pp. 230-231: Bertrand Rindoff Petroff/Getty Images; pp. 232-233: Peter White/Getty Images; p. 235: © Inez and Vinoodh/Trunk Archive.

Every possible effort has been made to identify and contact all rights holders and obtain their permission for work appearing in these pages. Any errors or omissions brought to the publisher's attention will be corrected in future editions.

© 2024 Assouline Publishing
3 Park Avenue, 27th floor
New York, NY 10016   USA
Tel: 212-989-6769   Fax: 212-647-0005
www.assouline.com
ISBN: 9781649803443

Front cover: © Man Ray 2015 Trust/Artists Rights Society (ARS), NY/ADAGP, Paris.
Back cover: © 2024 Artists Rights Society (ARS), New York, Photo Christian Bérard, *Vogue* © Condé Nast.

Art directors: Charlotte Sivrière, Jihyun Kim
Editorial directors: Esther Kremer, Marc Einsele
Editors: Amy L. Slingerland, Léana Esch
Photo editors: Elizabeth Eames, Ginger Ooi
Printed in Italy by Grafiche Milani.
All rights reserved. No part of this publication may be reproduced or transmitted in any form or by any means, electronic or otherwise, without prior consent of the publisher.